Criminal Justice Assessment and Classification of Prisoners, Probationers, and Parolees

Criminal Justice Assessment and Classification of Prisoners, Probationers, and Parolees

First Edition

Abu Mboka

California State University – Stanislaus

cognella
SAN DIEGO

Bassim Hamadeh, CEO and Publisher
Alisa Muñoz, Project Editor
Abbey Hastings, Production Editor
Emely Villavicencio, Senior Graphic Designer
Greg Isales, Licensing Associate
Natalie Piccotti, Director of Marketing
Kassie Graves, Vice President of Editorial
Jamie Giganti, Director of Academic Publishing

9781516515257

cognella® ACADEMIC PUBLISHING
3970 Sorrento Valley Blvd., Ste. 500, San Diego, CA 92121

Brief Contents

Detailed Contents

Introduction

PEOPLE WHO ASPIRE to build successful careers in corrections are expected to possess adequate knowledge about why offenders commit crimes, how to stop offenders from committing crimes, and how to prevent potential offenders from taking part in criminal activities. A science-based response to each of these questions is crucial to the achievement of correctional goals (Mboka, 2020). For example, the answers to why people commit crimes partly dictate the sentences given to each offender. The explanation of how to stop offenders from recidivating dictates the nature and type of specialized conditions that correctional agencies impose upon pretrial releasees, probationers, and parolees. Views on how to deter would-be offenders from engaging in criminal activities significantly inform the way correctional agencies and officers respond to offenders and criminal activities.

Throughout the history of modern American correctional systems, the answers to questions about why crimes occur, how to correct offending behaviors, and how to prevent future crimes have been informed by the claim that humans rationally gravitate toward crime because of the pleasure they associate with or the thrill they derive from wrongful acts; therefore, lawbreakers must be severely and swiftly punished to effect specific and general deterrence (Akers et al., 2017; Lilly et al., 2018; Williams & McShane, 2018). This view is firmly grounded in American laws and public policies and is accordingly well established within American criminal justice institutions. Consequently, it took decades of intense political lobbying plus legal and public debate among social scientists, politicians, social justice advocates, and other private entities who are interested in crime control and the rehabilitation of offenders to reach the current stage where evidence-based therapeutic interventions and informed risk, needs, and responsivity assessment and classification processes are now viewed as superior to the draconian emphasis on punishment. This shift in institutional responses to crime in general makes the discussions about therapeutic responses to crimes and criminality unavoidable in courses that express interest in pretrial release, probation, and parole, as well as questions of why people commit crimes, how to rehabilitate offenders who are already in the criminal justice system, and how to deter at-risk members of the public from engaging in criminal activity.

Historically, correctional institutions have emphasized punishment as a legitimate way to correct offenders' behaviors and to deter future criminality. This approach is generally characterized by an overt emphasis on incarceration and intensive pretrial release, probation, and parole (Abadinsky, 2012). In institutional settings, punitive isolation and close custody classification are usually motivated by the desire to punish as a way to compel offenders to adopt a particular prosocial behavior. Studies, however, show that these policies are not evidence-based interventions and do not reduce recidivism rates (Mann et al., 2016; Tullock, 1974). Instead, retributive policies actually increase the chances of recidivism and fail to explain or prevent crimes, rehabilitate offenders, or deter future crimes (Petersilia & Turner, 1991, 1993). This reality explains why in recent decades, correctional institutions have legally and publicly committed to the medical model, the view that crimes are symptoms of social and psychological pathologies that can be diagnosed and treated just like physical illness (Balch, 1975; Lehman, 1972; MacNamara, 1977; Simon, 2013).

Despite the focus on the medical model, existing books on pretrial services, probation, parole, and corrections principally devote chapters to the administration and politics of community and institutional corrections. Popular topics typically include issues relating to how probation and parole agencies are managed; the constitutional rights of pretrial releasees, probationers, and parolees; the history of the American prison system; the hiring process for probation and parole officers; institutional structures; and discussions of criminal justice institutions. Unfortunately, however, even the most popular textbooks in the field of corrections do not cover criminogenic risk factors, needs, and responsivity and do not provide in-depth discussions about factors that inform criminal and delinquent thinking and behavior, the clinical process of rehabilitating offenders, deterrence of at-risk persons from engaging in criminal activity, and ways of assessing and classifying offenders using risk-assessment tools. These and other issues present the need for this book.

First, this text is written with the understanding that knowledge of historical facts, institutional bureaucracy, and legal analysis of federal court cases are relevant constituencies of the type of knowledge correction officers are expected to possess but should not be the focal point of classroom discussions because there is no generic agency; each agency teaches its own history, policies, procedures, goals, aims, and style of operation. Second, knowledge about specific correctional agencies' unique and organic bureaucracies, politics, mandates, missions, histories, and human resource matters do not explain individual offenders' behaviors, how to rehabilitate offenders, or how to prevent future criminality. Third, correctional agencies invest significant resources in training their new hires about what they stand for, how to carry out their mission, and how to remain in compliance with policies and procedures. Fourth, the era of retributive policies as the only way to control and prevent crime is no longer as attractive as the medical model: the belief that crimes are symptoms of social, religious, political, cultural, socioeconomic, and/or political pathologies; therefore, crimes can be assessed, classified, and cured or managed using evidence-based interventions just like any other illness.

Fifth, this book is written with the understanding that success in corrections is now measured, at least in part, by the degree to which offenders are successfully rehabilitated and crimes are prevented from taking place, hence the need for anyone who is aspiring to become a successful pretrial, probation, corrections, or parole officer to devote significant academic preparation to the acquisition of knowledge and skills relevant to the assessment, classification, and management of risk, needs, and responsivity. In this respect, this book has five thematic sections: (1) foundations of community corrections, (2) criminal behaviors, (3) responding to offending behaviors, (4) classification of offenses and offenders, and (5) correcting and preventing criminal thinking and behavior.

Section I discusses the complexity and multiplicity of criminal laws and the difficulties for many people to completely avoid the breach of any of the 8,000–10,000 criminal laws on the books and thus argues that offenders should be viewed as humans who are destined to break laws. In this respect, Section I also briefly discusses criminological and sociological theories that generally inform criminal justice and public policies as well as explains why people commit crimes, how to rehabilitate offenders, and how to prevent future acts of criminality. This section concludes with a discussion of race and other factors that do not explain any particular criminal behavior or tendency.

Section II talks about the different types and categories of criminal behaviors with a specific emphasis on violent offending behaviors, substance-related offending behaviors, sex offending behaviors, general criminal behaviors, and mental health–related offending behaviors. In each chapter, special attention is paid to factors that inform specific criminal behaviors and patterns of offenders' lawbreaking behaviors, factors that distinguish one set of crimes and offenders from other behaviors and lawbreakers, and the challenges posed by offending behaviors for criminal justice practitioners, as well as law and correctional policy makers.

Section III broadly discusses four competing philosophies of corrections, specifically (1) retributive, (2) restorative, (3) procedural, and (4) distributive justice approaches to criminal and delinquent behaviors and the extent to which each of the approaches is relevant to correctional policies and practices. This section also broadly covers matters relating to pretrial service, probation, and parole systems; the historical background of risk-assessment tools; the logic of risk, needs, and responsivity assessment and classification; criminogenic risk and protective factors; and ethical guidelines that direct offenders' behaviors.

Section IV is devoted to the explanation of different classification systems used by courts, correctional institutions, and pretrial service, probation, and parole agencies to differentiate between and among offenders within and outside each category of offending behaviors. In other words, this section explains how criminal justice practitioners use risk-assessment and classification tools to differentiate one sex offender from another sex offender, one controlled substance user from another and how to differentiate between violent offenders and sex offenders and between high-risk offenders and low-risk offenders. In addition, this section also covers the various labels that courts, community corrections officers, and institutional corrections officers use to manage offenders' thinking and behavior.

Section V explains the process of writing presentence and pretrial investigative reports, the content and function of those investigative reports, and their history in terms of how they relate to evidence-based interventions. A chapter is specifically devoted to matters relating to pretrial, probation, and parole investigative reports and the use of evidence-based interventions. This section also broadly discusses the different clinical interventions and practices commonly used by correctional agencies to rehabilitate and manage sex offenders, violent offenders, controlled substance abusers, general offenders, and people who engage in antisocial behaviors as a consequence of mental illness. Collectively, these five sections provide a comprehensive understanding of why certain people commit certain crimes, how to rehabilitate offenders, and how to prevent at-risk persons from engaging in criminal and delinquent thinking and behavior using evidence-based interventions and practices.

REFERENCES

Abadinsky, H. (2012). *Probation and parole: Theory and practice*. Pearson.

Akers, R. L., Sellers, C. S., & Jennings, W. G. (2017). *Criminological theories: Introduction, evaluation, and application*. Oxford University Press.

Balch, R. W. (1975). The medical model of delinquency: Theoretical, practical, and ethical implications. *Crime & Delinquency, 21*(2), 116–130. https://doi.oeg/10.1177/001112877502100204

Lehman, P. E. (1972). The medical model of treatment: Historical development of an archaic standard. *Crime & Delinquency, 17*, 204–212.

Lilly, J. R., Cullen, F. T., & Ball, R. A. (2018). *Criminological theory context and consequences* (7th ed.). SAGE Publications.

MacNamara, D. E. J. (1977). The medical model in corrections requiescat in pace requiescat in pace. *Criminology & Social Integration Journal, 14*(4), 439–447. https://doi.org/10.1111/j.1745-9125.1977.tb00036.x

Mann, H., Garcia-Rada, X., Hornuf, L., & Tafurt, J. (2016). What deters crime? Comparing the effectiveness of legal, social, and internal sanctions across countries. *Frontiers in Psychology, 7*, 85–85. https://doi.org/10.3389/fpsyg.2016.00085

Mboka, A. K. (2020). *Assessment and classification of juvenile offenders: A treatment manual for criminal justice practitioners*. Cognella Academic Publishing.

Petersilia, J., & Turner, S. (1991). An evaluation of intensive probation in California. *Journal of Criminal Law and Criminology, 82*(3), 610–658.

Petersilia, J., & Turner, S. (1993). Intensive probation and parole. *Crime and Justice, 17*, 281–335. http://www.jstor.org/stable/1147553

Simon, J. (2013). The return of the medical model: Disease and the meaning of imprisonment from John Howard to Brown v. Plata. *Harvard Civil Rights-Civil Liberties Law Review, 48*, 217–256. https://scholarship.law.berkeley.edu/cgi/viewcontent.cgi?article=2928&context=facpubs

Tullock, G. (1974). Does punishment deter crime? *Public Interest, Summer* (36), 103–111.

Williams, F. P., & McShane, M. D. (2018). *Criminological theory* (7th ed.). Pearson.

SECTION I

Foundations of Community Corrections

CHAPTER ONE

The Context and Concepts of Criminal Behaviors

LARGE SECTIONS OF the American public view those who get caught up in the criminal justice system as people who are extremely dangerous and strange. People with arrest histories are sometimes perceived as exceptionally eerie and are regarded as "twisted" and mentally sick. Consequently, many offenders are socially rejected and discriminated against. In some jurisdictions, adult offenders are even prohibited from carrying out civic duties, such as serving on a jury and voting, and they are legally disqualified from taking up certain employments. These public policies are backed by a broad public sentiment that pushes the criminal justice system to emphasize tighter control over offenders by way of incarceration and intensive probation and parole with broad restrictions on where they can go, what they can do, and with whom they can socialize.

For the trained mind, the negative public view of people who get arrested and prosecuted raises many relevant questions, including whether people with criminal or delinquent histories actually pose more threats to public safety than those without such records and whether such people really differ from people with a so-called clean criminal record. Are some offenders more treatable than others? Is it possible to live a productive and meaningful life completely free from occasional, intentional, and unintentional commission of crimes? This chapter explains how every human being is a potential candidate for committing crimes. It begins with the discussion of the concept of punishment and crime, the roles of criminal laws, and why it is difficult for many people to live a crime-free life, as well as the role of crime and punishment as a regulating mechanism for human interaction or socialization. It is also designed to remind the criminal justice practitioner that arrests, charges, and convictions alone do not always predict future criminal tendencies because criminal behaviors and criminal laws are informed by many socioeconomic, environmental, political, cultural, and psychological factors that must be accounted for during the criminal justice assessment and classification process.

EVOLUTION OF HUMAN CRIMINALITY

Questions about the origin of penal laws are in part inquiries into the cosmological and biological evolution of humans: the origins of society and government, as well as the concept of justice. These ancient questions have so far produced multiple explanations, some scientific, others religious, and still others purely shared traditions and beliefs. Some of the religious explanations are that the universe and its contents, including humans, are a product of God's creation. This position is shared by Muslims, Jews, and Christians, whose holy books trace the history of crime and punishment to the creation of Adam and Eve and their subsequent punishment for eating from the "tree of the knowledge of good and evil" and thus acquiring sentience.

Some of the scientific explanations are quite different and hold that the universe evolved out of interactions among forces and matter billions of years old. According to the big bang theory, for instance, the universe is more than 13.73 billion years old and was born out of random interactions among atoms, energy, and subatomic particles, such as protons, neutrons, and electrons. That is, the origin and evolution of the universe can be traced to an initial state of high temperature and density between 13.73 billion (Ian, 2012) and 15 billion years ago (Peebles, Schramm, Turner, & Kron, 1994). In addition to the scientific and religious explanations, many ethnic and religious groups have developed their own notions of how humans came to be what they are today. Some speak of God as a supernatural force that resides in the sky from where he created the earth and humans and from where he regulates human behavior.

In the end, how humans came to be what they are today is still debatable and will likely continue to be a source of disagreement for centuries to come. Nevertheless, a lot has been learned about humans and of particular importance to this chapter is how the concept of crime and punishment came into existence as a natural consequence of human grouping. Indeed, regardless of what conditions informed neolithic culture, there is enough anthropological evidence to deduce that the first criminal laws were created out of the desire to guard units of families and defend collective interests, including the protection of property.

Humans are vulnerable to many natural conditions and victimization by other animals. They do not have many of the physical, psychological, and physiological capacities needed to survive on dry land, underwater, or in the air nor are they able to defend themselves against many of the other animals that can threaten their lives. For example, humans have to constantly ingest food and water to remain alive. Humans cannot survive underwater for too long, swim for too long, or swim fast enough to avoid getting drowned or falling victim to other water-based animals. Humans can easily die from extreme cold or heat. They do not have venom, claws, or teeth powerful enough to use as tools to defend themselves against other animal predators. Equally, humans cannot fly or outrun many animals, such as bears, tigers, and lions that have both the tendencies and capacities to threaten their lives. Their abilities to see, hear, and smell are also far weaker than other creatures. These natural constraints on humans probably gave birth to the concept of human grouping, society, property, and law and punishment.

To compensate for their natural weaknesses, humans had to live in groups—after all, it is more effective to fight off threats as a group than individually. The need for collective defense against natural forces like wildfires, extreme weather, and dangerous creatures made the idea of living in groups the best and perhaps the only option. The decision to live in groups also gave birth to the concept of society and consequently the idea of crime and punishment as a means to regulate and punish individual members' unwanted behaviors toward others.

The formation of communal life initially motivated by the need to mount collective defenses against natural threats also led to the creation of permanent residences and the consequential task of having to go to distant places in search of food to bring home. These developments, in turn, prompted the domestication of plants and animals. Vegetables and fruits did not suddenly spring up near human settlements. Someone had to have brought fruits like apples, mangos, and pears home, eaten them and thrown the seeds or remnants not far from their huts or caves. The seed from rotten or leftover fruits and vegetables that ultimately found their way to dumping grounds germinated and grew more fruits, which in turn produced more young plants. From this process, the idea of farming, or planting edible fruits, vegetables, and other sources of food likely developed. The successful domestication of plants and the invention of farming ultimately resulted in excess food which either attracted certain animals into human societies or made it easier to domesticate cubs captured during hunting expeditions and brought home. Such animals likely stayed around human settlements because of the availability of food and the protection human societies provided against other predators.

The formation of family and society; the development and acquisition of property, such as hunting and self-defensive tools; the domestication of plants and animals; and the emergence of farming land ownership collectively provided plenty of reasons for interpersonal conflicts, such as property disputes, as well as crimes like stealing and criminal destruction. The abundance of food also meant humans had more free time to devote to the pursuit of pleasure, which is one of the chief natural sources for all known human mischief. The obvious result was the immediate emergence of the need to regulate human behaviors with the aim of preventing harm to property, family, and society. The origin of criminal laws and the concept of criminal justice can, therefore, be traced to the inability of humans to survive as individual units, the idea of and the formation of family and society, the invention of tools, and the domestication of plants and animals. These and the concept of individual rights and the unique ability of humans to harm others in the pursuit of individual enjoyment necessitate penal law and the penal system.

THE RIGHTS OF INDIVIDUALS

Primates, in general, and especially humans, are naturally programmed to gravitate toward behaviors that reward their insatiable desire for pleasure. Even nature bribes humans with pleasure for doing activities that keep them alive, such as eating, sleeping, sex, and shooting the breeze. Indeed, if sleeping were more painful than the discomfort that comes with sleeplessness, then many people would have ended up suffering from insomnia. Similarly, if eating food was more painful than the pain of hunger, then many people would have occasionally chosen starvation unless they were prevented from doing so by the fear of starving to death. In a similar vein, if thirst were more pleasurable than drinking, then many people would have easily opted for dehydration unless they were persuaded by the thought of dying to avoid behaviors that would lead to desiccation-related complications.

It can be argued that humans derive pleasure from satisfying most of their biological needs. This includes the act of chasing pleasures associated with activities that further the pursuit of life, liberty, and happiness. The problem, however, is that unregulated pursuits of pleasure naturally create reasons for crimes, as many people would prefer to enjoy other people's labor and bodies using the natural power vested in them as humans. Such a condition, the 17th-century English philosopher Thomas Hobbes argued, leads to chaos, exemplified by what life must have been in the "state of nature"—a condition under which human societies existed prior to the formation and creation of the concept of a central regulating body or government and its institutions (Lloyd & Sreedhar, 2013).

In the state of nature, according to Hobbes, humans were said to have inherent rights and determinations to defend their self-preservation and to engage in activities that promoted their enjoyment of life, even at the expense of others. The desire for a central regulating body, in this case government, with absolute and unlimited sovereign authority was, therefore, born out of threats to individual self-preservation created by competing individual rights as each person was naturally pushed to engage in behaviors that led to the maximization of the pursuit of pleasure or self-satisfaction and preservation. The competing individual rights can be grouped into two categories: positive and negative rights.

Positive rights are those that cannot be enjoyed without the assistance of another person. In modern times such rights include the right to government protection, education, marriage, and nationality, as well as the right to equal treatment. In all of these cases, the person enjoying the rights relies on the efforts of other members of society. For protection, the individual relies on other people, such as police officers or soldiers. For education, the enjoyment of the individual right to education depends largely on the willingness of another individual to teach. In the case of marriage, a partner and someone to officiate at the marriage, as well as a system to register the marriage, are needed.

Unlike positive rights, negative rights morally and legally compel others to refrain from interfering with their exercise because in theory individual application of such rights can be achieved without harm or threat to humans or property. The most common of these rights include the right to life, sleep, opinions, mobility, and communications. These or any negative rights can be exercised without the assistance of others. However, if all people were to put their individual rights to use without any oversight, the likely result would be very chaotic. Surely, allowing people to walk anywhere, take anything they can, beat whoever they want, and destroy whatever they physically can would likely be tantamount to anarchy. Under such conditions, weaker members of society would have to live at the mercy of stronger members, and that would mean a sort of "war of all against all."

In an attempt to avert such imminent danger of anarchy, political scientists hypothesize that individuals chose to surrender many of their rights to a central governing body in exchange for more positive rights through a process known as a social contract—a sort of contract entered into by rational, free, and equal persons that entails giving up some natural rights and powers to a central regulating and sovereign body in exchange for the preservation and promotion of a greater good (Lloyd & Sreedhar, 2013). The criminal justice system can, therefore, be said to have come into existence by way of humans' trying to avoid social, economic, and political chaos, as well as trying to create specific rights through the creation of central agencies and charging those institutions with the responsibility of promoting and preserving the greater good through the protection of lives and property against natural and human-made threats and the promotion of liberty and happiness.

Social Contracts

The idea of an unregulated human society in the state of nature is troubling because such a society becomes one in which only the most powerful survive. That is, with humans and their lust for safety, pleasure, and socialization, an all-out exercise of natural rights is not a good option because an unregulated exercise of freedom increases the possibility of a solitary, poor, nasty, brutish, and shorter life. Thomas Hobbes (1588–1679), John Locke (1632–1704),

Hugo Grotius (1583–1645), and John Rawls (1921–2002), among many others, have written extensively about the state of nature. Hobbes describes the condition as one that "consisted of internecine wars" and "brut life" (Lloyd & Sreedhar, 2013; Reese, 1999, p. 732).

In the state of nature, according to Hobbes, each individual is born with unalienable rights and has the power and right to preserve his or her existence, even at the expense of others. However, the fullest pursuit of each person's rights will result in anarchy and threaten the lives of all. The fear of such pandemonium gave birth to the concept of the social contract, a social bond between individuals and governments wherein the individual promises to exercise his or her rights within the scope of the law, and in return, the government protects the individual against natural and human-made threats. The contract is symbolized by the formation of a regulatory body created by the social pact to which individuals surrender some of their natural or negative rights and agree to obey the contract.

The authority created by the social contract gives governments the power to enact criminal laws that bind their citizens. People participate in the creation of those laws by way of voting and paying taxes. The individual renews the contract through participation in elections, continuous payment of taxes, and consumption of public resources. The taxes pay the salaries of state employees, including criminal justice practitioners who perform many of the public services that the individual enjoys. Such services include the creation of laws that protect individual lives and properties and that facilitate the pursuit of liberty, as well as the assessment, classification, and management of criminal offenders. In addition, states are required to subject those who breach the contract to suitable and proportionate sanctions, such as incarceration, fines, probation, and, in some cases, execution. Unfortunately, however, it seems like those punitive measures have not had the deterrence effect that criminal sanctions, in general, are designed to produce. This result is not surprising given that the majority of contemporary penal laws are relatively too new, too complicated, and too many for the modern human ways of thinking and behaving.

MODERN PENAL LAWS

Though laws in general have been evolving with humans since the formation of family and society and the invention of property, including tools, domesticated plants, animals, and farming lands, complete abstinence from crime has not been compatible with human nature because humans have an insatiable desire for that which provides them pleasure. Fear of criminal punishment alone is not enough to stop the behaviors that produce the highest pleasure. Among other reasons, penal codes prohibit behaviors that humans have practiced for over 150,000 years, and many prohibited behaviors, such as the use of violence to resolve conflicts, have been used throughout the history of modern humans. Besides, contemporary penal laws are relatively too new and too complicated for many people.

Foreign Nature of Penal Codes

The majority of existing penal codes are relatively foreign to human nature because most modern laws were developed during the last 4,000 years and are, therefore, relatively too new. The oldest known penal law, the Hammurabi code, for instance, is known to have been created in 1752 BC, a relatively short time ago given that human grouping or societies have been in existence for over 150,000 years. If one traces the Christian and Jewish Bibles' Exodus to the 1440s BC, the Ten Commandments would also be less than 4,000 years old. Similarly, Quranic laws believed to have been revealed to the Islamic Prophet Muhammad are only 1,450 years old, as the first Quranic revelation is believed to have taken place in 611 AD, 41 years after the birth of the Prophet in 570 AD.

The relative newness of modern penal laws, therefore, means that modern humans have to unlearn many drug- or violence-related acts that their ancestors practiced for 150,000 years. For juveniles, this means that depending on the jurisdiction, they have to unlearn their natural human instincts to steal, fight, and violate many categories of penal law and a 150,000-year-long genetic coding process between the time they are born and the time they reach age 12.

Too Many Penal Laws

There is a shared belief among many Americans that criminal law is a fix for every social challenge. Further, the public firmly believes that those who are identified by the criminal justice system as "criminals" or "delinquent" pose a particular set of threats to public safety; therefore, the only way to mitigate the threat such people pose to society is to closely monitor and control them by way of incarceration, intensive probation, and parole. The assumption is that tighter control over offenders and, in some cases, harshly treating those offenders will further public safety. These mentalities inform public policies that are laced with the "get tough on crime" sentiment and that give legitimacy to countless laws.

The number of laws is also evidently too high for even the least antisocial members of society to obey. For example, an American Bar Association study concluded in 1998 shows that the number of federal offenses on the books at the time of the study was higher than 3,000. Another study done in 2008 by a Louisiana State University law professor puts the number of federal offenses on the books at 4,500 (Fields & Emshwiller, 2011a; Fields & Emshwiller, 2011b). As the number continues to go up and not down, the combined total of federal and state laws brings the estimated number of criminal laws each person in the United States has to navigate on a daily basis to a staggering 8,000 to 10,000 penal laws. The number is even higher if one adds county and municipal codes, the laws one has to obey at school, and the policies and procedures one has to follow in workplaces.

Complexity of Penal Codes

The majority of contemporary penal laws relate to drugs, sex, and violence, and many such laws are just too broad. The Comprehensive Drug Abuse Prevention and Control Act of 1970 perfectly supports this conclusion. The law, which primarily criminalizes the felonious act of trafficking or possessing controlled substances, goes far beyond those two acts. The 130-page law prohibits many additional behaviors, including the fraudulent mislabeling of a controlled substance; tampering with drug containers or labels; the use of communication tools, such as the Internet and phone to facilitate the commission of a felonious act; and the advertisement of controlled substances. Under this act, one can easily get in trouble with the law if he or she places a prescribed pill in any container other than the one labeled by the pharmacist.

Similarly, the strict application of the 1978 Sexual Exploitation of Children Act, the 1984 Child Protection Act, the 1988 Child Protection and Obscenity Enforcement Act, the 1996 Child Pornography Protection Act, and the 1998 Child Protector and Sexual Predator Punishment Act can easily turn teenagers and innocent Internet browsers into child pornography offenders. Section 2252 of Chapter 110 under Crimes and Criminal Procedure in the U.S.

Code punishes the sexual exploitation and other abuse of children. The law, which regulates "certain activities relating to materials involving the sexual exploitation of minors," broadly prohibits the possession, transmission, or participation in the production of obscene images or materials, sexually suggestive images, or images of a lascivious nature that depict anyone below the age of 18, and as such, it allows for the prosecution of innocent citizens.

The broad nature of this well-intended law (Sexual Exploitation and Other Abuse of Children, 2010a) can land many innocent citizens behind bars. This is evident by the fact that under sections of the law, particularly those that fall under the Sexual Exploitation and Other Abuse of Children law heading, the Federal Bureau of Investigation (FBI) has successfully raided and prosecuted people for attempting to possess child pornography by simply clicking on hyperlinks that claim to have child pornography (2010). In 2007, for instance, the FBI started posting fake hyperlinks, and when clicked on, the dummy links directed individuals to an FBI computer that would copy the Internet Protocol (IP) addresses and the date and time of each attempt to access the alleged child pornography. The FBI would later use the IP addresses to obtain warrants to search suspects' homes (2010). These tactics led to the successful indictment of Roderick Vosburgh when he clicked on a hyperlink (Gibbs, 2008). He was later charged with attempting to download child pornography and possessing child pornography when the FBI found two tiny thumbnails on his computer that depicted underage girls in sexually explicit positions (2010). Although computer experts argued during the trial that the picture could have been accidentally downloaded, Vosburgh was charged with and convicted of the possession of child pornography in violation of 18 U.S.C. § 2252(a)(4)(B) (Sexual Exploitation and Other Abuse of Children, 2010b) and for attempting to possess child pornography in violation of 18 U.S.C. § 2252(b)(2) (2010) (Sexual Exploitation and Other Abuse of Children, 2010c).

In Ohio, police arrested and charged a 13-year-old with felony pandering of obscenity because the boy used his phone to record sex acts between two of his friends and later showed the video off at a skating party (Feyerick & Steffen, 2009; WLWT.com, 2009). In the state of Pennsylvania, photos of a 12-year-old in a training bra, taken when the suspect in this case was 12 years old, landed her on the district attorney's list for possible prosecution on allegation of producing child pornography (*Patriot-News*, 2010). Similarly, a Floridian youth who received "sext" messages from his girlfriend containing naked pictures of herself and who later mass emailed the photos to friends in an attempt to "get back at her" was convicted of transmitting child pornography and ordered to register as a sex offender until he turns 43 years old.

CONCLUSION

The lesson from this chapter is that the number of people who have or who will likely commit serious and dangerous crimes, such as armed robbery, rape, arson, home invasion, premeditated murder, mass shootings, or terrorism, in their lives is very low. However, many upstanding citizens have engaged or will continue to engage in felonious acts, such as the possession of controlled substances, reckless driving, willfully lying on tax returns, use of the telephone or the Internet to further the commission of a felony, making false statements to law enforcement agents, tampering with evidence, engaging in insurance fraud, obstructing justice, child abuse, and/or endangering a child. A similarly high number of people have committed or will in their lives commit the crime of underage drinking, driving without a license, simple assault, theft, contributing to the delinquency of a minor, trespassing, engaging in malicious mischief, illegal gambling, aiding and abetting, and or driving under the influence (DUI) of alcohol or a controlled substance.

The lesson, therefore, is that the vast majority of offenders are no different than other humans and, therefore, do not pose any special threat to the public in any unique way. However, given the fact that laws are becoming more complex and continue to multiply at an alarming rate, it is much easier to explain why there is hardly anyone in the United States over the age of 18 who has not committed a punishable offense (Fields & Emshwiller, 2011a). People who involuntarily make contact with the criminal justice system as the result of criminal behaviors, therefore, deserve to be treated with the understanding that they are human. In this regard, response to their criminality must be guided by careful assessment and classification systems that are informed by evidence-based practices. Furthermore, it is important to remember that some behaviors occur accidentally, are influenced by circumstances beyond offenders' control, and that humans are human.

DISCUSSION QUESTIONS

1. Should the complexity of penal codes be taken into account when assessing an offender's risk or needs level?
2. In the context of risk and needs assessment and classification, how much weight should be given to the saying "ignorance of the law excuses not"?
3. The case can be made that every normal or abnormal person intentionally or unintentionally commits misdemeanors or felony crimes. Which criminal offenses do people more commonly commit, and why?
4. Have humans and human societies evolved enough to live crime-free lives?
5. In the absence of "law and order," which group of people would be affected most by criminal behaviors?

REFERENCES

Feyerick, D., & Steffen, S. (2009). *'Sexting' lands teen on sex offender list.* CNN's American Morning. https://www.cnn.com/2009/CRIME/04/07/sexting.busts/index.html

Fields, G., & Emshwiller, J. R. (July, 2011a). Many failed efforts to count nation's federal criminal laws. *The Wall Street Journal.*

Gibbs, M. (2008). Knock, knock, it's the FBI. *Network World, 25*, 58–58.

Ian, R. (2012). Big bang theory. In *A dictionary of astronomy* (2nd rev. ed.). Oxford University Press, p. 53.

Lloyd, S. A., & Sreedhar, S. (2013). Hobbes's moral and political philosophy. In *The Stanford encyclopedia of philosophy.* Retrieved September 20, 2013, from http://plato.stanford.edu/archives/sum2013/entries/hobbes-moral/

Patriot-News. (2010, February). Sexting: Make the punishment fit the 'crime' for teenagers. *The Patriot-News.* https://www.pennlive.com/editorials/2010/02/sexting_make_the_punishment_fi.html

Peebles, P. J. E., Schramm, D. N., Turner, E. L., & Kron, R. G. (1994). The Evolution of the Universe. Retrieved from https://www.scientificamerican.com/article/the-evolution-of-the-universe/

Reese, W. L. (1999). *Dictionary of philosophy and religion.* Humanity Books.

Sexual Exploitation and Other Abuse of Children, 18 U.S.C § 2252 (2010a).

Sexual Exploitation and Other Abuse of Children, 18 U.S.C. § 2252(a)(4)(B) (2010b).

Sexual Exploitation and Other Abuse of Children, 18 U.S.C. § 2252(b)(2) (2010c).

Titles II and III of the Comprehensive Drug Abuse Prevention and Control Act of 1970 (Public Law 91-513), (1970).

United States v. Vosburgh, No. 08-4702, 602 F.3d 512 (3rd Cir. 2010) (United States Court of Appeals for The Third Circuit 2010). Titles II and III of the Comprehensive Drug Abuse Prevention and Control Act of 1970 (Public Law 91-513), (1970).

WLWT.com. (2009). *Investigators say teen showed video to others.* http://www.wlwt.com/news/18963796/detail.html#ixzz1OfDlMH6J.

CHAPTER TWO

Theoretical Explanation of Crimes

KEY CONCERNS FOR criminal justice agencies and practitioners are how to bring down crime rates and the cost of managing offenders. The desire to achieve these goals is increasingly elevating the need to know why offenders become offenders in the first place. The answer to this question is crucial to any meaningful assessment and classification process. Luckily, however, plenty of sociological, psychological, and criminological theories explain the causes of crimes, the ways offenders learn to commit crimes, the opportunities and factors that aid criminal behaviors, the social factors that mitigate antisocial and prosocial behaviors, and the ways environmental structures and conditions generate illegal activities. These theories pinpoint characteristics, thinking, behaviors, histories, environments, family, and community and cultural issues that predict the likelihood of a particular future antisocial behavior. The theories also provide practitioners with means for helping offenders understand their own behavioral patterns and to identify factors that influence their criminal behaviors.

This chapter provides succinct overviews of nine theories: (1) differential association, (2) social learning, (3) social control, (4) social bond, (5) rational choice, (6) routine activity, (7) labeling, (8) social disorganization, and (9) subcultural theory. These key theories are cited by sociologists, criminologists, and psychologists when talking about criminal thinking, attitudes, and behaviors and when talking about causes and treatment of criminal behaviors and the contents of assessment and classification tools.

Collectively, these sociological, criminological, and psychological theories argue that certain conditions increase the chances of criminal behaviors and that the presence of criminal behaviors suggests the presence of certain factors that make the criminal behavior possible. These theories further identify certain kinds of thinking, attitudes, behaviors, histories, conditions, environments, and events that predict future anti- and prosocial thinking, attitudes, and behaviors.

Broad knowledge of these factors is necessary for identifying risk and protective factors that aggravate or mitigate criminal tendencies. Sufficient knowledge of these items can also significantly improve criminal justice practitioners' assessment and classification capabilities. At a minimum, during the assessment and classification process, such knowledge guides practitioners' actions as to what factors to look for when talking to offenders, when reading offenders' files and reports, and when planning treatment. Awareness of the factors also enhances public policy responses to criminality both in terms of those persons already in the criminal justice system and those at risk of ending up in it.

DIFFERENTIAL ASSOCIATION THEORY

Sociologists, criminologists, and social psychologists frequently cite differential association theory, which remains one of the best-known explanations of criminal behavior when talking about the causes of crime (Jeffery, 1965). The key argument advanced by this theory is that criminal behaviors are learned through social interactions in the company of intimate groups, especially peers, family members, and friends. It is through these social interactions that offenders learn the motivations, the techniques, the rationalizations, and the thinking and attitudes that drive the behavior. Criminal behaviors occur when there is an excess of acquired values, motives, drives, rationalizations, and attitudes favoring criminal behaviors as opposed to favoring conventional prosocial behaviors.

Differential association theory also argues that offenders are likely to choose criminal behaviors over noncriminal behaviors when they are in command of more criminal rationalization for criminal behaviors than the rationalization for noncriminal behaviors.

A well-developed antisocial rationalization reinforces an offender's tendencies to associate with other offenders who reinforce or reward antisocial behaviors. The reinforcement of behaviors occurs through praise and shows of respect for the actors. Rewards may also take the form of monetary compensation, such as buying stolen property from thieves. Such exposures reinforce the behaviors and further strengthen the offenders' desire to engage in similar behaviors.

The extent to which criminals' skills, values, motivations, and rationalizations are acquired and put into practice depends on the degree of connections, length, and frequency of the interactions, as well as the quality of relationship or intimacy, frequency of interaction with others, and connections' duration and intensity. Since the content and patterns of association and interaction with others generally differ from one individual to another, the consequence of the associations will be different. The longer and more frequent the contact with antisocial persons, the higher the risk level. If the criminals' associations possess high levels of criminal thinking, values, beliefs, attitudes, and behaviors, then the offenders' chances of participating in criminal activities are greater (Williams & McShane, 2014).

Differential association theory explains a number of criminal behaviors and in doing so advances several risk and protective factors. Chiefly, the theory explains why people who are sexually victimized early on sometimes sexually victimize others and why criminal justice policies heavily attempt to control sex offenders. It also explains why street gang members take pride in criminal behaviors and why offenders with long histories of criminal activity tend to recidivate more often than first-time offenders. The theory also allows for the measurement of criminal knowledge, reinforcement of criminal behaviors, and distorted thinking as predictors of future criminal behaviors and tendencies.

STRAIN THEORY

Premises advanced by strain theory are simple: strain—that is, individual failure to lawfully achieve respect and power because of the lack of adequate social resources—makes individuals think that there are no legitimate alternatives to crime; thus, potential offenders are pushed toward criminal behaviors (Akers et al., 2016). Strain is experienced through encounters with unfavorable social conditions, such as socioeconomic barriers and institutional biases. These conditions have the collective potential to prevent individuals from achieving their basic goals through legitimate means. In an attempt to correct for the difficulties, individuals may feel compelled to pursue their goals through illegal means. For many young people, gang membership comes in handy in this regard because, in addition to the facilitation of criminal activities, people join gangs to gain respect from their peers in their communities and to acquire power and authority that are lacking for them in mainstream societies.

Strain theory explains most survival-type crimes, such as armed robbery, drug trafficking, theft, and criminal trafficking. The notion that social pressure compels people to chase goals that most potential offenders lack the means to achieve puts additional pressure on individuals to engage in criminal behaviors (Polizzi, 2010). The strain theory perspective has the potential to give probation and parole officers reasons to connect offenders to social resources and opportunities. Recognition of the need to help offenders acquire legitimate means to live out prosocial behaviors is critical to the prevention of future criminality, as well as the maintenance of public safety. Indeed, evidence-based investment in offenders' educational, employment, and social capabilities can minimize the degree and impact of strains on a would-be offender's behaviors.

ROUTINE ACTIVITY THEORY

Routine activity theory suggests that when a motivated offender comes into contact with a suitable target in the absence of a guardian or authority capable of preventing victimization, the offender is more likely to victimize the target or engage in criminal or deviant behavior. Similarly, in the absence of a motivated offender or suitable target, a crime is unlikely to occur, even if there is no capable guardian or authority to prevent the behaviors. When a motivated offender acquires access to a suitable target without a suitable guardian or authority to prevent the offenses, the likelihood of criminal offending increases. The presence of all three elements (offender, target, authority) reduces the risk of successful completion of a criminal act but the absence of capable guardians significantly increases the possibility of criminal offending behaviors (Cohen & Felson, 1979; Osgood et al., 1996; Tilley et al., 2015).

Routine activity theory focuses on the environment and what and who is present in that environment. Hence, some risk assessment tools measure an offender's motivation level. Probation and parole officers also assess the level of exposure to risk and protective factors as they relate to certain criminal behaviors, offenders' access to potential victims, and whether offenders have suitable guardians in their lives to prevent them from engaging in criminal behaviors. Hence the framework of routine activity theory provides some explanation of existing policies relating to what offenders can and cannot do, as well as how to act in the community. For example, the theory explains why child molesters are prohibited from working with children or frequenting places where children congregate. This theory also explains why people with a history of writing fake checks are denied the opportunity to work as cashiers. In addition, it explains why police departments carefully screen people who want to become police officers.

Clearly, giving a sex offender unsupervised access to children means giving motivated offenders access to suitable targets without suitable guidance. Under such conditions, routine activity theory argues, the offender is bound to victimize such children. It is on that basis that probation and parole officers prohibit sex offenders from working with children, for such policies reduce sex offenders' access to suitable targets and opportunities for the offenders to victimize children. The same goes for police applicants—giving a motivated criminal a police uniform, gun, patrol car, and the inside knowledge of city crime management strategies would be a perfect example of how motivated offenders plus suitable targets and absence of suitable guidance increase the potential for criminal behaviors. People who write fake checks are also presumed to be motivated by illegitimate financial gain, and giving such offenders the duty to manage a cash drawer means providing a motivated offender with a suitable target.

LABELING THEORY

One of the tasks performed by public institutions and officials is to assign labels to behaviors. The criminal justice system labels people as felons, criminal addicts, and violent offenders. The labeling theory places such behaviors into two categories: primary and secondary criminality or deviance. The primary deviance is the initial criminal or delinquent act. The logic is that although every person in society engages in some form of deviant behaviors, those who are caught get labeled and consequently their status or standing in society becomes tainted, and as a result, they suffer severe consequences. Core assumptions are that deviance itself is a reaction to certain behaviors; therefore, criminality may have very little or nothing to do with the behavior itself. In other words, deviance is a matter of social definition or social meaning given to behaviors by others (Albrecht & Albrecht, 1978).

Use or possession of marijuana, consumption of alcohol, solicitation or patronization of prostitutes, and participation in illegal gambling, for example, are considered deviant or criminal acts in some jurisdictions while the same behaviors are completely acceptable and, in fact, socially rewarded in other societies. It is only in societies where these behaviors are perceived and labeled by the social audience as deviant that the individuals who engage in them are labeled deviant or criminal. Hence individual deviance or criminality in some cases depends purely on assigned labels and not on behavior. However, once an offender is labeled as a criminal, drunk driver, murderer, sex offender, or drug addict, the person internalizes the deviant labels and is also treated accordingly. See, for example, policies in certain areas that restrict the employment of felons and their access to certain privileges.

Labels have severe consequences. Once the labels are assigned, members of the public and social institutions, including schools and law enforcement agencies, tend to police the labeled individuals more closely and are likely to associate more deviance and criminality to those people. Consequently, the individuals may feel conditioned to act in accordance with the role of the assigned label. At the same time, the audience may view the individual as being what the label says he or she is (Akers et al., 2016; Williams & McShane, 2014;). For example, persons labeled as criminals are perceived to be first and foremost criminals. Consequently, the individual may begin to accept the label as a self-identity. This change in self-concept results in the internalization of deviant behaviors and attributes. Ultimately, the result is an increase in the risk of future criminal behaviors or secondary deviant behaviors.

The second or repeat criminal behaviors are made easier by the social and economic consequences imposed by labeling—consequences like limited employment that come with the labels attached to first acts by public institutions, such as schools and the criminal justice system. Hence, the secondary act of deviance or criminality occurs partly as a result of the first labels placed on the offender after the first behavior by public institutions like school and criminal justice authorities.

The labeling theory is a useful source of guidance for probation and parole officers. It reminds those criminal justice practitioners that the labels they assign to offenders have consequences for the effective management of offenders. It also requires practitioners to be careful when making decisions about assigning labels to offenders. In addition, the theory enhances criminal justice practitioners' capacity to detect and measure the effect of criminal justice labels on offenders' recidivism or future criminal behaviors. In short, the labeling theory cautions criminal justice practitioners to conscientiously use labels, including the labeling of offenders as minimum-, medium-, and high-risk offenders.

SOCIAL DISORGANIZATION THEORY

The central argument of social disorganization theory is that variations in social structure, culture, and the local ecology, along with a lack of resources, are factors that shape social order, levels of social control, and social integration in communities. Weakened social integration of neighborhoods renders self-regulatory mechanisms impotent and leads to the emergence of group cultures that reward criminality. In other words, social contexts of human interactions and experiences can influence future behaviors; therefore, one's presence in socially disorganized environments can increase the risk of future criminality (Akers et al., 2016).

Social disorganization theory views disorganized environments as risk factors because variations in disorganized societies weaken the "capacity of neighborhoods to constrain" residents from violating social norms (Markowitz et al., 2001, p. 293). Characteristics of such environments usually include high risk factors, such as poverty, criminal activities, and lack of good social institutions that would generally control criminal behaviors (Markowitz et al., 2001; Sampson and Groves 1989).

The focus of social disorganization theory on the ecological characteristics and residential locations of offenders is particularly useful for the assessment and classification of offenders' needs. This theory explains crime rates in poor and resource-depressed neighborhoods and provides explanations for why offenders are sometimes advised to move out of certain localities to minimize their chances of recidivism. The theory also explains why probation and parole officers are expected to pay attention to the physical environments in which probationers and parolees reside. The focus on localities also lends some validity to why some public policies are aimed at improving neighborhood institutions and social conditions with the goal of reducing the potential for criminal behaviors.

SUBCULTURAL THEORY

The strong relationship between membership in criminal gangs and criminal behaviors is well documented and understood by police, corrections, probation, and parole officers in every major American city. What is not so clear is why people join gangs or form antisocial subcultural groups. Subculture theory tries to provide answers to this important question. The theory does so by arguing that people join criminal-subcultural groups like gangs because they associate some perceived benefits that they lack in mainstream settings with membership in antisocial subculture groups. The main premise is that members of lower socioeconomic classes are often inadequately prepared to successfully compete with members of the middle class for opportunities because the rules that govern their interactions are set by the dominant values of society, which tend to favor those who are socioeconomically privileged. Consequently, the less-privileged or lower social class members of society may feel that they are being squeezed out of the mainstream and its privileges (Fischer, 1975; Williams & McShane, 2014).

Culture is defined as the means through which societies express beliefs and accumulate material things. Culture shapes language, values, gender roles, social norms, religions, and artistic expression. A subculture, therefore, represents values and norms that are characteristically distinct from those of the larger community. Members of subculture groups define themselves through symbolic resistance to conventional norms. Members hold common perceptions, share feelings of identity with one another, maintain a clear and sustained sense of group identity, and retain a relatively high level of autonomy. Examples of subcultural groups include street gangs, terrorist groups, and hate groups. Membership in these groups increases the possibility of criminal behaviors that arguably pave the way for the achievement of status and power that underprivileged members of society feel they have been wrongfully denied by the mainstream.

The framework provided by subcultural theory is particularly useful for crafting policies that aim toward crime prevention and recidivism reduction. The subcultural theory provides an understanding of risks associated with membership in antisocial groups like criminal gangs. It also explains why people join criminal gangs in the first place. Gang membership is seen as a risk factor because criminal gangs promote and reward criminal behavior. For example, criminal gangs expect their members to develop reputations for toughness and demonstrate through criminal activities that "they have nerve." It is also important to note that when the value system that defines a subcultural group is anti-conventional, the subcultural group tends to offer members opportunities to illegally gain status.

SOCIAL LEARNING THEORY

One of the most widely used theoretical frameworks for policy response to crimes and the shaping of thinking, attitudes, and behaviors of particularly young people is social learning theory. Obviously, the theory is an extension of the differential association theory. The two theories argue that criminal behavior is learned through exposure to criminals or behaviors and rationalizations that are favorable to criminal behaviors. However, unlike the differential association theory, social learning theory goes further to explain the process by which criminal behaviors are learned (Akers et al., 2016; Williams & McShane, 2014).

The major premise of social learning theory is that the probability of criminal behavior increases and the chance of prosocial behaviors decreases depending on whether a person associates with people who engage in criminal behaviors, possess thoughts and attitudes that favor or disapprove of prosocial behaviors, view criminal behaviors as justifiable or undesirable acts, and see antisocial behavior as a source of pleasure or discomfort. In other words, criminal behaviors are learned through association, definition, reinforcement, and initiation (Cullen & Agnew, 2011).

Association refers to direct interaction with people who engage in antisocial behaviors and/or the display of positive views of people who glamorize or celebrate antisocial behaviors. Definition is the meaning and attitudes that one develops and attaches to antisocial behaviors. The definition provides discriminative cues that certain antisocial behaviors espoused by antisocial values will be reinforced by perceived benefits associated with the behavior. Thus, if the definition is one that views antisocial behaviors as wrong and undesirable acts, the risk of antisocial behaviors decreases. The risk increases if the same behavior is viewed as normal.

Reinforcement refers to the anticipated consequences of antisocial behavior. If the perceived consequence is punishment, then the risk of antisocial behaviors decreases, but if the anticipated consequence is some form of material or moral reward, then the risk of antisocial behavior increases. The last element is the imitation of the behavior, which consists of the actual execution of the criminal or antisocial behavior. For substance abusers, this would be the initial experiment with a controlled substance. For sex offenders, this is the initial sex offense.

Social learning theory provides a wide range of ways to examine behavioral history critically during the process of assessment and classification of risks and needs. The theory highlights the thinking, attitudes, and behaviors of those with whom offenders interact. It also illustrates the importance of offenders' views of antisocial behaviors, particularly in terms of whether offenders fully comprehend the negative consequences of their behaviors. The theory also distinguishes between experimentation and repeat behaviors. The former predicts a decrease in risk if the offender comes out thinking that the perceived consequences of the experimented behavior outweigh the anticipated benefit and the later or repeat behaviors simply predict increases in the risk of future behavior. For correction, probation, and parole officers, social learning theory shines a light on the predictive ability of thinking, behaviors, and attitudes of people with whom offenders interact and those whose behaviors they imitate. It also explains the predictive values of offenders' attitudes toward antisocial behaviors and the perceived rewards they associate with criminal and delinquent behaviors.

SOCIAL CONTROL THEORY

Questions about why certain people refrain from committing certain crimes attract many answers, including the ones advanced by social control theories (Chriss, 2007). The phrase social control theories cover a range of theoretical perspectives that discuss social factors that control human behaviors under a variety of circumstances and conditions. Several theoretical frameworks fall into this category, but social bond theory is more useful for the purpose of criminal justice assessment and classification.

Social bond theory explains why people obey social rules, in this case criminal laws, by arguing that in one way or another, individuals are bonded to the dominant values system of the society in which they live. The level of bonding can be measured by the degree to which the individual is involved with, believes in, and is attached and committed to societal values. When that bond is neutralized, whether permanently or temporarily, individuals become "free" to engage in criminal behavior (Akers et al., 2016; Williams & McShane, 2014). The level of individual attachment, commitment, involvement, and belief in the common goals and moral values that define their relationships to public and social institutions, including peer groups, family, and public institutions, such as schools, can, therefore, influence the individual's behaviors under certain circumstances. At the very basic level, the theory argues that people who are committed, involved, and attached and who believe in their communities or social institutions are less likely to violate the norms that shape behaviors in their societies.

Commitment develops out of a mental calculation of the benefits and consequences of antisocial behaviors in relationship to future prosocial goals. Commitment, therefore, refers to the time and energy offenders may invest in the pursuit of social bonds in furtherance of their goals. Commitment is important because if a person is committed to the core objectives of their institutional relationships, their commitment to the relationship may reduce the opportunity for criminal or delinquent behaviors, especially if the party to their relationship disapproves of those antisocial behaviors. For example, people who do well in particularly public institutions, such as schools, may be persuaded to avoid criminal behaviors that would interfere with their performance and disrupt their favorable relationships with such institutions.

Attachment is the care an individual shows for prosocial institutions, such as schools, public authorities, and all that those institutions stand for. Chriss (2007) views attachment as "emotional closeness to family, peers, and schools" (p. 692). Cullen and Agnew (2011) define attachment as emotional "connections to another person" (p. 215). Such connections push offenders to refrain from criminality if the offenders believe that their behaviors would interfere with their relationships. For example, a student who is attached to school, family, and similar institutions is less likely to engage in criminal behaviors that would strain those relationships (Zahn et al., 2010, p. 10). In the same vein, when an attachment between a person and prosocial institution is strong and healthy, the image of the institution in the mind of the would-be offender can act as a protective factor. That is the person may think of the institutions to which they are attached when confronted with the opportunity to commit criminal acts.

Those who through their bonds with prosocial institutions harbor the belief that criminal behaviors are wrong are less likely to engage in such behavior because belief in prosocial peers, authorities, and, most importantly, family members often means possessing ideas that support prosocial thinking and behavior. Involvement in institutional relationships and tasks requires prosocial behaviors that further the conventional goals of the social and public institutions to which an individual is bonded. These behaviors signify the level of motivation and the degree to which the offender sacrifices to achieve core goals. Involvement reduces the possibility of idleness and thus the chance to get into trouble. The level of involvement can, therefore, be measured by the degree of time individuals spend on completing conventional or prosocial activities.

In short, social control theories suppose that the need for self-preservation, fear of punishment, and individual desire for social recognition push people to pursue goals that are self-serving; therefore, attachment, commitment, involvement, and belief in prosocial peers, family members, and public institutions can mitigate the chance of criminal behaviors. Those who invest more time, energy, and resources in the pursuit of healthy bonds are more likely to be concerned with losing their investment and thus are less likely to engage in behaviors that weaken their respective bonds. In the absence of such bonds, the chance for criminal behaviors increases. Consequently, probation and parole officers can use an offender's bond to society as a predictive factor to calculate the risk of future criminal behaviors and to measure the offender's likelihood of achieving social goals, especially in the areas of education and employment.

RATIONAL CHOICE THEORY

The theory most frequently cited when issues of crime control come up within the criminal justice system and elsewhere in the public spheres is rational choice theory. The core contribution of rational choice theory to the understanding of criminality is that humans are equal in their creation and their freedom, and everyone has the ability to choose between right and wrong. Hence, humans live in a world in which certain behaviors are determined by free will, and they make rational calculations that favor the seeking of pleasure and avoidance of pain. Since behaviors are, therefore, driven by the innate desire to achieve the greatest benefit and pleasure, criminal and delinquent behaviors are made possible when the perceived negative consequences of criminal acts are seen as inferior to the supposed benefits of criminality (Akers et al., 2016).

Criminal and delinquent acts always oppose established norms and laws (Williams & McShane, 2014). Therefore, the theoretical assumption that individuals base their decisions to engage or not to engage in criminal activities on rational calculations and thus act with the aim to increase their perceived pleasure creates a chain reaction of conditions that directly or indirectly increase the chances of criminal activities when the selected behaviors are antisocial in nature. This classical perspective is the core theoretical framework that informs many public policies that seek to address criminal behaviors in the United States. Consequently, rational choice theory is widely used by parole and probation officers as a basis for recommending penal interventions. The theory also serves as a good source of guidance for mostly penal and community supervision policies that emphasize harsh conditions of probation and parole with the goal allegedly to teach offenders that crime doesn't pay.

CONCLUSION

Theories discussed in this chapter drive research and criminal justice policies relevant to criminal justice operations. Furthermore, the social, psychological, and environmental factors these theories discuss provide a basic understanding of the kinds of information that in one way or another inform certain sexual, substance, violent, and general offending behaviors. The theories offer a wide range of explanations as to why certain people engage in criminal activities and why others refrain from such behaviors. Collectively, they address questions such as the following: *How do the thoughts, behaviors, and attitudes of people with whom offenders associate affect criminality? What are the effects of the environments in which offenders reside? How do social hardship and public policies inform criminal behaviors? What are the likely effects of policies that emphasize the targeting of offender needs with the aim of minimizing criminal behaviors?* More importantly, the theories discussed in this chapter enhance criminal justice practitioners' capacity to appreciate many of the items that are contained in criminal justice risk and needs assessment tools.

DISCUSSION QUESTIONS

1. Which of the theories discussed in this chapter better explain violent, sexual, substance abuse, or general offending behaviors?
2. If you had to pick one theory that more accurately addresses criminal behaviors in general, which theory would that be?
3. Which of these theories advances classical views, and which one makes positivist arguments?
4. Name a few criminal behaviors that are not adequately explained by any of the theories discussed in this chapter.

REFERENCES

Akers, R. L., Sellers, C. S., Jennings, W. G. (2016). *Criminological theories: Introduction, evaluation, and application*. Oxford University Press.

Albrecht, G. L., Albrecht, M. H. (1978). A critical assessment of labeling in the juvenile justice system. *Justice System Journal, 4*(1), 114–128.

Chriss, J. J. (2007). The functions of the social bond. *The Sociological Quarterly, 48*(4), 689–712.

Cohen, L. E., Felso, M. (1979). Social change and crime rate trends: A routine activity approach. *American Sociological Review, 44*(4), 588–608.

Cullen, F. T., & Agnew, R. (2011). *Criminological theory: Past to present: Essential readings*. Oxford University Press.

Fischer, C. S. (1975). Toward a subcultural theory of urbanism. *American Journal of Sociology, 80*(6), 1319–1341.

Jeffery, C. R. (1965). Criminal behavior and learning theory. *Journal of Criminal Law, Criminology, and Police Science, 56*(3), 294–300.

Markowitz, F. E., Bellair, P. E., Liska, A. E., & Liu, J. (2001). Extending social disorganization theory: Modeling the relationships between cohesion, disorder, and fear. *Criminology, 39*(2), 293–319.

Osgood, D. W., Wilson, J. K., O'Malley, P. M., Bachman, J. G., & Johnston, L. D. (1996). Routine activities and individual deviant behavior. *American Sociological Review, 61*(4), 635–655.

Polizzi, D. (2010). Agnew's general strain theory reconsidered. *International Journal of Offender Therapy and Comparative Criminology, 55*(7), 1051–1071.

Sampson, R. J., & Groves, W. B. (1989). Community structure and crime: Testing social-disorganization theory. *American Journal of Sociology, 94*(4), 774–802.

Tilley, N., Farrell, G., & Clark, R. V. (2015). Target suitability and the crime drop. In M. A. Andresen & G. Farrell (Eds.), *The criminal act: The role and influence of routine activity theory* (pp. 59–76). Palgrave Macmillan.

Williams, F. P., & McShane, M. D. (2014). *Criminological theory*. Pearson.

Zahn, M. A., Agnew, R, Fishbein, D., Miller, S., Winn, D-M., Dakoff, G., Kruttschnitt, C., Giordano, P., Gottifredson, D. C., Payne, A. A., Feld, B. C., & Chesney-Lind, M. (2010). *Causes and correlates of girls' delinquency. Girls study group understanding and responding to girls' delinquency*. Office of Justice Programs.

CHAPTER THREE

Dormant Factors

EVERY HUMAN SOCIETY deals with sex offenses, violent crimes, substance abuse problems, and other general criminal behaviors. Differences exist in how each society defines sexual, violent, substance abuse, and general offenses, as well as ways to respond to those behaviors. In most instances, however, crime control takes on the task of predicting offenders' next antisocial moves. This long-standing desire to predict future behaviors in an attempt to control criminal behaviors has led to many claims and assumptions about the relationship or lack thereof between race, nationality, religion, physiological characteristics and behaviors in general, and, more specifically, criminal and deviant behaviors.

In the United States in particular, claims about relationships between crime and nationality, race, religion, and even sexual orientation float around with relative ease. The most persistently challenged and cited, however, is race. Of course, the prominence of the notion that race predicts behavior has a long history in the United States where race has long been used as a reason to violate the bodies and exploit the labors of people and to exclude persons from public domains (Ngai, 1999, p. 502). Throughout the history of the United States, race has also been used as justification for many adverse socioeconomic and political policies that affect predominantly nonwhites.

RACIAL MARK

Race does not enhance the accurate prediction of individual criminal thinking and behavior; rather, it compromises the integrity of risk and needs scores. Its lack of predictive value is informed by the fact that skin color is useless. Race has no genetic basis, and no specific genetic characteristics can be used to distinguish one race from another. Race is not biological, and most variations exist within and not between races. Most human traits "are inherited independently of one another. The genes for skin color, for example, have nothing to do with the genes for hair texture, eye shape, blood type, musical talent, or athletic ability" (PBS, 2017).

Notwithstanding the fact that race is not a useful factor in predicting criminal behavior, there is a long history of claims that certain criminal behavior is more common among blacks, Asians, Hispanics, or whites and that thus race can accurately predict thinking, attitudes, and behaviors. Consequently, a superficial search of the

Internet using phrases such as race plus serial killers, mass shooters, child sex crimes, violent crimes against children, terrorism, gang crimes, or violent sex crimes against children would create the impression that certain racial groups are predisposed to commit certain crimes more often than other races. Similar conclusions could also be reached when one googles "white and crimes," "black and crimes," "Hispanics and crimes," or "Asians and crimes" (Wolak et al., 2005).

A recent report published by the New Century Foundation entitled the "Color of Crime: Race, Crime, and Justice in America," provides the following dubious summaries:

> In 2013, a black was six times more likely than a non-black to commit murder, and 12 times more likely to murder someone of another race than to be murdered by someone of another race.
>
> If New York City were all white, the murder rate would drop by 91 percent, the robbery rate by 81 percent, and the shootings rate by 97 percent.
>
> In an all-white Chicago, murder would decline 90 percent, rape by 81 percent, and robbery by 90 percent (Rubenstein, 2016, p. ii).

Wikipedia describes the source of these claims, the New Century Foundation, as a white supremacist group that advocates for segregation on the basis of race. Obviously, the report uses gun violence in New York as a basis for predicting levels of gun violence in any society with black residents, although evidence clearly shows that the nations with the most gun violence are not in sub-Saharan Africa where almost the entire population is black.

The New Century Foundation report does not explain why the United States, with its 61.6% white, 17.6% Hispanic or Latino, and only 13.3% black population is the "world leader in gun deaths" (U.S. Census, 2015). Also, the report does not explain why the United States' rate of violent gun deaths per 100,000 people in 2013 was 3.55 compared to the 3.12 combined total for Belgium, Cyprus, Finland, France, Italy, Malta, Netherlands, and Spain. The United States' rate of violent gun deaths per 100,000 people was also higher than the combined 3.54 gun violent death rate for Russia, Belarus, Croatia, Bulgaria, and Slovakia (Kelto, 2015). The New Century Foundation claims also fail to explain why the death rate in sub-Saharan countries is lower than the gun violence death rate in the United States. As Kelto (2015) noted, in "sub-Saharan Africa where there is not armed conflict, death rates from guns are relatively low. If the U.S. were on the continent, it would have the eighth-highest number of gun deaths," well ahead of war-torn countries like the Democratic Republic of Congo, Rwanda, Somalia and South Sudan (Kelto, 2015).

A cursory examination of even credible statistics on certain criminal activities can also give cause to an informed mind to conclude that race predicts criminal thinking and behavior. For example, a U.S. Department of Justice's national analysis of crime reports that while "nearly 70% of those serving time for violent crimes against children were white, whites accounted for 40% of those imprisoned for violent crimes against adults" (Greenfeld, 1996, p. iv). This implies that not only do whites victimize children more but also they commit some of the most violent crimes against children (Greenfeld, 1996, p. iv).

In a work entitled "Serial Killers—A Homicide Detective's Take" by a homicide detective veteran with 20 years of experience who claimed to have investigated six serial murder cases, the author wrote that there "is a consensus of the majority of criminal profilers, based on actual cases they have investigated" that "serial killers tend to be mostly white males;

between 20 and 40 years of age" (Andreu, 2014). In the same vein, the U.S. Bureau of Justice Statistics reported that in 2014 "6% of all black males ages 30 to 39 were in prison, compared to 2% of Hispanic and 1% of white males in the same age group" (Carson, 2015). Approximately, 27.3% of adult offenders arrested in a given year are African American, although the group represents about 13% of the U.S. population (FBI, 2016; Free & Ruesink, 2012). When taken narrowly, these claims and figures may sound like blackness is a predictor of criminal behavior.

Although the figures cited thus far can cause even an informed mind to conclude that race predicts criminal behaviors, first, a simple comparative examination of the extent to which race dictates criminal behaviors would show that for the purpose of risk or needs assessment and classification, race is a useless category. For example, an examination of national data reveals that even when accounting for race, between 20% and 39% of the racial disparity in criminal justice statistics remains unexplained (Free & Ruesink, 2012). This means that mere skin color does not explain the high rate of African Americans who involuntarily make contact with the criminal justice system—although skin color may be exploited in some cases.

Second, the rate of blacks who participate in the American criminal justice system compared to the rate of blacks who participate in criminal justice systems in societies outside the United States would not support the notion that race predicts criminal behaviors. Third, if skin pigmentation were a reliable biological marker for how people think and act under a given circumstance, then the entirety of African countries would have the highest number of recorded criminal activities and would have the highest prison populations. If race truly predicts behavior, then the type of crime people associate with blacks would be more common in sub-Saharan Africa, where almost the entire population is black.

Similarly, if race were a reliable predictor of behaviors, then the crimes people associate with particularly white males would be more visible throughout Europe where the number of white males is more concentrated. If claims about particularly black crimes mean being black is a risk factor for engaging in certain antisocial behaviors at a rate higher than other races, then such criminal activities would be much higher in places like West Africa where almost the entire population is black. Even in instances where race might seem capable of predicting behavior, there are factors other than race that explain behavior.

Factors and events that inform good and bad behavior are not inherent in the genetics that make people black, white, or brown. On the contrary, what humans encounter in their environments and through contact with cultures, traditions, beliefs, and laws inform and predict their behaviors. Historically, however, the concept and label "race" has been used far too often as a basis for creating and applying unjust public policies, including the advancement of social inequality and the determination of who has rights over what. For example, race has normalized the extermination of Native Americans, the exclusion of Asian immigrants, and the exploitation and victimization of blacks in various forms (PBS, 2017).

There are factors and logical explanations for why, compared to white offenders, African Americans and Hispanics are disproportionately found among the wrongfully convicted and why they are more likely to be incarcerated, to receive longer and harsher sentences, and to be sentenced to life without parole. There are also factors that explain why Hispanics and blacks account for 56.4% of offenders serving sentences of life without parole, why they account for 42% of offenders on death row, and why they have made up 35% of all prisoners executed since the death penalty was reinstated in 1976 (Free & Ruesink, 2012). Indeed, not only does skin color fail to predict criminal or noncriminal thinking, attitudes, and behavior, any race can produce the likes of Adolf Hitler, Martin Luther King Jr., Nelson Mandela, Mother Theresa, or Osama bin Laden.

NATIONALITY

Nations have well-established norms, traditions, histories, values, and political and legal frameworks within which national decisions are made and actions are taken. These characteristics are formed and nourished for years, making them difficult to change over a short period. In addition, there are less than 200 nations. Hence it is possible to predict certain nations' behaviors under a given circumstance. However, for several distinct reasons, the same cannot be said about the individuals who reside within the borders of each nation.

First of all, unlike nations, there are over seven and a half billion persons who purposefully organize their behavior around the seeking of pleasure and the avoidance of pain. Second, each person can change his or her thinking, attitudes, and behaviors in a matter of minutes. Third, many of the values and motives that guide individual behaviors are hard to establish because each person is unique, with the full ability to publicize only those behaviors that they want others to know. So, belonging to or having the nationality of any particular nation does not predict future thinking and behavior. Yet nationality is frequently used at even national levels as something by which individual behaviors can be predicted. For example, in January 2017, President Donald J. Trump signed an executive order banning people from Iraq, Syria, Iran, Libya, Somalia, Sudan, and Yemen from entering the United States for at least 90 days and permanently banned Syrian refugees from entering the United States (Bier, 2017). This executive action taken on behalf of the United States follows an old American tradition (National Archives, 2017; Ngai, 1999).

History shows that the United States has used nationality or national origin to restrict the movement of and to ban Chinese, Japanese, and all Asians from the Asiatic Barred Zone from entering the United States on the basis that such nationals posed a particular risk to national security. The so-called Asiatic Barred Zone included much of the continent of Asia, with the exclusion of current Japan and Eastern China, and the islands adjacent to the continent of Asia (Asiatic Barred Zone Act, 1917).

In 1924, the U.S. Congress created a "national-origins system" that benefited only Western Europeans and excluded most Eastern Europeans, as well as almost all Asians and Africans. During World War II, the internment of Japanese Americans relocated, or led to the incarceration of, 110,000 to 120,000 Japanese Americans. In 1942, an executive order by President Franklin D. Roosevelt was used to deport and detain persons of Japanese, German, and Italian ancestry as a way to allegedly protect "against espionage and against sabotage to national-defense material, national-defense premises, and national-defense utilities" (Executive Order No. 9066, 1942).

Not surprisingly, however, policies that target nationality as a risk factor have no established relevance as far as crime control and risk assessment and classification are concerned. However, it is important to note that national policies such as the aforementioned reinforced a shared belief that the place of birth or possession of a country's nationality was a good predictor of certain criminal behaviors.

Even in cases where studies persistently show a particular criminal behavior being dominated by a particular nationality, national origin is not a reliable source for predicting any particular criminal behavior or even any individual thinking and behavior. For instance, Nigerians are known for 419 scams, which refer to the 419 section in the Nigerian penal code. The scam typically involves Nigerians who live in the United Kingdom and Benin contacting potential victims in the United States and tricking them into paying a certain amount of money under the promise of a future larger payoff (Isacenkova et al., 2014).

Similarly, studies show that most of the men who participate in child sex tourism come from the United States, United Kingdom, Canada, Germany, and Australia (Mattar, 2007; Zaf & Tidball, 2010). Child sex tourism refers to traveling to different jurisdictions solely to engage in sexual behavior with children. Noticeably, the common trends among these countries are that their citizens possess strong economic stability, enjoy advanced Internet and cell phone communication technologies, and have access to the means to travel to distant places like Cambodia, Philippines, Thailand, and Kenya where economic hardships and weak criminal justice systems make it easier for child sex tourists to engage children in sexual acts for money.

Clearly, it would be fruitless to assume that all Nigerians are at higher risk of committing scam-related crimes and all or most men from the United States, United Kingdom, Canada, Germany, and Australia are at higher risk of pursuing children for the purpose of sexual behaviors. What is supported by most theories and studies is that many factors explain the behavior of people from a particular region or country, including Nigeria, the United States, United Kingdom, Canada, Germany, and Australia. In the case of child sex tourism, factors that attract pedophiles from wealthy countries include weakened criminal justice systems at destination countries, feeble law enforcement resources, and corruption. At the same time, the ease of travel, fear of strict domestic laws, functioning criminal justice systems, and harsh prosecution of sex crimes, especially crimes against children, push pedophiles in places like the United States, Canada, Australia, United Kingdom, and Germany to travel abroad for the sole purpose of engaging in criminal activities (Johnson, 2011).

Pedophiles with the means to travel or live in countries where they are less likely to be prosecuted harshly or at all for sexual acts involving children than they would in their home countries find these to be adequate reasons for pursuing sex tourism. At least these conditions provide some explanation of why pedophiles travel from places like the United States, United Kingdom, Germany, and Australia to destinations such as Cambodia, Philippines, and Thailand. Similarly, although 419 fraud points to specific nationals, in this case Nigerians, in reality, the fraud does not explain anything about nationality. Rather, the behavior highlights some of the adverse consequences of poor economic conditions, ineffectiveness of local and criminal justice systems, and relative ease of Internet access and phone technology that facilitate the contact between offenders and victims.

RELIGION

Nationality can be easily confused with religion because certain countries are known for specific religions, such as Islam, Hinduism, or Judaism, and thus people from such countries can be easily mischaracterized as Muslims, Hindus, or Jews irrespective of their actual religious preference and practices. Consequently, the more people are led to believe that nationality predicts behavior, so will they be persuaded to assume a connection between nationality and religion and thus between religion and antisocial behaviors. Such calculations lead to the postulation that people from certain countries are at high risk of committing particular sets of crimes—for example, people from particularly Muslim countries may be taken as Muslims and thus viewed as being at high risk of committing terrorist crimes.

There is no doubt that religion can be used to predict certain behaviors. For instance, Rastafarians may be at increased risk of being arrested for possession of marijuana or marijuana-related paraphernalia. Equally, it is rational to assume that practicing Muslims are less likely to be arrested for driving under the influence of alcohol or to shoplift pork from a grocery store. After all, Christians, Muslims, Hindus, and other mainstream religious groups are more likely to avoid behaviors that are inconsistent with their respective values and religious teachings and practices.

In the end, however, there is no well-established link between the practice of a particular religion and criminal activities that would warrant the use of religiosity as a risk factor for the purpose of risk calculation. Indeed, although scholars have tried to draw a link between religiosity and less serious behaviors, a mere affiliation with atheism, Christianity, Hinduism, Islam, or Judaism does not predict the likelihood of an individual committing sex crimes, violent crimes, substance abuse-related offenses, or participating in any general category of crime. If anything, religiosity may serve as a protective factor.

Generally speaking, the major religions of the world teach peace and promote prosocial behaviors. So logically, religion could be a useful protective factor in some cases, although not impactful enough to alter a risk level. For example, scholars have suggested that a lack of religious commitment is "a major cause of crime (including delinquency)" (Ellis, 1985, p. 501). Some scholars have also argued that there "has been mounting evidence since 1970 that an inverse relationship does exist between at least some forms of religiosity and criminality" (Ellis, 1985). Consequently, many criminal justice institutions, such as correctional facilities, encourage offenders to actively practice religion by facilitating, for example, "church attendance as part of crime and delinquency prevention and rehabilitation programs" (Ellis, 1985, p. 502). The assumptions are that as a person's religiosity increases, the likelihood of criminal activity will decrease. It is, however, difficult to defend this position in the face of a well-documented history of religious leaders committing heinous crimes.

According to the Royal Commission into Institutional Responses to Child Sexual Abuse, for example, "seven percent of Catholic priests in Australia between 1950 and 2010 allegedly sexually abused children, according to data provided by church authorities in a major investigation" (Kennedy, 2017). Similarly, self-proclaimed leaders of Al Qaeda, the so-called Islamic State, and other radical religious groups and their members around the world commit their crimes in the name of their respective religions. If religions were reliable sources of risk and needs assessment, one would expect that at a minimum those who head such institutions would be at low risk of committing the types of crimes with which they are frequently associated.

GENDER

Anatomically males and females show sex differences. Women have the ability to bear children, something that men lack. Males, however, dominate all criminal activities. In other words, the majority of violent offenders, sex offenders, substance abusers, and general offenders are males. The 2016 FBI reports also indicate that out of the 4,158,264 victims recorded in 2015, more than half (50.9%) were female. However, 63.3% of the offenders were males, and only 25.7% were female with 11% failing to declare their gender—note that gender is socially constructed while sex is biological. Most of the arrestees (63.3%) recorded by the FBI in 49 states were also male, and only 25.7% were female (FBI, 2016). The majority of youth who make contact with the criminal justice system for engaging in delinquent behaviors are boys. As Free and Ruesink (2012) observed, 90% of offenders arrested for murder and manslaughter, 98.7% of those charged with forcible rape, and 88.2% of persons detained for robbery are also men.

Even in instances where male and female behaviors are characteristically similar, men still outnumber women. For instance, according to the National Institute on Drug Abuse, men are more likely than women to use almost all types of illicit drugs. Men are also more likely to end up in the emergency department for overdoses than women, although women have the same likelihood as men to become addicted. This raises the question of whether being male increases the risk of committing violent, sexual, substance abuse, and general offenses and whether sex should form part of the calculation of an offender's risk and needs levels. Answering yes to this question would mean that biological differences between males and females contribute to prosocial and antisocial thinking, attitudes, and behaviors.

Few theoretical frameworks have attempted to explain gender differences in criminal behaviors. The most prominent are the biological and feminist explanations—namely, the testosterone and liberation theories. The testosterone theory contends that primitive "residues of aggressive behavior prevailing in animal life, determined by testosterone, remain attenuated in man and suppressed through familial and social inhibitions" (Batrinos, 2012, p. 564). However, this throwback to animal states still manifests itself in various intensities and forms from "thoughts, anger, verbal aggressiveness, competition, dominance behavior, to physical violence" (Batrinos, 2012, p. 567). Thus "testosterone levels are higher in individuals with aggressive behavior," and those with high levels of testosterone are at higher risk of committing violent crimes (Batrinos, 2012, p. 564).

The liberation theory attributes female criminality to the "emergence of the women's liberation" movement, which is believed to have increased criminal opportunities and support for illegal behavior and weakened social controls that traditionally regulated women's behaviors (James & Thornton, 1980, p. 230). That is, the liberation theories contend that the increasing participation of females in particularly street crimes is a result of the departure from female dependence on males in favor of female self-reliance. These theories argue that we live in paternalistic societies where men are independent, and women are dependent on men, and where public laws and policies favor views that empower males and promote the dominance of men and the subordination of women. Hence, as the gender gap narrows as a consequence of the liberation movement, the behaviors of both women and men, both legitimate and illegitimate, become more alike (Williams & McShane, 2014).

Whether or not testosterone induces violent criminal thoughts, anger, verbal aggressiveness, dominant behavior, or physical violence, this theory does not explain other criminal behaviors, such as substance abuse, sexual abuse, and general offending behavior. Similarly, the connection between liberation and nonsurvival crimes remains blurry. Evidently, there are no established differences with regard to thinking, attitudes, and criminal behaviors between women and men or girls and boys. Social learning, social disorganization, and social control theories can explain many of the factors that facilitate criminal behaviors.

PHYSIOLOGICAL CHARACTERISTICS

The science of measuring body parts, such as the size and shape of skulls, in an effort to classify people as high risk for committing crimes is not new. Throughout the history of criminology, some have argued that biological and personality traits reliably predict criminal thinking and behavior. Consequently, the size or shape of the head, facial asymmetry, jaw size or shape, ear size, shape of the nose, and the length of arms have either been looked at or cited as a marker of future criminality (Lombroso & Ferrero, 1898).

In 1898, Caesar Lombroso and William Ferrero argued that "the criminal woman is consequently a monster" who lacks the virtues that cause many "normal" women to live crime-free lives (1898, p. 151). Indeed, women who commit crimes, they argued, possessed the characteristics of men. Accordingly, most female crimes could be attributed to women with visible masculinity; hence, women with visible masculinity were at risk of committing crimes. Nevertheless, apart from factors such as mental health, which can set the trajectories of criminal careers, there is no established evidence to support a link between biological and personality traits and criminal thinking and behavior (Cauffman, 2008).

CONCLUSION

The process of predicting and calculating risk and needs is a complex undertaking that involves the assessment of various forms of ecological factors, economic opportunities, psychosocial histories, mental health statuses, life experiences, attitudes and behaviors, and individual relationships with vital social institutions, such as family and learning and employment establishments. For these reasons, only certain factors, and not race, religion, nationality, gender, or physical characteristics, are useful for the purpose of risk and needs assessment. Factors such as mental health disorders, weak cognitive ability and moral reasoning, inability to recognize consequences of behaviors, environmental conditions, life circumstances, and psychological abnormality are critical in this process. In many cases, these factors explain why certain racial groups, nationalities, genders, and religious groups are overrepresented in certain categories of criminal behavior.

DISCUSSION QUESTIONS

1. What are some of the key factors that make local criminal justice systems incapable of protecting children from child sex tourism?
2. Every now and then throughout the history of the United States, politicians manage to win the support of voters using race as a definitive predictor of criminal behavior. Why do these sorts of appeals work in the United States but fail in other countries?
3. What is the best way to address child sex tourism if the goal is to end the practice?
4. The rate of women making involuntary contact with the criminal justice system has been steadily rising, faster than the rate of males, in the past decades. What are some of the key factors responsible for these changes?

REFERENCES

Andreu, N. (2014). *Serial killers—a homicide detective's take.* Expert Law. https://www.expertlaw.com/library/investigators/serial_killers.html

Asiatic Barred Zone Act of 1917, 39 Stat. 874, 8 U.S.C.0. (1917).

Batrinos, M. L. (2012). Testosterone and aggressive behavior in man. *International Journal of Endocrinology and Metabolism, 10*(3), 563–568. https://doi.org/10.5812/ijem.3661

Bier, D. J. (2017, January 27). Trump's immigration ban is illegal, *The New York Times.* https://www.nytimes.com/2017/01/27/opinion/trumps-immigration-ban-is-illegal.html

Carson, E. A. (2015). Prisoners in 2014. *Bulletin.* http://www.bjs.gov/content/pub/pdf/p14.pdf

Cauffman, E. (2008). Understanding the female offender. *The Future of Children, 18*(2), 119–142.

Ellis, L. (1985). Religiosity and criminality: Evidence and explanations of complex relationships. *Sociological Perspectives, 28*(4), 501–520. http://doi.org/10.2307/1389231

Executive Order 9066 (1942).

FBI. (2016, December 12). *FBI releases 2015 crime statistics from the national incident-based reporting system, encourages transition* [Press release]. https://www.fbi.gov/news/pressrel/press-releases/fbi-releases-2015-crime-statistics-from-the-national-incident-based-reporting-system-encourages-transition

Free, M. D., & Ruesink, M. (2012). *Race and justice: Wrongful convictions of African American men.* Lynne Rienner Publishers.

Greenfeld, L. A. (1996). *Child victimizers: Violent offenders and their victims.* Bureau of Justice Statistics. https://www.bjs.gov/content/pub/pdf/CVVOATV.PDF

Isacenkova, J., Thonnard, O., Costin, A., Francillon, A., & Balzarotti, D. (2014). Inside the scam jungle: A closer look at 419 scam email operations. *EURASIP Journal on Information Security, 4*(1–18).

James, J., & Thornton, W. (1980). Women's liberation and the female delinquent. *Journal of Research in Crime and Delinquency, 17*(2), 230–244.

Johnson, A. K. (2011). International child sex tourism: Enhancing the legal response in South East Asia. *International Journal of Children's Rights, 19*(1), 55–79. https://doi.org10.1163/157181810x499367

Kelto, A. (2015). *The U.S. is a world leader in gun deaths.* NPR. Retrieved January 3, 2017, from http://www.npr.org/sections/goatsandsoda/2015/12/07/458815891/the-u-s-is-a-world-leader-in-gun-deaths

Kennedy, M. (2017). *Australian Catholic Church: 7 percent of priests sexually abused kids over decades.* NPR. http://www.npr.org/sections/thetwo-way/2017/02/06/513745513/australian-catholic-church-alleges-7-of-priests-sexually-abused-kids-over-decade

Lombroso, C., & Ferrero, W. (1898). *The female offender.* Appleton and Company.

Mattar, M. (2007). *International child sex tourism: Scope of the problem and comparative case studies.* The Protection Project, Johns Hopkins University. http://www.protectionproject.org/wp-content/uploads/2010/09/JHU_Report.pdf

National Archives. (2017). *World War II enemy alien control program overview: Brief overview of the World War II enemy alien control program.* National Archives. Retrieved January 31, 2017, from https://www.archives.gov/research/immigration/enemy-aliens-overview.html

Ngai, M. M. (1999). The architecture of race in American immigration law: A reexamination of the Immigration Act of 1924. *Journal of American History, 86*(1), 67–92. https://doi.org/10.2307/2567407

PBS. (2017). *What is race?* PBS. Retrieved January 4, 2017, 2017, from http://www.pbs.org/race/001_WhatIsRace/001_00-home.htm

Rubenstein, E. S. (2016). *The color of crime: Race, crime, and justice in America* (rev. ed.). New Century Foundation.

U.S. Census. (2015). *Quick facts*. Retrieved January 3, 2017, from https://www.census.gov/quickfacts/table/PST045216/00

Williams, F. P., & McShane, M. D. (2014). *Criminological theory* (6th ed.). Pearson.

Wolak, J., Finkelhor, D., & Mitchell, K. J. (2005). *Child-pornography possessors arrested in Internet-related crimes: Findings from the national juvenile online victimization study.* National Center for Missing & Exploited Children. http://www.missingkids.com/en_US/publications/NC144.pdf

Zaf, C. R., & Tidball, S. (2010). *A survey of child sex tourism in the Philippines* [Paper presentation]. Second Annual Interdisciplinary Conference on Human Trafficking, University of Nebraska-Lincoln, Lincoln, NE, United States.

SECTION II

Criminal Behaviors

CHAPTER FOUR

Violent Offending Behaviors

A HIGH PROPORTION of offenders in the criminal justice system fall into the category of violent offenders. Indeed, while violent crimes in general have been trending downward for more than two decades (James, 2015), over half of states' male prison populations are classified as violent offenders (Carson, 2015a). As the Bureau of Justice Statistics (BJS) reported, more than half (54%) of male offenders in state prisons in 2013 were doing time for violent crimes (Carson, 2015b). In 2015, about 2.7 million or 0.98% of all persons age 12 or older experienced at least one violent victimization (Truman & Morgan, 2016). During the same period, 7.3% of 192,663 prisoners under federal correctional authority were violent offenders. Reports also show that 53.2% of 1,325,305 prisoners under state jurisdiction in 2013 were classified as violent offenders. This figure includes 12.5% of sex offenders who have committed the act of rape.

It is, therefore, extremely important for criminal justice professionals to develop good knowledge about the proportion, characteristics, and trends of violent crimes generally committed by offenders. The ability to identify and classify violent behaviors is also vital in determining the types and levels of scrutiny, as well as the interventions each violent offender deserves in order for them to fully benefit from the key services offered by corrections, probation, and parole departments. The FBI defines violent crimes as offenses that involve the use or threat of force. The list of criminal behaviors that fall under this definition is long, but many of the violent behaviors fit into one of five categories: (1) sexual, (2) gang, (3) domestic, (4) terrorism related, or (5) general violence. Obviously, each of these categories of violence poses a significant threat to public health and safety.

This chapter briefly discusses the typologies of violent crimes and violent offenders and the trend of each category of violence. Violent crimes typically include threatening victims or causing them physical harm. The worst of these behaviors include violent crimes, such as rape and certain forms of sexual assault, robbery, physical assault, and all forms of homicidal behaviors. Generally, however, it is difficult to separate violent offenders from nonviolent offenders using arrest or incarceration figures because some crimes, such as vandalism and arson, may fall either within or outside the definition of violent crime. In some cases, the circumstances surrounding the crimes, as well as the manner in which such crimes are committed, can make the difference. Criminal offenses such as setting an occupied structure on fire, willful destruction of property, and acts of vandalism can also qualify as violent crimes.

TYPOLOGY OF VIOLENT OFFENDERS

Knowledge of the types of violent crimes that often pull offenders into the criminal justice system is as important as the types of violent offenders. Of importance to criminal justice practitioners are the motives, reasons, or goals behind each violent crime. Such motives could be characterized in six ways: (1) thrill, (2) mission, (3) visionary, (4) lust, (5) retaliatory, and (6) financial gain–driven violence. Thrill violent offenders engage in violent behaviors because they enjoy or derive gratification from engaging in violent acts. Missionary violent offenders act with the mindset that they have a duty to cleanse society of unwanted or undesirable persons. These offenders generally target people who fall under specific labels, such as street prostitute; gay; disabled; those who belong to certain religious, racial, or ethnic groups; or people viewed as abnormal or seen as immoral stains on society.

Visionary violent offenders tend to have severe mental health needs and thus claim to engage in violent acts because they have allegedly seen visions or heard voices from demons, angels, the devil, or from some sort of contact with a supernatural force or authority commanding them to engage in specific violent acts. Lust violent offenders actually derive sexual gratification from the infliction of pain on another person. This category of offender engages in specific violent acts, such as torturing their victims for the pleasure and excitement they derive from such acts. Retaliatory offenders act in the name of vengeance or payback for perceived acts of injustice with the goal to create in their minds a sort of equalization for the wrong. Financial gain–motivated violent offenders use violence to achieve unique criminal objectives that further the acquisition of material wealth. For instance, the robber who kills innocent customers during a bank robbery does so to complete the robbery successfully. Offenders who murder their spouses to claim life insurance money also do so to acquire insurance proceeds.

TYPOLOGY OF VIOLENT CRIMES

Irrespective of whether an offender's criminal behavior falls under one or more of the clinical typologies of violent offenders (thrill, mission, visionary, lust, retaliatory, or financial gain), violent behaviors can be legally grouped under one of these criminal behavior categories: sexual, gang, domestic, property, terrorism related, and general violence. Except for crimes such as terrorism, these categories of violent criminal behavior account for a large number of the offenders in jails and prisons and those on probation or parole. Hence it is critically important for people who work with such offenders to have broad knowledge of the prevalence of each criminal behavior. At the least, knowledge of whether the trend of a particular crime is going up or down can help with the planning of interventions for that particular criminal behavior.

Street and Gang Violence

The U.S. Department of Justice defines a gang as an association of three or more individuals who collectively identify themselves as a group and whose goals include in part the use of violence or intimidation to achieve criminal objectives (NGR, 2015a). Gangs use unique characteristics and symbols, such as common names, signs, colors, hand signs, tattoos, and or other physical markings, which set them apart from other gangs. Each of the thousands of gangs that exist in the United States can, however, fit into one of three key categories of criminal gangs: (1) street, (2) prison, and (3) outlaw motorcycle gangs. Seven years ago, there were an estimated 29,400 of these gangs throughout 3,500 jurisdictions across the United States (Egley & Howell, 2012). Today, there are more than 33,000 active gangs with 1.4 million active street, prison, and outlaw motorcycle gang members in the United States. Members of these gangs are responsible for an average of 48% of violent crimes in most American jurisdictions (NGIC, 2011).

The American public has been dealing with criminal gang problems for over 2 centuries. Although gangs in the late eighteenth century were less dangerous compared to many contemporary gangs, the presence of gangs has been felt by the public, and particularly law enforcement agencies, as a major threat to public safety and health (Howell et al., 2011; Howell & Moore, 2010). Even today, gangs and gang violence remain a major concern for police, corrections probation, and parole officers in every American county (NGIC, 2011). Gang-related homicides account for most of the intentional violent deaths in major American cities.

Some well-established street, prison, and motorcycle gangs are active both in prison and on the street; hence, many would qualify as both prison and street gangs. For example, the 18th Street gang qualifies as both a prison and street gang. Similarly, Bloods, Crips, Latin Kings, and Gangster Disciples are active prison and street gangs. The same is true for gangs such as Barrio Azteca, Bloods, Crips, Mexican Mafia, MS-13, Norteños, Tango Blast, Texas Syndicate, and Sureños. Gangs particularly known for their involvement in street prostitution and human trafficking are the Bandidos, Bloods, Brown Pride, Crips, Folk Nation, Latin Kings, MS-13, Mexican Mafia, Norteños, Sureños, and 18th Street (NGIC, 2013).

Table 4.1 shows examples of key categories of gangs active in the United States. The list is based on the place of gang origin, the gang size, and whether the gang is active on the streets or in prisons or jails. The most recent estimate shows that nationally two thirds of these gangs and more than 80% of the gang members are located in larger cities and suburban counties. Members of these gangs are responsible for an average of 48% of violent crimes in most American jurisdictions (NGIC, 2011).

Despite the seemingly clear distinctions, it is almost impossible in some cases to distinguish between street and prison gangs. The process is complicated by the fact that federal prisons, each of the 50 states, and many large county jails, have their own regulations and classification systems that designate a gang as a street or prison gang based on their own criteria. Further, prison gangs operate both within and outside the walls of prisons, and some gangs designated as prison gangs did not originate in prison. Also, while certain states base their classification of a gang as a prison gang on whether the gang was formed in prison or jail, many states look at whether a particular gang is active in prison or jail. Some states use the origin of a gang, while others look at the size of a gang or where a gang is most active (on the street or in prison or jail) (Nathan, 2017).

Notwithstanding the different categorizations, the National Gang Intelligence Center and the National Alliance of Gang Investigators' Associations define a prison gang as "a criminal organization that originates in the penal system" (NGR, 2015b, p. 15). Members of prison gangs use violence to maintain control over their environments, other prisoners, and illicit activities both within and outside the walls of prisons and jails. Prison gangs call some of the most critical shots on the streets. They dictate street-level criminal activities and set the rules of engagement with other gangs and responses to police actions.

TABLE 4.1 *Active Gangs in the United States*

STREET GANGS	PRISON GANGS	OUTLAW MOTORCYCLE GANGS
18th Street Gang	Almighty Latin King	Bandidos
38th Street gang	Aryan Brotherhood	Black Sabbath
Armenian Power	Aryan Circle	Brother Speed
Black Disciples	Aryan Nations	Chosen Few
Black Mafia	Barrio Azteca	Devil's Disciples
Bloods	Black Guerilla Family	Diablos
Crips	Border Brothers	El Forastero
East Side Longos	Dead Man Inc	Galloping Goose
Folk Nation	Dirty White Boys	Gypsy Joker
Four Corner Hustlers	Gangster Disciples	Hells Angels
Fresno Bulldogs	Hells Angels	Highwaymen
Friends Stand United	Ku Klux Klan	Iron Horsemen
Jackson Street Boys	Mexican Mafia	Mongols
Latin Kings	MS-13	Moonshiners
Luzon Visayan Mobsters	Murder Inc.	Outlaws
Maniac Latin Disciples	Nazi Low Riders	Pagans
Menace of Destruction	Ñetas	Phantom
Mexican Posse 13	Northern Ryders	Rock Machine
Norteños	Northern Structure	Sin City Disciples
Simon City Royals	Nuestra Familia	Sons of Satan
Spanish Cobras	Peckerwoods	Sons of Silence
Sureños	Tango Blast	Vagos
Tall Arabian Posse	Texas Syndicate	Warlocks
Varrio Nuevo Estrada	Warrior Society	Wheels of Souls

Prison gangs' involvement in street criminal activities are driven primarily by the desire to generate cash revenue and to exercise control over territories. In other words, street gang members commit criminal acts, including murder, drug and human trafficking, and other criminal activities, at the request of prison gangs and "then forward revenue and contraband gained from the commission of their crimes into prison. In exchange, incarcerated gang members provide protection to the street gang members when they are incarcerated" (NGR, 2015b, p. 15).

Street gangs are formed on the street, and members carry out criminal activities in their neighborhoods throughout the United States. Some street gangs are neighborhood based and thus generally confined to specific territories or jurisdictions. Other street gangs have national profiles and thus maintain a presence and operate in multiple jurisdictions. However, both neighborhood-based and national-level street gangs, such as the MS-13, Latin Kings, Crips, and Bloods collaborate with prison gangs at many levels to effectively organize and carry out a variety of criminal activities, including drive-by shootings, intimidation, aggravated assault, hit and runs, robberies, home invasions, and homicides. They also commit nonviolent crimes, such as weapons trafficking, street-level drug trafficking, prostitution, theft, and certain categories of sex or human trafficking (Battin-Pearson et al., 1998; Miller, 1992; NGR, 2015b).

Outlaw motorcycle gang members are approximately 44,000 nationwide, are affiliated with roughly 3,000 gangs (NGIC, 2011). Outlaw motorcycle gangs consist of three or more motorcycle owners and riders who share common interests or who engage in criminal undertakings. It is important to note that there are perhaps more recreational motorcycle riders than outlaw motorcycle gangs. However, those who ride under the banner or patches of groups like the Hells Angels, Pagans, Vagos, Sons of Silence, Outlaws, Bandidos, and Mongols commit a variety of violent and nonviolent crimes. Members of this category of gangs are known for crimes such as robbery, homicide, assaults with weapons, and assaults resulting in serious bodily injury. Beyond violent crimes, members have a well-earned reputation for racketeering, bribery, credit card fraud, insurance fraud, motor vehicle theft, and drug dealing, notably methamphetamine, cocaine, and marijuana. Outlaw motorcycle gangs also traffic in weapons, humans, large-scale drugs, and child sex (NGIC, 2013).

Many gang members join street, prison, and motorcycle gangs purely for the personal benefit realized through illicit activities and the direct proceeds derived from criminal activities, such as the trafficking and sale of stolen goods, prostitution, and similar acquisitive crimes. Some gang members join gangs for the sake of physical protection against other criminal gangs or gang members. Certain gang memberships are also motivated by specific factors, such as the desire to maintain honor, defend local turf, acquire a sense of belonging, and retain control over people within so-called territories. No matter what, however, membership in any criminal gang suggests that at a minimum an offender is most likely committing gang-related crimes and thus has a high probability of continuing to commit petty or serious crimes, including violent ones.

Domestic Violence

The U.S. Department of Justice's *2015 Criminal Victimization Report* showed that 3.0% or 806,050 of 5,006,620 violent crimes reported to law enforcement in 2015 were intimate partner violence (Truman & Morgan, 2016). The National Coalition Against Domestic Violence defines domestic violence as "the willful intimidation, physical assault, battery, sexual assault, and/or other abusive behavior as part of a systematic pattern of power and control perpetrated by one intimate partner against another" (NCADV, 2017). Domestic violence is a very dangerous and sometimes deadly offending behavior that affects many vulnerable members of society. The behavior produces extensive financial, psychological, and physical pain and suffering for victims. For instance, it is estimated that on average, victims of intimate partner violence spend $948 on emergency care for each domestic violence–related incident (Vagianos, 2015). Despite the psychological, financial, and physical costs, domestic violence remains highly underreported.

On average, 20 people in the United States suffer some form of abuse by their domestic partners each minute. That is more than 10 million victims in a single year. Reports also show that about 15% of all violent crimes recorded by criminal justice officials are committed by domestic partners. Estimates also show that 1 in 3 female murder victims and 1 in 20 male murder victims are killed by domestic partners (NCADV, 2017). Between 2001 and 2012, about 11,766 American women were murdered by male current or ex-partners. At least three women are murdered every day in the United States, and at least 38 million women have suffered some form of domestic violence in their lifetimes. In 2011 alone, 926 women were murdered by domestic partners (Vagianos, 2015).

Much of the underreporting of domestic violent behaviors can be explained by factors such as a lack of trust in the criminal justice system, fear of offender retaliation, and concern for the harm the offender would suffer. Hence a significant proportion of victims (32%) conceal their victimization in an effort to preserve offenders' privacy, 21% of the victims do so to protect their victimizers from possible legal and financial consequences of their actions, 19% are held back from reporting their victimization by fear of reprisal from the offender, and 20% think the domestic victimization is a minor offense that does not warrant criminal justice intervention (Reaves, 2017). The desire to preserve family unity and feelings of shame, self-blame, and genuine fear of their abusers are also common barriers that domestic violence victims encounter when they are faced with the dilemma of reporting their victimization (Othman et al., 2014).

Sexual Violence

Violence is a known extension of sex offenses. Consequently, sex crimes, such as rape and sexual assault, are almost synonymous with violence. In fact, rape and sexual assault are common types of sexually violent acts that take place but are not reported to law enforcement. Indeed, about 30.6% of sex offenses qualify as rape, and sexual assault with objects accounts for 4.7% of all documented sex offenses (Finkelhor et al., 2009). About 1 in 5 women and 1 in 59 men become victims of rape in the United States at least once in their lives. Also, 9.4% of women in the United States have a history of being raped by an intimate partner (NCADV, 2017). Many other serious sexual offenses, such as child molestation and the production of child pornography, are also unquestionably violent acts.

Reports from the National Sexual Violence Resource Centers (NSVRC) show that 12.3% of women were raped at age 10 or younger, 30% of women were raped between the ages of 11 and 17, about 27.8% of male victims were raped at age 10 or younger, and more than one third of women who were raped before the age of 18 are also assaulted during their adulthood (NSVRC, 2015). An estimated 19.3% of women, more than 23 million, become victims of rape during their lifetime. Another 43.9% of women experienced other forms of sexual violence. Also, a troubling percentage (8.8%) of women suffer rape at the hands of an intimate partner, and an estimated 15.8% of women suffer other forms of sexual violence at the hands of an intimate partner (Frieden et al., 2014). Similarly, an estimated 1.7% of men, or almost 2.0 million, suffer similar victimization during their lifetimes. The number of males who experience other forms of sexual violence is, however, lower, at about 23.4% compared to the 48.9% of women who suffer similar experiences. These figures do not account for sexual coercion or other forms of unwanted sexual contact.

Domestic and International Terrorists

Terrorism is a leading source of public safety and health concerns. With the exception of Antarctica, terrorists are active in every corner of the globe. Between 1980 and 2005 alone, 17,216 people fell victim to both international and domestic violence, of which 3,178 people were killed and 14,038 wounded (FBI, 2017). Since September 12, 2001, the United States has witnessed more than 90 attacks by violent extremists, resulting in more than 300 deaths in addition to the 9/11 terrorist attacks, which claimed 3,000 lives. Unfortunately, the casualty figures from terrorism have also drastically increased in the last 2 years (GAO, 2017).

Of course, this is not surprising because the number of lone wolves and extremist groups who see terrorist behavior as the best way to resolve their social, political, and personal conflicts seems to also be on the rise.

Terrorist groups carry out indiscriminate mass killing or engage in mass destruction of life and property without regard for innocent lives or people who die or suffer injuries as a consequence of their actions. Instead, terrorists tend to care most about what message their atrocious behavior allegedly communicates to those in power or opposition or how they are viewed by others. The concern tends to be on how many lives are destroyed and how much destruction is achieved.

Some terrorist acts are motivated by personal grievance or by a sense of wrongdoing by governments, individuals, or groups of people. Other terrorist acts are committed on behalf of organizations or political institutions or because of personal grievances. Another set of terrorists, visionary or missionary offenders, believe that they are doing God's work by killing people they considered disobedient to their God. Some believe that they will receive certain rewards or comforting treatment after death.

Violent extremist groups support or commit violent crimes as a way to achieve political, ideological, religious, or social goals. Often, this category of terrorist group espouses a particular ideology or political and social issues. In this respect, some of the most common groups that have produced extremist-related violence are racial supremacy and radical Islamist groups. The list of terrorist groups, however, include abortion rights, animal rights, and environmental groups. The extremists who seem to be causing the most harm to Americans are domestic terrorists, commonly referred to as homegrown or lone-wolf terrorists. Since September 11, 2001, these extremists have killed more Americans than jihadist organizations, such as the Islamic State or Al-Qaeda (Nakashima, 2015). In fact, the majority of post-September 11 terrorist attacks in the United States have been carried out by non-Muslims (Sampathkumar, 2017).

Although most acts of terrorism in the United States are local, international or internationally influenced acts of terrorism remain one of the most serious public safety health and safety issues. Unfortunately, however, there is no internationally agreed-upon definition of what constitutes "terrorism" (Setty, 2011). For example, the U.S. government defines terrorism as any "unlawful use of force and violence against persons or property to intimidate or coerce a government, the civilian population, or any segment thereof, in furtherance of political or social objectives" (Judicial Administration, 2003). Although both domestic and international terrorism fit into this definition, the absence of a universally accepted definition makes it difficult to assess and classify acts of international terrorism effectively. Obviously, part of the problem has to do with the fact that there is no consensus among nations about why people become terrorists or what constitutes an act of terrorism.

Some countries argue that terrorism is a consequence of political and socioeconomic inequality. Others argue that the root causes of terrorism are the United States' foreign policies, particularly as they relate to the Middle East, Arabs, or Islam. Some countries view terrorism as acts of extremism or fanaticism kept alive by Islam or at least Islamic communities. Other countries believe that terrorist acts are unfortunate products of broader prevailing political and socioeconomic injustices around the world. Other nations fear that a universal definition of terrorism would unavoidably establish a permanent link between the phenomenon and religion, particularly Islam, and thus serve as a reason for future profiling of Muslims (UN-Sixth-Committee, 2005).

GENERAL VIOLENT CRIMES

The U.S. Department of Justice's *2015 Criminal Victimization Report* showed that 0.98% of persons (about 2.7 million) age 12 or older suffered serious violent crime that year. In the same period, about 7.6% of households (10 million) were victims of violent property crimes—that is, about 110.7 per every 1,000 households in a single year (Truman & Morgan, 2016). It is estimated that at least 1,248,185 serious violent crimes occurred in the United States in 2016, or about 386.3 violent crimes per 100,000 inhabitants. In the same year, 64.3% of the violent crimes reported to law enforcement were aggravated assaults, and 26.6% were robbery offenses, while rape accounted for 7.7% and murder 1.4% (FBI:UCR, 2017).

Certain types of violent crimes do not, however, automatically fit into any particular category of violence and thus can be best described as general violence—a group of violent behaviors that fall outside the definition of terrorism, gang, domestic, or sexual violence. General categories of violence account for most violent crimes reported to law enforcement. Obviously, there are more general crimes, both serious and minor, than any other category of criminal behavior. The most common types of violence that fall under the general category of criminal behaviors include non-domestic aggravated or simple assaults, destruction of property, kidnapping, disorderly conduct, armed robbery, certain types of arson cases, and other non-domestic, terrorist related, and sexually violent acts against other persons. Arson or the crime associated with setting structures on fire is a unique general violent crime because the offense can fall into one or more categories of violent offenders, particularly visionary, thrill, lust, and acquisitive or financial gain motivated.

Violent Arson

Irrespective of the motive, arson involving occupied structures is considered an act of violence. Obviously, the individual setting the fire does so with little regard for human life. Such a mindset is indicative of a willingness to cause another person suffering. It is, therefore, important to distinguish between those who set fires for the sake of the pleasure they associate with flames (lust) and those who set fires for the sole purpose of concealing their criminal behaviors (financial gain). It is also useful to separate those who set fire to avenge a perceived act of injustice (retaliatory) from those who do so purely because of alleged visionary or missionary reasons.

An arsonist who sets bushes on fire is also different from the arsonist who sets a dwelling on fire. The former does so with no apparent intention to cause human death, and the latter does so with the intention to cause death, or at least with no concern for human lives. In the end, however, the assessment and classification of arsonists in general require a great deal of information gathering and analysis because arsonists come from a variety of criminal backgrounds (Häkkänen et al., 2004). Studies also show that about 18% of arsonists suffer some form of mental retardation (Burton et al., 2012).

CONCLUSION

Victims of violent crimes suffer a variety of harms. In particular, victims of serious violent crimes, such as rape and aggravated assault, suffer significant financial, psychological, and socio-emotional problems. They face problems with work and experience difficulties with social interaction, including difficulties getting along with and trusting family members and peers. The majority (91%) of violent crime victims also experience one or more physical symptoms long after experiencing the initial victimization (Langton & Truman, 2014). The consequences of sexual violence in particular are felt in various ways. For instance, the Centers for Disease Control and Prevention (CDC) noted that some of the consequences of sexual violence include rape-induced pregnancy; gynecological complications; sexually transmitted infections; immediate and chronic psychological consequences, such as symptoms of post-traumatic stress disorder, shame, or guilt; strained relationships with friends and significant others; and drug and alcohol abuse behaviors (CDC, 2017).

The proper assessment and classification of violent offenders can produce benefits for victims, offenders, and society as a whole. Accurate identification of violent offenders makes it easy to identify appropriate interventions and services for both the offenders and their victims. Similarly, it makes it easier for corrections, probation, and parole officers to devise the most appropriate and effective services and security levels for offenders. The alternatives, misclassification and misidentification, results in mistreatment of offenders, application of scarce resources, or the allocation of resources to the wrong offenders at the expense of those who most need such help. In this scenario, the offenders, society, victims, and future would-be victims directly benefit.

DISCUSSION QUESTIONS

1. What characteristics differentiate visionary violent offenders from other types of violent offenders, such as thrill, lust, or acquisitive violent offenders?
2. Which factors lead to an increased number of people who perpetrate violence in the United States?
3. Which is more dangerous, prison gangs, street gangs, or outlaw monocycle gangs?
4. What factors motivate people to become domestic or international terrorists?
5. Why do offenders think violence is an effective tool for solving many social, domestic, political, and financial problems?

REFERENCES

Battin-Pearson, S. R., Thornberry, T. P., Hawkins, J. D., & Krohn, M. D. (1998). Gang membership, delinquent peers, and delinquent behavior. *Juvenile Justice Bulletin*. https://www.ncjrs.gov/pdffiles/171119.pdf

Burton, P. R. S., McNiel, D. E., & Binder, R. L. (2012). Firesetting, arson, pyromania, and the forensic mental health expert. *Journal of the American Academy of Psychiatry and the Law Online*, *40*(3), 355–365.

Carson, E. A. (2015a). Prisoners in 2014. *Bulletin, 1–19.* https://www.bjs.gov/content/pub/pdf/p14.pdf

CDC. (2017). *Sexual violence: Consequences*. https://www.cdc.gov/

Egley, A., & Howell, J. C. (2012). Highlights of the 2010 national youth gang survey. *Juvenile Justice Fact Sheet*, 1–3.

FBI. (2017). *Terrorism 2002–2005*. https://www.fbi.gov/stats-services/publications/terrorism-2002-2005

FBI:UCR. (2017). *2016 crime in the United States*. Retrieved October 13, 2017, from https://ucr.fbi.gov/crime-in-the-u.s/2016/crime-in-the-u.s.-2016

Finkelhor, D., Ormrod, R., & Chaffin, M. (2009). Juveniles who commit sex offenses against minors. *Juvenile Justice Bulletin*. https://www.ncjrs.gov/pdffiles1/ojjdp/227763.pdf

Frieden, T. R., Jaffe, H. W., Cono, J., Richards, C. L., & Iademarco, M. F. (2014). Prevalence and characteristics of sexual violence, stalking, and intimate partner violence victimization—national intimate partner and sexual violence survey, United States, 2011. *Surveillance Summaries, 63*(8), 1–18. https://www.cdc.gov/mmwr/pdf/ss/ss6308.pdf

GAO. (2017). *Countering violent extremism: Actions needed to define strategy and assess progress of federal efforts*. http://www.gao.gov/assets/690/683984.pdf

Häkkänen, H., Puolakka, P., & Santtila, P. (2004). Crime scene actions and offender characteristics in arsons. *Legal & Criminological Psychology, 9*(2), 197–214.

Howell, J. C., Egley, A., Tita, G. E., & Griffiths, E. (2011). U.S. gang problem trends and seriousness, 1996–2009. *National Gang Center Bulletin, May 2011*(6), 1–23. https://www.nationalgangcenter.gov/Content/Documents/Bulletin-6.pdf

Howell, J. C., & Moore, J. P. (2010). History of street gangs in the United States. *National Gang Center Bulletin, May 2010*(4), 1–25. https://www.nationalgangcenter.gov/Content/Documents/History-of-Street-Gangs.pdf

James, N. (2015). *Is violent crime in the United States increasing?* Congressional Research Service. https://fas.org/sgp/crs/misc/R44259.pdf

Judicial Administration, 28 C.F.R., Chapter I Department of Justice (2003).

Langton, L., & Truman, J. (2014). *Socio-emotional impact of violent crime. Special Report*. U.S. Department of Justice, Office of Justice Programs. https://www.bjs.gov/content/pub/pdf/sivc.pdf

Miller, W. B. (1992). *Crime by youth gangs and groups in the United States*. Office of Juvenile Justice and Delinquency Prevention, https://www.ncjrs.gov/pdffiles1/Digitization/156221NCJRS.pdf

Nakashima, E. (2015, October 18). Domestic extremists have killed more Americans than jihadists since 9/11. How the government is responding. *The Washington Post*, Post Nation https://www.washingtonpost.com/news/post-nation/wp/2015/10/15/how-the-justice-department-is-stepping-up-its-response-to-domestic-extremists/

Nathan, M. D. (2017). *White supremacist prison gangs in the United States, a preliminary inventory*. ADL. https://www.adl.org/sites/default/files/documents/assets/pdf/combating-hate/CR_4499_WhiteSupremacist-Report_web_vff.pdf

NCADV. (2017). *Domestic violence*. https://ncadv.org/assets/2497/domestic_violence.pdf

NGIC. (2011). *2011 national gang threat assessment; emerging trends*. https://www.fbi.gov/stats-services/publications/2011-national-gang-threat-assessment

NGIC. (2013). *2013 national gang report*. https://www.fbi.gov/file-repository/stats-services-publications-national-gang-report-2013/view

NGR. (2015a). *2015 national gang report (NGR)*. https://www.fbi.gov/file-repository/stats-services-publications-national-gang-report-2015.pdf/view

NGR. (2015b). *The 2015 national gang report (NGR)*. https://www.fbi.gov/file-repository/stats-services-publications-national-gang-report-2015.pdf/view

NSVRC. (2015). *Statistics about sexual violence*. https://www.nsvrc.org/sites/default/files/publications_nsvrc_factsheet_media-packet_statistics-about-sexual-violence_0.pdf

Othman, S., Goddard, C., & Piterman, L. (2014). Victims' barriers to discussing domestic violence in clinical consultations. *Journal of Interpersonal Violence, 29*(8), 1497–1513.

Reaves, B. A. (2017). *Police response to domestic violence, 2006–2015. Special Report.* Bureau of Justice Statistics. https://www.bjs.gov/content/pub/pdf/prdv0615.pdf

Sampathkumar, M. (2017, June 23). Majority of terrorists who have attacked America are not Muslim, new study finds. *Independent.* https://www.independent.co.uk/news/world/americas/us-politics/terrorism-right-wing-america-muslims-islam-white-supremacists-study-a7805831.html

Setty, S. (2011). What's in a name? How nations define terrorism ten years after 9/11. *University of Pennsylvania Journal of International Law, 33*(1), 1–63.

Truman, J. L., & Morgan, R. E. (2016). Criminal victimization, 2015. *Bulletin.* https://www.bjs.gov/content/pub/pdf/cv15.pdf

UN-Sixth-Committee. (2005). *Agreed definition of term 'terrorism' said to be needed for consensus on completing comprehensive convention against it.* (2005 [GA/L/3276]). https://www.un.org/press/en/2005/gal3276.doc.htm

Vagianos, A. (2015). 30 shocking domestic violence statistics that remind us it's an epidemic. *HuffingtonPost.* https://www.huffingtonpost.com/2014/10/23/domestic-violence-statistics_n_5959776.html

CHAPTER FIVE

Substance-Related Offending Behaviors

IN 2015, THERE were as many as 171,245 people in jails and 206,300 in state prisons for drug-related offenses. During the same period, there were 185,917 people in federal prisons serving time for drug offenses (Carson, 2015a). These figures are higher than the 2014 figures. For example, the U.S. Department of Justice's reports show that at the end of December 2014, of the 1,316,409 prisoners under states' correctional authorities, 15.7% were serving time for substance-related offenses. In the same period, more than 50% of male and 59% of female prisoners in federal institutions were serving time for drug-related offenses (Carson, 2015b). This means that controlled substance-related offenses create serious public safety and health challenges for police, corrections, probation, and parole officers.

Given the high number of people who make contact with the various branches of the criminal justice system as a result of controlled substance-related offenses, it is important to have good knowledge about the scope and prevalence of substance use, misuse, and related behaviors. Such knowledge enhances the process of identifying the types and levels of needs and services that each offender deserves to fully benefit from available correctional resources. Indeed, knowledge about the degree and scope of substance abuse and related offenses is helpful in formulating and asking questions relevant to the successful assessment and classification of offenders' substance-related criminal behaviors. In this respect, this chapter discusses the scope of controlled substance use, abuse, misuse, and related offenses by people who involuntarily come into contact with the criminal justice system. The list of controlled substance and alcohol use, abuse, and related behaviors includes acts of physical consumption or use of certain controlled or prohibited substances, as well as the physical possession, transportation, and sale of such substances.

Compared to other categories of criminal behaviors, various private and government agencies gather and disseminate a lot of information about substance abuse-related behaviors and crimes. For example, the U.S. Department of Health and Human Services (DHHS) and its affiliates and subsidiaries, such as the Substance Abuse and Mental Health Services Administration, the National Institute on Drug Abuse (NIDA), the Office of National Drug Control Policy (ONDCP), the Substance Abuse and Mental Health Services Administration (SAMHSA), and the CDC collectively and individually gather rich and current information about the trends and consequences of controlled substance abuse, use, and related offenses.

A report by the National Survey on Drug Use and Health (NSDUH), which is a product of the collective efforts of the DHHS, ONDCP, NIDA, SAMHSA, and CDC, is particularly helpful. Generally, the survey samples about 67,500 people who are 12 years old or older. The report contains national and state-level data on the use of tobacco, alcohol, and illicit drugs, including the nonmedical use of prescription drugs by persons aged 12 years old or older. The report, therefore, offers a reliable glimpse into the world of substance abuse, use, and related crimes (Bose et al., 2016). The NSDUH annual survey does not, however, sample people living in group shelters, such as boarding houses, college dormitories, camps, and halfway houses. The study also does not survey people without a fixed address, including homeless people, active military personnel, inmates, and residents of nursing homes, mental institutions, and hospitals.

SCOPE OF DRUG AND ALCOHOL ABUSE BEHAVIORS

The 2014 BJS reports showed that 50% of males and 59% of females in federal prisons in September 2014 were serving time for drug-related offenses, of which 3.6% were for drug possession (Carson, 2015a, p. 17). In the previous year, Puzzanchera (2013) estimated that about 58% of the 258,500 offenders who were serving time during the period were doing so for drug and liquor law violations (34%), and only 4% were there for DUI. Results of the 2015 NSDUH show that about 27.1 million people or 1 in 10 Americans (10.1%) used an illicit drug in the 30 days that preceded the survey, and 22.2 million Americans aged 12 or older were current marijuana users (Bose et al., 2016). The different types of controlled substances frequently abused are briefly discussed (Table 5.1).

Illicit Drugs

The most common types of illicit drugs are marijuana, cocaine, heroin, hallucinogens, methamphetamines, and prescription medications, including psychotherapeutics. In 2015, there were about 22.2 million marijuana users, 3.8 million persons who misused prescription pain relievers, 1.9 million users of cocaine, and 1.9 million users of prescription tranquilizers and other psychotherapeutic medications. The least commonly used substance is heroin, with as low as 0.3 million users (Bose et al., 2016). Nonmedical use of prescription drugs, therefore, remains a key problem and, unfortunately, a common behavior in the United States (Bose et al., 2016; NIDA, 2016).

Street names of controlled substances regularly change—see Table 5.1. These drugs get frequently abused, especially pain relievers, tranquilizers, stimulants, and sedatives. Tranquilizers consist of benzodiazepines, meprobamate products, and muscle relaxants. Stimulants include methamphetamine, amphetamine, dextroamphetamine, and phentermine products, as well as mazindol, methylphenidate, and dexmethylphenidate. Sedatives cover temazepam, flurazepam, and triazolam, and any barbiturates (Bose et al., 2016; Burwell, 2016). As shown in Table 5.2, of these four categories of prescription drugs, the misuse of pain relievers is most common, totaling about 3.8 million users aged 12 or older. In addition, three fifths of those who misused psychotherapeutic drugs also reported misusing pain relievers, which generally include synthetic, semi-synthetic, and nonsynthetic opioid medications, such as fentanyl, codeine, oxycodone, and hydrocodone. In fact, some studies have reported that prescription pain reliever misuse is more common than the use of any illicit drug in the United States except for marijuana (Volkow, 2014).

TABLE 5.1 *Common Street Drugs*

DRUGS OR ALCOHOL	STREET NAMES
Alcohol	Booze, Brew, Liquor
Anabolic Steroids	Juice, Roids
Bath Salts	Bloom, Cloud Nine, Vanilla Sky, White Lightning
Cocaine	Blow, Bump, C, Charlie, Coca, Coke, Flake, Rock, Snow, Toot
Cough and Cold Medicines	Candy, Dex, Drank, Robo, Robotripping, Skittles, Triple C, Tussin, Velvet
Heroin	Black Tar, H, Horse, Junk, Ska, Smack
Inhalants	Bold, Laughing Gas, Poppers, Snappers, Whippets
Marijuana	Grass, Herb, Mary Jane, Pot, Reefer, Skunk, Weed
MDMA (Ecstasy or Molly)	Adam, Beans, Clarity, E, Hug, Love Drug, X, XTC
Methamphetamine (Meth)	Chalk, Crank, Crystal, Fire, Glass, Go Fast, Ice, Speed, Tina
Prescription Depressant Medications	A-minus, Barbs, Candy, Downers, Phennies, Red Birds, Reds, Sleeping Pills, Tooies, Tranks, Yellow Jackets, Yellows, Zombie Pills
Prescription Drugs	Barbs, Candy, Oxy, Percs, Reds, Speed, Tranks, Vikes
Prescription Pain Medications (Opioids)	Happy Pills, Hillbilly Heroin, OC, Oxy, Oxycotton, Percs, Vikes
Prescription Stimulant Medications (Amphetamines)	Bennies, Black Beauties, Hearts, Roses, Skippy, Speed, The Smart Drug, Uppers, Vitamin R
Salvia	Maria Pastora, Sally-D, Salvia divinorum, Shepherdess's Herb, Ska Pastora
Spice	Fake Weed, K2, Moon Rocks, Skunk, Yucatan Fire

Source: National Institute on Drug Abuse for Teens (NIDA, 2017)

Table 5.2 also shows that stimulants are widely used and abused, with a total of 1.7 million people aged 12 or older having a history of misusing such controlled substances. Stimulants consist of methamphetamine, amphetamine, dextroamphetamine, and phentermine products; mazindol products; and methylphenidate or dexmethylphenidate products. The latter are typically used by medical doctors to treat neurological disorders, asthma, and other respiratory problems. According to the NIDA (2016), stimulants increase alertness, attention, and energy. Stimulants also elevate blood pressure, heart rate, and respiration.

Common types of tranquilizers include benzodiazepines, meprobamate products, and muscle relaxants, which are prescribed to treat attention deficit hyperactivity disorder and a variety of other conditions (Bose et al., 2016; Burwell, 2016). As the name suggests, tranquilizers and similar prescription drugs induce tranquility in a person or animals. Tranquilizers are used to treat anxiety, insomnia, and severe or acute pain and are often used for end-of-life care.

An estimated 400,000 or about 0.2% of people aged 12 or older have some history of misusing sedatives, which consist of a wide variety of drugs that sedate or cause depression of the central nervous system. This drug category covers temazepam, flurazepam, triazolam, and barbiturates. When ingested, sedatives slow brain activity. About 1.9 million or 0.7% of respondents who completed the survey abused tranquilizer-type prescription drugs. In addition, an estimated 6.4 million people aged 12 or older misused psychotherapeutic

TABLE 5.2 *Illicit Drug Use Among Persons Aged 12 or Older in 2015 and 2016*

	YEAR 2015		MONTH 2015		YEAR 2016		MONTH 2016	
In Thousands	**1,000s**	**%**	**1,000s**	**%**	**1,000s**	**%**	**1,000s**	**%**
Illicit Drugs	47,730	17.8	27,080	10.1	48,501	18.0	28,564	10.6
Marijuana	36,043	13.5	22,226	8.3	37,570	13.9	23,981	8.9
Cocaine	4,828	1.8	1,876	0.7	5,071	1.9	1,874	0.7
Crack	833	0.3	394	0.1	882	0.3	432	0.2
Heroin	828	0.3	329	0.1	948	0.4	475	0.2
Hallucinogens	4692	1.8	1,240	0.5	4,903	1.8	1,390	0.5
Lysergic acid diethylamide (LSD)	1,535	0.6	352	0.1	1,896	0.7	374	0.1
Phencyclidine (PCP)	120	0.0	25	0.0	103	0.0	21	0.0
Ecstasy	2,560	1.0	557	0.2	2,485	0.9	619	0.2
Inhalants	1,759	0.7	527	0.2	1,660	0.6	600	0.2
Methamphetamine	1,713	0.6	897	0.3	1,391	0.5	667	0.2
Psychotherapeutics	18,942	7.1	6,365	2.4	18,671	6.9	6,207	2.3
Pain Relievers	12,462	4.7	3,775	1.4	11,517	4.3	3,350	1.2
Tranquilizers	6,050	2.3	1,874	0.7	6,060	2.2	1,953	0.7
Stimulants	5,251	2.0	1,653	0.6	5,647	2.1	1,735	0.6
Sedatives	1,511	0.6	446	0.2	1,531	0.6	497	0.2
Opioids (Heroin and Pain Reliever)	**12,693**	**4.7**	**3,963**	**1.5**	**11,824**	**4.4**	**3,649**	**1.4**

Source: 2016 National Survey on Drug Use and Health: Detailed Tables (CBHSQ, 2017)

medication in 2015, which amounts to about 2.4% of people (Bose et al., 2016). These medications are having a considerable negative effect on public health and safety in every major American city.

Alcohol Misuse and Abuse

The misuse and abuse of alcohol is a serious public health and safety issue. With this fact in mind, the NSDUH classifies alcohol use and abuse in three categories: (1) alcohol use, (2) binge drinking, and (3) heavy alcohol use. Alcohol use is defined as any use of alcohol in the 3 days that preceded the survey. Binge drinking is defined as the consumption of five or more standard alcoholic drinks by men and four for women on the same occasion on at least 1 day within a 30-day period. Heavy drinking refers to the consumption of eight or more drinks per week for women and 15 or more drinks per week for men (Burwell, 2016). Reports show that of the 51.7% of people aged 12 or older who are alcohol users, 66.7% are confirmed binge alcohol users and 17.3% meet the criteria for "heavy" alcohol use. In 2015, alone a total of 138.3 million Americans aged 12 or older used alcohol, 66.7 million engaged in binge drinking, while 17.3 million reported heavy alcohol use (Bose et al., 2016).

In addition, although underage drinking is prohibited in all 50 states and the District of Columbia, an estimated 7.7% of people between the ages of 12 and 20 engage in underage alcohol-related violations, 5.1% reported participation in binge alcohol use, and 1.3% in heavy alcohol use, respectively (Bose et al., 2016). Consequently, approximately 20.8 million people have a substance use disorder because of the use or abuse of alcohol or illicit drugs, and 15.7 million people used alcohol while 7.7 million people had illicit drug use disorders or used those drugs.

CONSEQUENCES OF CONTROLLED SUBSTANCE-RELATED OFFENSES

The nonmedical use of prescription or psychotherapeutic medication, along with cocaine use, seems to be on the rise with devastating consequences. The Commission on Combating Drug Addiction and the Opioid Crisis report recognized the extent to which the opioid crisis has heightened some of those consequences. Among other pronouncements, the report declared that an estimated 142 Americans die every day from drug overdoses. The report argued that between 1999 and 2015, more than 560,000 people died in the United States from drug overdoses. In other words, "drug overdoses now kill more people than gun homicides and car crashes combined" (Christie et al., 2017, p. 115; Commission Members, 2017).

The sentiments expressed in the commission's report were equally expressed during a hearing conducted by the Senate Caucus on International Narcotics Control. Speaking on behalf of the NIDA at the Senate hearing, Dr. Nora D. Volkow (2014) stated, "The abuse of and addiction to opioids such as heroin, morphine, and prescription pain relievers is a serious global problem that affects the health, social, and economic welfare of all societies." According to Volkow, "An estimated 2.1 million people in the United States have substance use-related disorders related to prescription opioid pain relievers alone" (Volkow, 2014, p. 1). This high rate of controlled substance use and abuse is a serious public safety and health problem. The gravity of the problem explains why in October 2017 the U.S. federal government declared the opioid crisis as a nationwide public health emergency, arguing that the epidemic kills more people than alcohol.

Effect of Substance Use or Abuse Disorder

Each year, the misuse of alcohol, illicit drugs, prescription medications, and other controlled substances costs the United States more than $400 billion, mainly because of the loss of workplace productivity, health-care expenses, and law enforcement responses to substance-related crimes. These behaviors also produce direct and indirect medical and mental health consequences for individuals. In addition, the misuse of alcohol or drugs can seriously harm the user or people who surround the user. Controlled substances also seriously affect individual behaviors and attitudes (Burwell, 2016).

At minimum, alcohol and drug misuse lead to alcohol and drug use disorders that currently affect millions of Americans. Substance use disorders are medical conditions caused by the repeated misuse of a controlled substance or substances. The conditions become serious when the abused substances begin to clinically impair the health and social functioning of the user or causes the individual to fail to satisfactorily fulfill his or her social and legal responsibilities. These consequences are generally caused by compulsive or uncontrolled use of one or more substances.

In 2015, over 7.8% or 20.8 million people aged 12 or older had diagnosable forms of substance use disorder, and about 21.7 million needed substance abuse treatment. The majority of such persons or 15.7 million (5.9%) of the population suffered from alcohol use disorders.

A sizable number (2.9% or 7.7 million) of the population had illicit drug use-related disorders. Marijuana use disorder accounted for only four million or 1.5% of the population, and pain reliever use disorder affected up to two million or 0.8% of the population (Bose et al., 2016).

Another obvious consequence of substance use and abuse is the heavy burden the habit places on public resources, such as costly hospital emergency department visits (Alber et al., 2015). According to Drug Enforcement Administration reports, in 2010, there were an estimated 53,542 emergency department visits associated with just PCP use. In 2011, there were 1.2 million emergency department visits involving the nonmedical use of all prescription drugs, and approximately 488,000 emergency room visits were for opioid pain relievers (DEA, 2013). These figures represent a significant change, considering that 7 years earlier (in 2014), only 173,000 of such cases were recorded (Volkow, 2014). Undoubtedly, these visits put significant pressure on public resources.

Obviously, the number one consequence of substance abuse disorder is addiction, which typically leads to serious consequences, such as death and disease. The list of long-term medical and mental health consequences is extensive and consists of liver and pancreatic diseases, hypertension, stroke, and cardiovascular and cardiopulmonary diseases, as well as human immunodeficiency virus (HIV), hepatitis, and other infectious diseases, plus cancers of the oral cavity, esophagus, larynx, pharynx, colon, and rectum (Bose et al., 2016; Burwell, 2016). In addition, each year, more than 2,200 alcohol overdose deaths occurred in the United States. Another 9,967 people are killed in motor vehicle crashes each year, and 31% of all traffic-related fatalities in the United States are associated with DUI (Burwell, 2016). Furthermore, the rate of drug overdose deaths in 2015 was 16.3 per 100,000 U.S. residents, 2.5 times more than the 6.1 rate in 1999 (Hedegaard et al., 2017).

Controlled substances alter human brain functions under certain conditions and thus compromise an individual's ability to recognize and prioritize needs. Controlled substances also increase compulsive behaviors, which either increase the frequency of contact with law enforcement or make interactions between law enforcement and offenders more difficult and cumbersome. These effects are felt within every criminal justice institution. At the very least, the fact that the mere possession of certain controlled substances constitutes a felony in many instances and that most offenders commit particularly acquisitive crimes to finance their habits means more headaches for law enforcement agencies.

Substance abuse and use also impair offenders' ability to think rationally. It is, therefore, not surprising that 49.5% of the 185,917 prisoners under federal correctional jurisdiction at year-end in 2015 were incarcerated for drug-related offenses, although the majority were there for non-drug-use or abuse-related behaviors. Similarly, 15.7% of 1,316,409 persons under state correctional jurisdiction at year-end in 2015 were there for substance-related offenses. Of that number, drug possession accounted for 3.5%, while 12.2% accounted for other drug-related offenses. In addition, 2.1% of public order offenses in 2015 were for DUI, and 12.1% were for other substance-related offenses (Carson & Anderson, 2016). In fact, 31% of all traffic-related fatalities in the United States were caused by alcohol-related behaviors.

CONCLUSION

Unlike violent, sexual, and general offending behaviors, some categories of substance abuse offenders can be classified as victimless offenders because their behaviors primarily harm them. When an assessment is heavily informed by such a background, the tendency for the needs level to rise above the risk level can be greater.

Some people may, however, disagree that the actual victims of victimless crimes are the offenders' relatives, friends, and the public at large who must deal with the long list of consequences associated with drug use. In addition, the controlled substance-related financial burden incurred by the public to mitigate the safety and health risk associated with such behaviors diverts critical resources away from other needed public services. It is, therefore, difficult to sustain the argument that drug use is a victimless crime.

Another unique characteristic of controlled substance abuse that should be taken into account is the fact that the pattern and scope of abuse are constantly changing. That is, the street names, types, and makes of controlled or illegal substances and the effects of controlled substances constantly change. The pace of change is sometimes too fast for an effective policy response. For these reasons, it is critically important for police, corrections, probation, parole, and criminal justice classification officers to update their knowledge constantly, particularly regarding the types of drugs or controlled substances available, as well as the effects of such drugs on offenders' medical and mental health and their social and economic responsibilities.

DISCUSSION QUESTIONS

1. Why are the use and abuse of drugs and other controlled substances so common in places like the United States?
2. Why does it take five or more alcoholic drinks for a male to qualify as a binge drinker, but it only takes four alcoholic drinks for a female to qualify as a binge drinker?
3. What factors best explain the rise in drug overdose or the heightened opioid misuse?
4. What is the best way to calculate the total financial cost of substance abuse and related criminal behaviors for the public?
5. What are the most productive ways to reduce the frequent abuse of drugs or alcohol?

REFERENCES

Alber, M., McCaig, L. F., & Uddin, S. (2015). *Emergency department visits for drug poisoning: United States, 2008–2011.* Centers for Disease Control and Prevention. https://www.cdc.gov/nchs/data/databriefs/db196.pdf

Bose, J., Hedden, S. L., Lipari, R. N., & Park-Lee, E. (2016). *Key substance use and mental health indicators in the United States: Results from the 2015 national survey on drug use and health.* Substance Abuse and Mental Health Services Administration. http://www.samhsa.gov/data/

Burwell, S. M. (2016). *Facing addiction in America: The surgeon general's report on alcohol, drugs, and health.* Surgeon General.gov. https://addiction.surgeongeneral.gov/surgeon-generals-report.pdf

Carson, E. A. (2015a). Prisoners in 2014. *Bulletin, 1–19.* https://www.bjs.gov/content/pub/pdf/p14.pdf

Carson, E. A., & Anderson, E. (2016). Prisoners in 2015. *Bulletin.* https://www.bjs.gov/content/pub/pdf/p15.pdf

CBHSQ. (2017). *2016 national survey on drug use and health: Detailed tables.* Center for Behavioral Health Statistics and Quality. https://www.samhsa.gov/data/sites/default/files/NSDUH-DetTabs-2016/NSDUH-DetTabs-2016.pdf

Christie, C., Baker, C., Cooper, R., Kennedy, P. J., Madras, B., & Bondi, P. (2017). *The president's Commission on Combating Drug Addiction and the Opioid Crisis.* The White House. https://www.whitehouse.gov/sites/whitehouse.gov/files/images/Final_Report_Draft_11-1-2017.pdf

Commission Members. (2017). *Interim report prepared by the Commission on Combating Drug Addiction and the Opioid Crisis.* The White House. Retrieved from https://www.whitehouse.gov/sites/whitehouse.gov/files/ondcp/commission-interim-report.pdf

DEA. (2013). *Phencyclidine (street names: PCP, angel dust, supergrass, boat, tic tac, zoom, shermans).* Drug and Chemical Evaluation Section. https://www.deadiversion.usdoj.gov/drug_chem_info/pcp.pdf

Hedegaard, H., Warner, M., & Miniño, A. M. (2017). Drug overdose deaths in the United States, 1999–2015. *NCHS Data Brief.* https://www.cdc.gov/nchs/data/databriefs/db273.pdf

NIDA. (2016). *National Institute on Drug Abuse (NIDA): Misuse of prescription drugs.* https://www.drugabuse.gov/

NIDA. (2017). *Teen drug facts.* https://teens.drugabuse.gov/drug-facts

Puzzanchera, C. (2013, December). Juvenile arrests 2011. *Juvenile Offenders and Victims: National Report Series Bulletin.* https://www.ojjdp.gov/pubs/244476.pdf

Volkow, N. D. (2014). *America's addiction to opioids: Heroin and prescription drug abuse.* Department of Health and Human Services, National Institutes of Health. https://www.nih.gov/sites/default/files/institutes/olpa/20140514-house-testimony-volkow.pdf

CHAPTER SIX

Sex Offending Behaviors

SEX OFFENDERS EVOKE perhaps more fear in citizens and concern among policy makers and criminal justice practitioners than any other group of offenders (Carter & Morris, 2007). This category of offenders is also extremely difficult to manage or rehabilitate. However, knowledge about the prevalence of key sexual offending behaviors and the characteristics of offenders is necessary for the assessment and classification of particularly offenders' social, clinical, and criminal histories, as well as how to manage offenders' behaviors. Broad knowledge about the various types of sexual offending behaviors and the characteristics of certain offenders can also help criminal justice practitioners identify useful questions to ask, go after specific information, and pinpoint effective ways to monitor certain offenders. After all, one of the key requirements for the successful classification of offenders is the ability to develop a good sense of what an offender has done and is capable of doing.

This chapter discusses the scope, typology, and trend of deviant sexual behaviors, illegal sexual acts, and sexual misconduct in general, as well as the characteristics of sex offenders. To that end, this chapter discusses the characteristics of sex offenses and sex offenders that police, court, corrections, probation, and parole officers typically encounter in their normal functions. The gist of the discussion will focus on child pornography, child sex tourism, child molestation, and sexual assaults and rape.

SEX OFFENDERS AND OFFENDING BEHAVIORS

Most sex crimes are committed against children or people under the age of 18. In fact, estimates show that 1 out of every 6 U.S. women and 1 out of every 33 U.S. men have experienced at least one attempted or completed rape as a child and/or adult (Carter & Morris, 2007). However, it is almost impossible to articulate the exact scope of sexual offending behaviors because most sex offenders do not come to the attention of the police. It is always interesting to ask people with limited knowledge about sex offenders questions such as where to find sex offenders. Generally, the immediate response to such a question is an image of an adult male sex offender lurking in the bushes or behind fences around schools or parks, or in shopping malls trying to lure or grab potential child victims for sexual assault. What is entertaining about this common response is the fact that the overwhelming number of adult sex offenders are acquaintances and family members, not strangers hiding in bushes.

Most juvenile victims of adult sex offenders are personally known by their victimizers, and, in fact, most offenders sleep under the same roof as their victims. They are acquaintances, relatives, friends, siblings, and parents or guardians. More precisely, 39.1% of sex offenders are acquaintances, and 51.8% are family members. Only 4.4% are strangers (Finkelhor et al., 2009). In 80% of rape and sexual assault cases, the victim is also known to the offender (Sinozich & Langton, 2014). Consistently, because of the ties that exist between victims and offenders, some victims may refuse to report their abuse to authorities. In some cases, victims may fear that they will destroy their relationship with their offenders. This is very important given that most offenders have some degree of control over their victims, making it harder for the victims to come forward. In cases where power over victims is not apparent, some offenders may use intimidation tactics and direct threats of physical or psychological harm to the victims or victims' loved ones to prevent the victims from reporting the offense to a third party.

Many victims also do not trust law enforcement agencies. Some may assume that if they report their victimization to officers, they will not believe them, or officers will take measures that will have a far-reaching effect on the victims, as well as the offenders. Some victims may even fear that contact with law enforcement will expose them to other criminal allegations. This is particularly true in cases where the victim is an undocumented resident or has had prior contact with the criminal justice system. Others may be simply too afraid of being harmed by the offender or may not want to make their victimization public because of shame, guilt, and or embarrassment.

DEFINING SEX OFFENDERS

The Center for Sex Offender Management (CSOM) provides a comprehensive definition of which behaviors constitute sex offenses or crimes. The agency defines sex offenses as the "unwanted sexual contact between two or more adults or two or more minors; or any sexual contact between an adult and a minor; or any unwanted sexual contact initiated by a youth toward an adult; or sexual contact between two minors with a significant age difference between them" (Gilligan, 2008). CSOM acknowledges that while some sex crimes involve physical contact, others, such as Internet crime, usually do not involve physical contact. Further, although CSOM's definition does not address deviant sexual behaviors that do not include another person or human victims, it broadly covers all penal violations that typically come under the control of criminal justice practitioners.

Sex offenders are categorized based on the means of sexual gratification, the types of sexual acts, and the statutory violations or labels. For instance, the "child molester" is derived from the legal label of child molestation, which refers to sexual misconduct involving children. However, the same behavior is sometimes referred to as pedophilia, and the victimizers as pedophiles, meaning persons who are sexually aroused by sexual acts involving children.

CHARACTERISTICS OF SEX OFFENDERS AND OFFENSES

Sex offenders and their offending behaviors are very diverse in terms of the degree of offending and the patterns, motivations, and individual risk and needs levels, as well as the factors that trigger the urges for sex offenses (Carter, 2009). Hence, few characteristics set apart certain populations of offenders from other groups. For example, according to the National Center for Victims of Crime, sex offenders are overwhelmingly male (adults and juveniles), with female offenders accounting for just 14% of sexual abuse cases involving boys and 6% of cases involving girls.

The list of crimes committed by sex offenders is long, but the most common sex crimes that come to the attention of police, courts, corrections, probation and parole officers are rape, sexual assault, child molestation, child sex tourism, and child pornography-related crimes. Although participation in any of these behaviors does not predict some automatic future sex crime, the occurrence of each category of sex crime serves as indisputable evidence that someone suffered physical, psychological, and financial harm and that the behavior poses a significant challenge for the successful management of the offenders who commit such crimes. There is, therefore, a need to know about the characteristics, breadth, and depth of sex offending behaviors, as well as the characteristics of the offenders.

Rape, Child Molestation, and Sexual Assaults

The sex offender population is quite heterogeneous. At the same time, certain categories of sex offenders share common characteristics. Child molesters, rapists, and sexual assault offenders are good examples of the distinctiveness of certain sex offenders and offending behaviors. The FBI defines rape as the "penetration, no matter how slight, of the vagina or anus with any body part or object, or oral penetration by a sex organ of another person, without the consent of the victim" (FBI:UCR, 2017). The U.S. Department of Justice defines sexual assault as "any type of sexual contact or behavior that occurs without the explicit consent of the recipient" (DOJ, 2017b). Sexual assault behaviors consist of forced sexual intercourse, forcible sodomy, child molestation, incest, fondling, and attempted rape. Child molestation involves any sex crime or indecent sexual activity between an adult and a younger child, generally below the age of 14.

Rapists who jump through their victims' windows or who murder or torture their victims are more likely to offend strangers (Craissati & Beech, 2004). In addition to the fact that rape itself is a violent act, rapists use greater levels of aggression and force against their victims than child molesters (Musu-Gillette et al., 2017). Of course, rape and sexual assaults are predominantly perpetrated by men; therefore, victimizers are more likely to assault females than males. Thus an offender with a rape history should be treated seriously. At the very least, what sets a rapist apart in terms of seriousness from other sex offenders is the fact that it is not uncommon for a rapist to murder his victim either to silence the person or because the killing is part of the sexual ritual.

Child Pornography

Another distinct category of sex offenses is the production and consumption of child pornography. Evidently, it is difficult to access a reliable empirical summation of the true nature and depth of child pornography production and consumption due in part to the strictness of the statutory criminalization of child pornography possession. Indeed, both state and federal laws prohibit the possession of child pornography, even in cases where the purpose of possession is strictly for conducting research. Despite these facts, a close examination of the limited information available on the phenomenon shows that child pornography is widespread and has serious consequences for child victims and society as a whole.

Of course, not all child pornography possession cases are the result of pedophilia, hebephilia, and ephebophilia desires nor do such cases always involve people with manifest patterns of sexual attraction to children. Pedophiles are people who exhibit persistent sexual interest in prepubescent girls between the ages of 10 or 11 and boys aged 11 or 12 years. Hebephiles are sexually interested in early adolescents, typically between the ages of 11–14 years old. Ephebophiles are offenders who harbor a persistent sexual interest in children between the ages of 15–19 years old.

Child pornography-related crimes are extremely serious, particularly in terms of the physical pain and suffering associated with the production of child pornography images and videos. For example, an examination of the records of 1,713 arrestees charged with child pornography-related offenses shows that 83% of the offenders possessed images of prepubescent children, and 80% of those images graphically depicted sexual penetration. Precisely 1 in 5 offenders (21%) had images depicting extreme violence against child victims. The types and degrees of the violence ranged from bondage and rape to children being gagged, bound, and blindfolded, as well as images showing children being subjected to acts of torture and forced to endure sadistic sexual acts (Wolak et al., 2005, p. 21).

According to the National Center for Missing and Exploited Children, Crimes Against Children Research Center, the Office of Juvenile Justice and Delinquency Prevention, and the National Juvenile Online Victimization survey, almost all offenders arrested for possession of child pornography were male, 91% were white, 86% were older than 25, and only 3% were younger than 18. Unfortunately, about 40% of offenders in possession of child pornography also had a history of sexually victimizing children and previously possessing child pornography (Wolak et al., 2005, p. vii). This data is not surprising because even the National Juvenile Online Victimization study concluded that child pornography offenders are sexually interested in prepubescent children or young adolescents and thus use images of child pornography for sexual fantasy and gratification.

Of course, not everyone in possession of child pornography qualifies as being clinically at risk of victimizing children sexually in the future. Indeed, many offenders charged with possession of child pornography are not necessarily pedophiles, hebephiles, or ephebophiles. On the contrary, some child pornography possessors commit the crimes out of a curiosity that evolves into downloading pornographic images of children. Other child pornography possessors are motivated by financial gain or simply by the desire to profit financially from the production or trading of child pornography (Wolak et al., 2005).

The production, possession, and distribution of child pornography is a serious global problem and a major challenge for any criminal justice practitioner charged with managing sex offenders, particularly pedophiles, hebephiles, or ephebophiles. The main difficulties are how to manage the various roles modern communication plays in both the facilitation and concealment of sexual exploitation of children. Communication technologies have also made it easier for sex offenders, particularly pedophiles, hebephiles, and ephebophiles, to move across national borders. Technology has provided sex offenders with access to victims in far localities. Child sex tourism is one example of how the development in communication technology has made it harder for courts and probation and parole officers to supervise pedophiles, hebephiles, and ephebophiles.

Child Sex Tourism

The World Tourism Organization defines child sex tourism as trips organized with the primary purpose of having a commercial sexual relationship with underage residents at the destination (WTO, 1995). The United Nations Office on Drugs and Crime (UNODC) defines child sex tourism as "the sexual abuse and exploitation of children by those who do not normally live in the location where the abuse takes place" (UNODC, 2014). The U.S Department of Justice defines child sex tourism as "the act of traveling to a foreign country and engaging in sexual activity with a child in that country" (DOJ, 2017a). Thus, broadly speaking, a child sex tourist is a person who engages in the sexual exploitation of children while away from a normal place of residence. These definitions cover children who are abused or exploited through prostitution, pedophilia, hebephilia, and ephebophilia-related activities, including acts involving child pornography (Blanchard et al., 2009; UNODC, 2014).

Child sex tourism involves physical sexual exploitation and abuse of children. The dreadful acts of producing, trafficking, and consuming child pornography are an active extension of the child sex tourism phenomenon because many child sex tourists are pedophiles (people who exhibit exclusive sexual attraction to children 11 years old or younger), hebephiles (offenders who possess a strong sexual interest in 11-to 14-year-old children), or ephebophiles (offenders with a sexual interest in 15-to 19-year-olds). These groups actively promote and get involved in the production, collection, and distribution of child pornography (ECPAT, 2008), and with the aid of communication technologies, such as cell phones and Internet-based tools, it is relatively easy for them to make contact with vulnerable children in foreign countries that are either too poor to police such offenders or who have inadequate legal systems to regulate the industry.

Reports show that many child sex tourists video record their sexual encounters with children for their own consumption, for sharing with other child pornographers, or for placing child pornography materials on the Internet in exchange for money or some other consideration, such as the exchange of child pornography for pornographic materials featuring other children. It is, therefore, not uncommon for pedophiles, hebephiles, or ephebophiles to hold membership in child pornography networks that distribute child pornography (ECPAT, 2008).

Certain groups of child sex offenders simply organize the crimes, while others only facilitate child sexual abuse. There are also those who travel internationally for the sole purpose of engaging in sexual activities involving children, while others do the same just to engage in similar behaviors out of curiosity. Thus not all child sex tourist offenders who make sexual contact with children are child molesters. Some offenders are sexually indiscriminate or are constantly looking for new and different sexual experiences. Others commit these types of sex offenses out of sexual curiosity that evolves into downloading child pornography images or physically participating in sexual acts with children. Lastly, there are offenders whose dealings with child pornography are motivated by an interest in financially profiting from the enterprise (Wolak et al., 2005).

Some child sex tourists' participation in child sex activities is situational, preferential, or experimental. Situational or opportunistic offenders may not have a true sexual preference for children but may engage in sex acts with them simply for the sake of having the opportunity to engage in sexual relationships and may do so without care for age. For instance, someone from a country where sexual behavior with children is criminalized and customarily condemned may be tempted to engage in such behavior if they find themselves in places where it is only mildly frowned upon by the public. The case can, however, be made that those who are not predisposed to such behaviors even at home are less likely to go from having no sexual interest in children to having sudden bursts of interest in engaging in sexual acts with children.

Experimental offenders primarily want to experience participation in sexual acts. The preferential offenders have a special preference for engaging in sexual acts with children and thus may actively seek out children for sexual activities. A person in the preferential category qualifies as a pedophile, or a person who is at least 16 years old and who suffers from recurrent sexual arousal fantasies or sexual urges or who engages in sexual activities with one or more prepubescent children aged 13 or younger (UNODC, 2014). Pedophile labels denote a clinical or psychiatric disorder. Unfortunately, however, most child sex tourism offenders fall into this category.

Most male tourists who want to engage in commercial sexual exploitation of children typically visit Southeast Asian countries, mainly Cambodia, the Philippines, Thailand, and Vietnam. These countries have historically been popular destinations for child sex tourists and thus are the world's prime child sex tourism destinations for western European, American, and Australian men who seek sexual acts with children (ECPAT, 2008; Montgomery, 2008; Thomas, 2016). Most victims of child sex tourists are children from the aforementioned and other disadvantaged countries where many children are economically vulnerable because of unstable or unfavorable economic and political conditions or the lack of effective legal systems to prosecute these types of crimes (Montgomery, 2008). It is worth noting that child sex tourism is an internationally growing billion-dollar industry that financially benefits many local economies and at the same time causes significant harm to millions of people, mainly children and young female adults. However, since this type of tourism serves as a critical source of revenue for poor destination countries, such places do not prioritize the enforcement of local anti-sex tourism laws.

In the period between 2003 and 2013, over 56% of all child sex offenders who traveled to Cambodia came from the United States (17%), United Kingdom (9%), and western Europe (30%). During the same period, 79% of the 210 known perpetrators that year who visited Thailand came from the United Kingdom (30%), Germany (19%), and United States (12%). Over 14% came from other European countries, mainly France (5%), Italy (5%), and Sweden (4%) (UNODC, 2014, p. 7).

Europeans and North Americans (mainly Canadian and American citizens and residents) have the economic means to travel to remote places in the world and pay for sexual encounters with children. A typical offender is a "dedicated paedophile that invests significant time and energy into coercing children into situations of sexual abuse" (UNODC, 2014, p. 9). These offenders groom vulnerable children and their parents by offering them money, presents, or invitations to their residences or hotel rooms, dinners out, or trips (UNODC, 2014). The exploitation takes place almost anywhere, including in brothels, on beaches, hotel rooms, parked cars, and in private homes in urban and rural or coastal settings.

ATTEMPTS TO PREVENT CHILD SEX TOURISM

The widespread phenomenon of child sex tourism, the various forms of abuse that are associated with such behavior, the challenges in apprehension created by communication technologies, and the ease with which offenders can travel abroad to engage in sexual acts with children create difficulties for police, courts, and corrections, probation, and parole officers. Consequently, more than 50 countries have legislated extraterritorial child sex tourism laws that seek to punish child sex tourists (Perrin, 2008). Unfortunately, however, very few child sex tourists are arrested or successfully tried and convicted under any of the countries' laws, including the British extraterritorial legislation (Niven, 2014), the Australian Child Sex

Offences Outside Australia (Ireland-Piper, 2010), and the American Extraterritorial Sexual Exploitation of Children Act (Andrews, 2004, Fraley, 2005, and PROTECT Act, 2003). The United States serves as a good example of what extraterritorial legislation generally tries to achieve and the common obstacles they face.

To prevent child sex tourism, the U.S. Extraterritorial Sexual Exploitation of Children Act allows for the prosecution of American citizens and residents who engage in sexual activities involving minors in any territories outside the borders of the United States. Of course, the act of traveling from one jurisdiction to another for the purpose of engaging in commercial or other forms of glorified prostitution involving adults is not a crime under U.S. law. It is, however, a very serious crime under U.S. law for any U.S. citizen or resident to travel abroad "with intent to engage in illicit sexual conduct" with a person under 18 years of age (Transportation of Minors Act, 2002b), or to engage in "illicit sexual conduct in foreign places" (Transportation of Minors Act, 2002a), or to participate in the "production of child pornography outside of the United States."

The Extraterritorial Sexual Exploitation of Children Act gives the United States extraterritorial jurisdiction over sex crimes committed against children by U.S. citizens or residents in foreign countries (Sex Trafficking of Children or by Force, Fraud, or Coercion Act, 2015). The law also punishes anyone who helps organize or assist another person with traveling for the purpose of engaging in sexual acts with a minor (Cole, 2011). To identify and successfully prosecute child sex tourists under this law, the U.S. government relies on the expertise of the High Technology Investigative Unit, the FBI, Immigration and Customs Enforcement/Homeland Security Investigations, the U.S. Attorney's Offices, and foreign governments' law enforcement personnel. Success in detecting, arresting, and prosecuting child sex tourists is, however, very tricky and rare.

It is extremely difficult to supervise sex offenders, especially those who are attracted to children and who derive pleasure from producing or consuming child pornography or participating in child sex tourism. One of the main sources of frustration is the role played by communication technologies and the vast economic differences that exist between child sex tourism and the countries noted for child sex tourists, such as the United States, Europe, and Australia. The fact that the government must prove beyond a reasonable doubt that a child sex tourist left the United States with the intention of engaging in sexual conduct with a person under 18 years of age in a foreign country makes it almost impossible for the government to act.

The United States is not the only country having difficulty enforcing extraterritorial laws. Given the power of modern communication and the ease of traveling abroad, it is practically impossible for any government or probation and parole officers to prevent a determined offender from traveling to engage in sexual exploitation of minors. Furthermore, improvement in modern communication technologies, especially cell phone and Internet technologies, makes it easier for sex offenders to frequently travel to foreign places for the sole purpose of sexually exploiting children. At the same time, the requirement of the government under section 2423(c), 2251(c) and 2260(a) of the Extraterritorial Sexual Exploitation of Children law to prove that a suspect travelled with the intent to engage in illicit sexual conduct or produce child pornography outside the United States makes it extremely difficult for governments to enforce extraterritorial laws, in part because those conversations and transactions are out of reach of the surveillance of the countries.

In addition to the high legal bar, there is obviously an abundance of online venues for gathering and disseminating information about places where child sex tourism flourishes. The

Internet also facilitates contact with local intermediaries who are always eager to arrange a child sex tourist's access to potential victims. Of course, the entire trip can be arranged and paid for from the comfort of one's home. There are also plenty of airlines that facilitate travel from origination countries, such as the United States, Canada, Australia, and United Kingdom to destination countries, including Cambodia and Thailand. Further, most Western and American child molesters and pornographers have the economic means to take full advantage of all the opportunities globalization and modern communities' technologies offer and to exploit the legal and economic conditions of destination countries.

OTHER SEXUAL BEHAVIORS

Child molestation, rape, child pornography, and sexual assault–related offenses are not the only sexually deviant behaviors handled by police, courts, and corrections, probation, and parole officers. Other sexual behaviors to consider when assessing and classifying sex offenders include voyeurism, frotteurism, and exhibitionism. These acts of sexual deviancy are tough to detect and difficult to prove and thus are rarely brought to the attention of authorities. Consequently, these kinds of sex crimes are hardly found in official criminal justice records. Yet voyeurism, frotteurism, and exhibitionism are very common, and the perpetrators are certainly at high risk of recidivating.

Voyeuristic behaviors represent sexual interest in, preferences for, and buildup fantasies about spying on people who are naked or engaged in sexual behaviors. Offenders with voyeuristic disorders, therefore, get sexually aroused by watching unsuspecting people in compromising positions. Exhibitionists derive sexual pleasure from exposing their genitals to unsuspecting persons. Typically, exhibitionists target specific groups of victims, particularly in terms of age and gender. The behaviors usually take place in public places, such as buildings or public parks. Frotteurs derive sexual pleasure from rubbing their clothed genitals or bodies against nonconsensual persons. Frotteurs typically act out their deviant sexual fantasies and urges in public places, most commonly on crowded public transportation, in dance clubs, and while standing in crowded lines. Some frotteurs engage in frotteuristic behaviors in private places, such as hallways.

Among the three paraphilic disorders, frotteurism is the least likely to come to the attention of law enforcement. This is, however, expected because many of the typical victims of frotteurism are children who are either too young to understand that they are being molested or who may innocently think that the offender accidentally bumped into them, or they accidentally made contact with the offender. Because the abuse often takes place with both the offender and victim clothed, the possibility is much greater for the victim to either not notice their victimization or to easily dismiss any bodily contact as something purely accidental. Even in situations where the victim becomes aware of their victimization, it is always difficult to legally prove beyond a reasonable doubt that the offender committed a crime.

CONCLUSION

Most sex offenders and offending behaviors never come to the attention of authorities. Consequently, what is known about sex offenders generally comes from the fewer than 20% of sex offenders who come to the attention of law enforcement authorities. This means that most sex offenders have a history of offending and participating in deviant, criminal, or delinquent sexual acts far beyond what is usually reported. It is, therefore, very helpful to pay close attention to both documented and undocumented histories of deviant and criminal behavior.

The accurate calculation of sex offenders' risks and needs is critical for the prevention or minimization of future sexual offending behaviors. Thus, for the purpose of classification, any history of sexual victimization should be treated as a critical risk factor for future sexual misconduct, irrespective of whether the offender being assessed is the victim or the perpetrator of the sexual behaviors. By carefully assessing every piece of information relating to past sexual misconducts, a corrections, probation, or parole officer should be able to direct offenders to suitable risk and needs management resources that could help the offender control his or her unwanted sexual misconduct.

DISCUSSION QUESTIONS

1. Which of the sexual offending behaviors discussed in this chapter is more difficult to assess, classify, and/or to manage?
2. What percentage of people who currently produce, consume, possess, or sell child pornography despite the long-standing effort to end the behavior?
3. What are some of the key factors that keep child sex tourism flourishing?
4. Besides child sex tourism, which behaviors should be regulated by extraterritorial laws?
5. How difficult or easy will it be to prosecute a sex offender for the act of frottage?
6. Is the rate of sexual victimization of children falling or increasing?

REFERENCES

Andrews, S. (2004). U.S. domestic prosecution of the American international sex tourist: Efforts to protect children from sexual exploitation. 94(2), 415–454. doi:10.2307/3491375

Blanchard, R., Lykins, A. D., Wherrett, D., Kuban, M. E., Cantor, J. M., Blak, T., Thomas, B., Dickey, R., & Klassen, P. E. (2009). Pedophilia, hebephilia, and the DSM-V. *Archives of Sexual Behavior, 38*(3), 335–350. https://doi,org/10.1007/s10508-008-9427-9

Carter, M. M. (2009). *Twenty strategies for advancing sex offender management in your jurisdiction.* Center for Sex Offender Management (CSOM), Center for Effective Public. https://cepp.com/wp-content/uploads/2015/12/twenty-strategies-for-advancing-sex-offender-management-in-your-jurisdiction.pdf

Carter, M. M., & Morris, L. (2007). *Enhancing the management of adult and juvenile sex offenders: A handbook for policymakers and practitioners.* Center for Sex Offender Management (CSOM), Center for Effective Public. Retrieved April 23, 2020, from Policy. http://forensiccounselor.org/images/file/CSOM%20Enhancing%20the%20Management%20of%20Adult%20and%20Juvenile%20Sex%20Offenders.pdf

Cole, J. (2011). Extraterritorial sexual exploitation of children [Paper presentation]. National Strategy Conference on Combating Child Exploitation, San Jose, California, United States. https://www.justice.gov/criminal-ceos/extraterritorial-sexual-exploitation-children

Craissati, J., & Beech, A. (2004). The characteristics of a geographical sample of convicted rapists: Sexual victimization and compliance in comparison to child molesters. *Journal of Interpersonal Violence, 19*(4), 371–388. https://doi.org/10.1177/0886260503262078

DOJ. (2017a). *Extraterritorial sexual exploitation of children.* Retrieved January 1, 2017, from https://www.justice.gov/criminal-ceos/extraterritorial-sexual-exploitation-children

DOJ. (2017b). *What is sexual assault?* Retrieved November 5, 2017, from https://www.justice.gov/ovw/sexual-assault

ECPAT. (2008). *Combating child sex tourism: Questions and answers.* Bangkok, Thailand End Child Prostitution, Child Pornography and Trafficking of Children for Sexual Purposes. Retrieved April 1, 2020, from https://www.ecpat.org/wp-content/uploads/2016/04/cst_faq_eng.pdf

FBI:UCR. (2017). 2016 crime in the United States. Retrieved October 13, 2017, from https://ucr.fbi.gov/crime-in-the-u.s/2016/crime-in-the-u.s.-2016

Finkelhor, D., Ormrod, R., & Chaffin, M. (2009, December). Juveniles who commit sex offenses against minors. *Juvenile Justice Bulletin.* https://www.ncjrs.gov/pdffiles1/ojjdp/227763.pdf

Fraley, A. (2005). Child sex tourism legislation under the PROTECT Act: Does it really protect? *St. John's Law Review, 2*(79), 445–484. Retrieved from https://scholarship.law.stjohns.edu/cgi/viewcontent.cgi?article=1242&context=lawreview

Gilligan, L. (2008). *Fact sheet: What you need to know about sex offenders.* Center for Sex Offender Management. http://www.csom.org/pubs/needtoknow_fs.pdf

Ireland-Piper, D. (2010). Extraterritoriality and the sexual conduct of Australians overseas. *Bond Law Review, 22*(2), 16–40.

Montgomery, H. (2008). Buying innocence: Child-sex tourists in Thailand. *Third World Quarterly, 29*(5), 903–917.

Musu-Gillette, L., Zhang, A., Wang, K., Zhang, J., & Oudekerk, B. A. (2017). *Indicators of school crime and safety: 2016* (NCES 2017-064/NCJ 250650). National Center for Education Statistics. https://nces.ed.gov/pubs2017/2017064.pdf

Niven, D. (2014, December 19). We have the legislation to convict British citizens who abuse children abroad—why don't we use it more? *The Guardian.* https://www.theguardian.com/social-care-network/2014/dec/19/simon-harris-british-citizens-child-abuse

Perrin, B. (2008). Our child sex offender laws should cross borders. *The Lawyers Weekly, 15.* https://sppga.ubc.ca/news/child-sex-offender-laws-cross-borders/

PROTECT Act (2003). "Prosecutorial Remedies and Other Tools to end the Exploitation of Children Today Act of 2003" or "PROTECT Act". Pub. L. No. Public Law 108–21—APR. 30, 2003 (2003).

Sex Trafficking of Children or by Force, Fraud, or Coercion, 18 U.S.C. § 1591 (2015).

Sinozich, S., & Langton, L. (2014). *Rape and sexual assault victimization among college-age females, 1995–2013. Special Report.* Bureau of Justice Statistics. https://www.bjs.gov/content/pub/pdf/rsavcaf9513.pdf

Thomas, T. (2016). *Policing sexual offences and sex offenders.* Palgrave Macmillan.

Transportation of Minors Act, 18 U.S.C. § 2423(c) (2002a).

Transportation of Minors Act, 18 U.S.C. § 2423(d) (2002b).

UNODC. (2014). *Protecting the future: Improving the response to child sex offending in Southeast Asia* (August 2014 ed.). United Nations Office on Drugs and Crime.

Wolak, J., Finkelhor, D., & Mitchell, K. J. (2005). *Child-pornography possessors arrested in Internet-related crimes: Findings from the national juvenile online victimization study.* National Center for Missing & Exploited Children, and Office of Justice Programs, U.S. Department of Justice.

WTO. (1995). WTO Statement on the prevention of organized sex tourism adopted by the General Assembly of the World Tourism Organization at its eleventh session, Cairo, Egypt. UNWTO Declarations, 5(6), 1–7.

CHAPTER SEVEN

General Criminal Behaviors

MORE PEOPLE END up in handcuffs in the United States than in any other country. On a typical day in 2015, for instance, there were an estimated 721,300 inmates confined in county and city jails. In the same year, there were 10.9 million admissions to jails. About 68% of that population had been taken into custody for felony-type offenses, 32% of the offenders were serving time for misdemeanors, and 27% were in detention for other offenses (Minton & Zeng, 2016). In the same year, as many as 3,789,800 people were on probation, 870,500 on parole, 728,200 in jail, and 1,526,800 in prison (Kaeble & Glaze, 2016a).

Some reports put the rates of incarceration in the United States at 670 per 100,000 persons, compared to 439 in Russia, 434 in Rwanda, 307 in Brazil, 114 in Canada, 76 in Germany, and only 30 in India. It is, therefore, not surprising that in 2015, more than 2.2 million people occupied the nation's prisons and jails (Sentencing Project, 2017; Walmsley, 2016). Of the persons who make contact with the various United States' criminal justice systems, 19% do so as a result of property crimes, and 11.6% do so as a result of public disorder and other general crimes (11.6%) (Carson & Anderson, 2016).

Indeed, the rate of violent crime and sexual and substance abuse offenses are well documented and classified accordingly during institutional and community corrections risk and needs assessment processes. However, the trends of general crimes and victimization and their effects on treatment outcomes are less documented. This chapter, therefore, describes the scope and trends of nonsexual, violent, and substance abuse–related offenses for which people commonly make contact with various branches of the American criminal justice system.

Broadly, general offenses include criminal behaviors such as shoplifting, wire fraud, human trafficking, narcotics trafficking, illegal possession of weapons, and other financial, street level, and public order crimes. Although these and similar crimes are not sexual, substance abuse related, or violent in nature, each of the behaviors can be easily grouped under immediate thrill-seeking behaviors or acquisitive offenses. Immediate thrill-seeking offenses include criminal behaviors motivated not by physical materials but rather some derivable mental comfort or pleasure. Acquisitive offenses are motivated by the desire to acquire physical material results.

Depending on the circumstances, some general crimes can, however, be classified as sexual, violent, or substance abuse–related offenses. For example, shoplifting can be an extension of violent, sexual, or substance abuse–related behaviors. If an offender shoplifts with the intention of using the proceeds of the stolen merchandise to acquire a weapon for the purpose of criminally harming a person or animal, then the shoplifting can be treated as a symptom of violent tendencies. Similarly, if someone shoplifts and uses the proceeds to buy a controlled substance, then the act of stealing can be a crucial extension of substance abuse behaviors. The same is true about a shoplifter who steals to acquire material goods that can be used to win the trust of potential sexual victims. Similarly, depending on the circumstance, certain types of arson, offenses against family, and acts of disorderly conduct can fall under the category of violence.

TRENDS OF ARRESTS, INCARCERATION, AND COMMUNITY CORRECTIONS

The BJS, the FBI, the Office of Juvenile Justice and Delinquency Prevention, and the Office of Justice Programs as a whole provide a wide range of data on the number of people who make unwanted contact with law enforcement agencies for a variety of delinquent and criminal behaviors (FBI-UCR, 2017; Puzzanchera & Kang, 2017). Reports generated by these agencies cover only about three fourths of the offenders who interact with law enforcement agencies around the nation. Nevertheless, the figures help form a healthy understanding of the trend of general criminal behaviors that fall outside the scope of sexual, violent, or substance abuse behaviors.

The Trends

Collectively, crime figures published by criminal justice agencies show a fluctuating pattern of arrest and detention, at least in the last seven years. Thus, a fixed trend of general criminal behaviors has yet to be established. For example, the FBI's 2017 reports estimate that in 2016, law enforcement agencies nationwide made 10.7 million arrests, excluding traffic violations (FBI-UCR, 2017). This figure represents a significant drop from the 14 million arrests reported for 2008. Table 7.1 further shows that the rate of arrests has consistently decreased each year, at least since 2008. The biggest decreases in the rate of arrests were in 2011 (5.7%) and 2013 (7.9%). The least changes occurred in 2012 and 2014, with drops of only 1.7% and 0.8%, respectively.

The gradual drop in estimated numbers of arrests from nearly 14 million in 2008 to about 11.2 million in 2014 is similar to the decline in the rate of arrests for specific general offenses, as well as the number of people who were under state and federal supervision during the same period. Specifically, Table 7.2 demonstrates that the 2015 U.S. correctional population reports by the Department of Justice's BJS show that the number of people who lived in correctional institutions and under the supervision of community corrections has hovered between 6.4 and 7.3 million. This represents a slight decrease in the overall rate of offenders under the supervision of the criminal justice system (Kaeble & Glaze, 2016b).

In 2015, there were 6,741,400 persons under the supervision of U.S. adult correctional systems. Of that number, 4,650,900 persons (68.9.8%) were on state or county probation or parole. Another 2,173,800 persons (32.2%) were in local jails or state prisons. Also, the total number of adults (6,741,400) under criminal justice supervision in 2015 represents a 4.2% increase from 2000, about a 1.8% increase in the number of adults on state and county

TABLE 7.1 *Estimated Arrests of All Persons 2008–2014*

YEAR	2008	2009	2010	2011	2012	2013	2014
Total Arrests	**14,005,600**	**13,687,200**	**13,120,900**	**12,408,900**	**12,197,000**	**11,302,100**	**11,205,800**
Property crime	1,687,300	1,728,300	1,644,000	1,639,900	1,646,200	1,559,300	1,554,000
Burglary	308,500	299,400	289,800	296,700	283,600	252,600	238,000
Larceny-theft	1,266,700	1,334,900	1,271,400	1,265,000	1,282,400	1,231,600	1,238,200
Vehicle theft	98,000	81,800	71,500	66,400	68,800	64,600	68,400
Arson	14,100	12,200	11,300	11,800	11,400	10,500	9,400
Forgery	90,100	85,800	78,100	70,200	67,000	61,000	56,800
Fraud	234,200	210,300	187,900	168,200	153,500	143,500	141,300
Embezzlement	21,400	17,900	16,600	16,200	16,000	15,700	16,200
Stolen property	111,300	105,300	94,800	93,200	97,700	92,700	88,900
Vandalism	285,000	270,400	252,800	237,600	228,500	201,200	198,400
Weapons	179,700	166,300	159,000	153,500	149,300	137,800	140,700
Prostitution	75,000	71,400	62,700	57,300	56,600	48,600	47,600
Gambling	9,800	10,400	9,900	8,600	7,900	6,000	5,600
Family victimization	118,400	114,600	111,100	116,700	107,000	101,200	102,300
Disorderly conduct	686,000	655,300	615,200	582,200	544,000	468,000	436,000
Vagrancy	33,900	33,400	32,000	29,200	27,000	25,800	27,400
All other offenses	3,835,100	3,764,700	3,720,400	3,532,200	3,448,900	3,282,700	3,274,400

Source: Easy Access to FBI Arrest Statistics 1994–2014 (Puzzanchera & Kang, 2017)

TABLE 7.2 *Correctional Populations in the United States, 2011–2015*

YEAR	ANNUAL TOTAL	PROBATION AND PAROLE		JAIL AND PRISON	
		TOTAL	%	TOTAL	%
2000	6,467,800	4,564,900	70.5	1,945,400	30
2005	7,055,600	4,946,600	70.1	2,200,400	31.1
2006	7,199,600	5,035,000	69.9	2,256,600	31.3
2007	7,339,600	5,119,000	69.7	2,296,400	31.2
2008	7,312,600	5,093,400	69.5	2,310,300	31.5
2009	7,239,100	5,019,900	69.3	2,297,700	31.7
2010	7,089,000	4,888,500	69.9	2,279,100	32.1
2011	6,994,500	4,818,300	68.8	2,252,500	32.2
2012	6,949,800	4,790,700	69.4	2,231,300	32.1
2013	6,899,700	4,749,800	68.8	2,222,500	32.2
2014	6,856,900	4,713,200	68.7	2,225,100	32.4
2015	6,741,400	4,650,900	68.9	2,173,800	32.2

Source: Correctional Populations in the United States, 2015 (Kaeble & Glaze, 2016b). Note that BJS estimates are rounded to the nearest 100 and in most cases may not be comparable to previously published BJS reports because of updated information or rounding.

probation and parole and an 11.7% increase in the number of adult offenders in county jails or state prisons around the country (Kaeble & Glaze, 2016a).

Despite the fluctuating rates of arrest in the past 7 years, figures for specific general offenses shown in Table 7.3 indicate that between 2007 and 2015, there was a steady drop in the rates of certain general categories of criminal activity. For example, on average, about 4,037 persons per 100,000 fell victim to general offenses, 407.7 persons per 100,000 were victims of larceny, and 525.5 of property crimes, excluding the general offenses listed in Table 7.3. During each year, an estimated 90.4 persons per 100,000 were arrested for burglary, 77 for vandalism, and 1,140.8 for other offenses, excluding nonsexual, violent, and substance abuse-related offenses and those crimes listed in Table 7.3.

TABLE 7.3 *All Arrest Rate per 100,000 Persons, 2008–2014*

YEAR	2008	2009	2010	2011	2012	2013	2014
Total All Arrests	**4,606**	**4,462**	**4,241**	**3,981**	**3,883**	**3,572**	**3,514**
Property crime	555	563	531	526	524	493	487
Burglary	101	98	94	95	90	80	75
Larceny-theft	417	435	411	406	408	389	388
Motor vehicle theft	32	27	23	21	22	20	21
Arson	5	4	4	4	4	3	3
Forgery	30	28	25	23	21	19	18
Fraud	77	69	61	54	49	45	44
Embezzlement	7	6	5	5	5	5	5
Stolen property	37	34	31	30	31	29	28
Vandalism	94	88	82	76	73	64	62
Weapons	59	54	51	49	48	44	44
Prostitution	25	23	20	18	18	15	15
Gambling	3	3	3	3	3	2	2
Offenses against family	39	37	36	37	34	32	32
Disorderly conduct	226	214	199	187	173	148	137
All other offenses	1,261	1,227	1,203	1,133	1,098	1,037	1,027

Source: Easy Access to FBI Arrest Statistics 1994–2014 (Puzzanchera & Kang, 2017)

Each year between 2007 and 2015, about 11 million people on average were arrested for various types of general offenses. The total rate, however, seemed to decrease each year, although with occasional fluctuation. For instance, in 2008, there were 11.9 million arrests of persons 18 and older, but by 2014, that number had gone down to just about 10.1 million arrests for various categories of general offending behaviors. These noticeable drops, as reflected in Table 7.4, also show that larceny-theft remained relatively high compared to other general offenses. For instance, in 2008, total arrests for theft or larceny offenses were less than a million (945,200), but that figure rose to above a million (1,061,100) in 2014. Although the recorded increase between 2007 and 2015 was moderate, any decrease in criminal behavior is positive for any law enforcement agency, and a flat rate is much better than any increase, no matter how slight.

TABLE 7.4 *Estimated Arrests of Persons > 18, 2008–2014*

YEAR	2008	2009	2010	2011	2012	2013	2014
Total All Arrests	**11,904,800**	**11,780,900**	**11,478,400**	**10,938,900**	**10,877,300**	**10,220,700**	**10,182,000**
Property crime	1,251,000	1,310,600	1,277,400	1,305,200	1,350,800	1,315,100	1,320,500
Burglary	225,000	224,600	224,600	234,700	229,800	209,700	197,400
Larceny-theft	945,200	1,017,300	990,300	1,011,200	1,058,200	1,045,600	1,061,100
Vehicle theft	73,200	61,900	55,700	52,400	55,800	52,900	55,700
Arson	7,700	6,900	6,700	6,900	7,100	6,800	6,200
Forgery	87,500	83,700	76,400	68,600	65,600	59,900	55,600
Fraud	227,000	204,100	182,100	163,000	148,800	139,000	137,000
Embezzlement	20,200	17,300	16,200	15,800	15,600	15,300	15,800
Stolen property	90,600	86,600	80,200	80,000	84,700	82,300	78,600
Vandalism	178,200	180,000	175,700	169,700	168,500	154,400	153,200
Weapons	139,900	132,500	127,700	125,300	124,600	117,400	119,900
Prostitution	73,500	70,000	61,600	56,400	55,800	47,900	46,900
Gambling	8,200	8,600	8,600	7,600	6,900	5,300	5,100
Family victimization	112,700	110,100	107,300	113,200	103,700	98,400	99,000
Disorderly conduct	497,500	485,200	459,200	443,000	423,900	372,600	355,400
All other offenses	3,474,900	3,441,400	3,423,600	3,267,300	3,209,200	3,087,500	3,088,200

Source: Easy Access to FBI Arrest Statistics 1994–2014 (Puzzanchera & Kang, 2017)

Increases in arrest rates of adult offenders were more visible between 2007 and 2015 compared to juvenile offenders during the same period. Unlike the rate of adults that shows fluctuation with moderate increases in some years, Table 7.5 shows that in 2008, adults represented 85% of the 14 million arrests. In 2014, the rate of adult offenders who were arrested was 90.8% of the 11.2 million arrests for that year, 90.4% for 2013, and 89.1% for 2012. At the same time, the rate of arrestees under 18 has been gradually dropping. During the same period, the rate of juvenile arrests dropped from 14.9% of the estimated 14 million arrests in 2008 to only 9.1% of the 11.2 million arrests in 2014. Similar reductions were recorded each year beginning in 2008.

TABLE 7.5 *Distribution of Arrest Figures*

YEAR	2008	2009	2010	2011	2012	2013	2014
Total of all arrests	**14,005,600**	**13,687,200**	**13,120,900**	**12,408,900**	**12,197,000**	**11,302,100**	**11,205,800**
Adult %	85	86	87.4	8.1	89.1	90.4	90.8
Juveniles %	14.9	13.9	12.5	11.8	10.8	9.5	9.1

While adult offending behaviors have been trending down, the patterns are higher compared to juveniles and continue to creep up in each behavioral category (Table 7.6). For example, adult offenders committed over 90% of the offenses of fraud, forgery, crimes against family, embezzlement, prostitution and 80% of property crime, burglary, larceny-theft, motor

TABLE 7.6 *Percent of All Arrests Involving Persons Age 18 and Over*

YEAR	2008	2009	2010	2011	2012	2013	2014
Total Arrests	**85.00%**	**86.10%**	**87.50%**	**88.20%**	**89.20%**	**90.40%**	**90.90%**
Property crime	74.10%	75.80%	77.70%	79.60%	82.10%	84.30%	85.00%
Burglary	72.90%	75.00%	77.50%	79.10%	81.00%	83.00%	83.00%
Larceny-theft	74.60%	76.20%	77.90%	79.90%	82.50%	84.90%	85.70%
Vehicle theft	74.60%	75.70%	78.00%	78.90%	81.00%	82.00%	81.50%
Arson	54.20%	56.30%	59.60%	58.30%	61.90%	65.00%	66.40%
Forgery	97.10%	97.50%	97.80%	97.80%	97.90%	98.30%	97.90%
Fraud	96.90%	97.10%	96.90%	96.90%	96.90%	96.90%	97.00%
Embezzlement	94.20%	96.60%	97.30%	97.40%	97.30%	97.50%	97.20%
Stolen property	81.40%	82.20%	84.60%	85.80%	86.80%	88.80%	88.30%
Vandalism	62.50%	66.50%	69.50%	71.40%	73.80%	76.80%	77.20%
Weapons	77.90%	79.60%	80.30%	81.60%	83.50%	85.20%	85.20%
Prostitution	98.00%	98.10%	98.30%	98.30%	98.60%	98.40%	98.40%
Gambling	83.40%	82.80%	86.40%	88.60%	87.80%	88.10%	89.90%
Family victimization	95.10%	96.10%	96.60%	97.00%	96.90%	97.20%	96.70%
Disorderly conduct	72.50%	74.00%	74.70%	76.10%	77.90%	79.60%	81.50%
All other offenses	90.60%	91.40%	92.00%	92.50%	93.10%	94.10%	94.30%

vehicle theft, stolen property, weapons crimes, disorderly conduct, and gambling. The same pattern is observed for all the years preceding 2014, with a steady pattern of increase beginning in 2008. In 2008, the adult population was responsible for 74.10% of the property crime reported for that year, and in 2014, the same population was responsible for 85.0% of the total arrests for property crime. Similarly, in 2008, adults accounted for 90.60% of arrests for all other offenses, and in 2014, the rate of adults arrested for the same behaviors was 94.30% of the total arrests for that year.

The differences between the rates of adult and juvenile offending are not, however, surprising. Evidence shows that in the past decades, public and institutional emphasis on juvenile rehabilitation has gradually overshadowed calls for detention and punishment. Consequently, juvenile correctional institutions, including secure care and community programs, have established a healthy history of commitment to treatment, training, education, and provision of somewhat balanced clinical, social, and legal services while at the same time holding youth accountable for the poor choices they make. Meanwhile, adult correctional institutions continue to focus primarily on incarceration, supervision, segregation, and accountability in ways that are often not guided by established clinical reasoning. At a systemic level, the adult correctional system's commitment to treatment has either remained stagnant or diminished.

ACQUISITIVE AND IMMEDIATE THRILL-SEEKING OFFENSES

One basic premise of classical criminology is that people choose to commit crimes after a conscious calculation of the likely benefits and costs of the offense if they are caught (Akers et al., 2017). That is, the pleasure generated by impulsive thrill-seeking crimes leads many people to engage in criminal activity (Callie & Ronald, 2013). Such calculations can lead to both acquisitive and thrill-seeking offenses, although these two categories of criminal behaviors generate specific benefits and, therefore, require unique responses. Acquisitive crimes are penal violations motivated primarily by the desire to acquire material benefits, often in the form of money or property, which the offenders use to achieve the desired gratification. Crimes such as theft, shoplifting, burglary, and robbery fall under this category.

Thrill-seeking offenses are criminal behaviors that produce some sort of immediate mental satisfaction or gratification. That is, the rewards that motivate the offending behavior tend to be nontangible gains or materials. Crimes in this category include the patronization of prostitution, illegal car racing (when no monetary gain is involved), certain categories of arson (those for fun), disorderly conduct, and acts of vandalism not overtly violent in nature. Offenders who engage in these behaviors derive personal satisfaction from the actual acts.

Knowledge of the distinction between thrill-seeking and acquisitive offenses can enhance the assessment and classification of particular need levels because acquisitive criminal behaviors often point to a lack of financial and material resources, although not always. For instance, immediate thrill-seeking motivated offenses can be associated with irrational thinking or the inability to empathize with victims or to wholly comprehend the full consequences of the behaviors. Hence offenders who fall into this category could significantly benefit from services that support cognitive behavioral change. Obviously, it is not normal to derive pleasure from vandalizing another person's property, hacking into or destroying another person's computer, or creating fear in people through acts such as cyberstalking or harassment. Indeed, such mindsets or behaviors can only be sustained by the constant use of distorted thinking.

Irrespective of whether an offense is acquisitive or thrill seeking, most general crimes are committed against property and public order. Persons who commit crimes against property affect another person's right of ownership by taking possession of the property, altering the condition of the property, or making use of the property without prior approval from the owner. Typical examples of crimes against property include burglary, theft, criminal damage, and vandalism. Public order offenses, on the other hand, are committed against society. These types of offenses include illegal behaviors intended to impede the smooth running of public institutions. Common offenses under this category include disorderly conduct, obstruction of justice, interference with lawful government operations, and similar offenses.

Cybercrimes

Many types of general offenses can be categorized as property or cyber-motivated crimes. Continuous advancements in technology and the Internet have made it possible for many of the general crimes to be electronically committed—cybercrimes cover a wide range of Internet or phone-aided illegal behavior (Rantala, 2008). According to the BJS, cybercriminals use computer viruses, worms, Trojan horses, spyware, adware, and other malware to infect and destroy; deliberately and maliciously vandalize, sabotage, damage, deface; or alter electronic files, data, web pages, or programs. The most common cybercrimes are cyber-hacktivism, espionage, terrorism, extortion, warfare, stalking, and cyberbullying. These behaviors seem to pose challenges for all law enforcement agencies across the globe because they can be committed across national and international borders and thus have no jurisdictional limitations.

Cyberattacks are normally carried out by activists against government institutions and large businesses or organizations. Generally, attackers will compel a government or institution to revise a policy or law or correct a perceived act of injustice. Most recently, hackers launched a cyberattack against the state of Michigan to draw attention to the Flint water crisis. Similarly, hackers attacked North Carolina's government websites to protest the state law requiring transgender people to use bathrooms that matched their gender at birth (Bergal, 2010). Cyberespionage is sometimes referred to as cyber-spying. The act involves the use of the Internet and phone communication technologies to obtain secret information from and about another country in violation of that country's laws. The act sometimes involves the use of surveillance viruses to eavesdrop on unsuspecting victims. In 2014, the United States indicted five Chinese military hackers for espionage. The five men, Wang Dong, Sun Kailiang, Wen Xinyu, Huang Zhenyu, and Gu Chunhui, are still on the FBI's most wanted list.

Cyberterrorism refers to the use of the Internet and phone technologies to illegally take over or gain access to governments' computer networks and misuse such systems to intimidate or coerce governments to act in a way that would further the terrorist's political, economic, or social objective. Cyberextortion takes place when an offender uses the Internet or phone technologies to demand money or other goods or to coerce specific behavior from other persons using the threat of harm toward those persons or their property. Common examples of cyberextortion include malicious attackers disabling a system and repeatedly demanding money or using ransomware that encrypts a victim's data and then demanding money for the decryption.

Cyberstalking is obsessive, repetitive, and unwanted contact with victims using the Internet and phone technologies. In addition to the unwanted contact, a cyberstalker typically uses false accusations, threats, extortion, and exploitation aimed at dominating victims. Stalkers may also use emails, instant messages, phone calls, and other communication methods to make or attempt to make inappropriate contact. Cyberbullying is the use of the Internet and phone media, such as chatrooms or text messaging, to bully another person. Common forms of cyberbullying include persistent electronic harassment and hateful or frightening threats. Cyberbullies do use various means that include impersonation, insults, and sharing or threatening to share embarrassing or compromising photos of their victims.

Each year, the Department of Justice and the Department of Homeland Security prosecute various types of cyber-based or aided criminal activities pursuant to the Prioritizing Resources and Organization for Intellectual Property Act of 2008. The crimes range from copyright infringement, smuggling and trafficking of medications, theft of trade secrets or intellectual property, economic espionage and/or computer hacking, and trafficking in counterfeit merchandise or cell phone parts (DOJ, 2016).

An early National Computer Security Survey by the BJS assessed 7,818 businesses around the country. The study found that 67% of the respondents claimed to be victims of cybercrimes. In the same study, about the same number of people reported having more than one cyberattacker, and nearly 60% detected one or more types of cybercrimes, while 11% reported cyber theft. The most common types of documented cybercrimes are theft and illegal use of personal or financial information, theft of intellectual property, destruction of property using adware or other malware, and use of spyware. In some cases, companies experienced offenders who hacked into their computer systems with the intention to steal vital information or to corrupt systems operations (Rantala, 2008).

Property Crimes

Most acquisitive offenses involve property crimes, such as shoplifting, motor vehicle theft, and burglary. It is, therefore, not unexpected that the arrest rate for property crime in 2016 was 420.6 per 100,000 inhabitants. In 2015, about 7.6% of U.S. residents suffered property crimes. Three million of the victims had their property burglarized, half a million had their vehicles stolen, and 11 million people suffered some type of theft. In the same year, about 7.6% or 10 million households were victims of one or more property crimes. Another 14.6 million persons, or 110.7 per every 1,000 households, were victims of burglary (2,904,570), motor vehicle theft (564,160), or theft (11,142,310) (Truman & Morgan, 2016). Percentage-wise, the most common crimes were burglary (10.1%), larceny-theft (3.5), motor vehicle theft (0.8%), fraud (2.3%), and other acquisitive crimes (2.2%). In the same period, of the 185,917 prisoners under the jurisdiction of the federal correctional authority, 6.0% were for property crimes, with fraud accounting for 4.7%, burglary 4.7%, and 1.1% for others (Carson & Anderson, 2016).

In the previous year (2014), about 11.6% of the 1,316,409 prisoners under state correctional control on December 31, 2014, were incarcerated for public order crimes, 3.9% of which were for weapons and 5.6% for other offenses. On the same date, 36.3% of the 185,917 people under federal correctional jurisdiction served time for public order offenses consisting of weapon-related offenses (16.3%), immigration violations (8.0%), and other offenses (12.0%). Furthermore, 19.0% of the estimated 1.3 million prisoners under state correctional authority on December 31, 2014, were there for property crimes such as shoplifting and vandalism. These figures are troubling considering that most property crimes do not end in incarceration (Carson & Anderson, 2016).

Property crimes, and indeed general offenses, also consist of financial crimes, which actually account for a large segment of general offenses (FBI-UCR, 2017; Puzzanchera & Kang, 2017). The list of financial crimes is long, but at the top of the list are falsification of financial information, false accounting entries, misrepresentations of financial condition, fraudulent trades, illicit transactions designed to evade regulatory oversight, self-dealing by corporate insiders, individual tax violations, fraud in connection with an otherwise legitimately operated business, and insider trading, bribing, or kickbacks. Financial crimes also cover health-care fraud, international and domestic public corruption, Ponzi schemes, money laundering, and securities and commodities fraud. The estimated cost to victims of property crimes, excluding arson, is about $15.6 billion per year (FBI-UCR, 2017). These pieces of information are, therefore, useful to criminal justice professionals charged with classifying and clinically responding to criminal, deviant, and delinquent behaviors.

CONCLUSION

It is important to stay abreast of how some general offenses relate to other categories of behaviors or how certain general offenses are informed by violent tendencies, deviant sexual desires, and or substance abuse behaviors. Of course, the important clue to watch for is any direct or indirect relationship between a general offense and other categories of behavior, including those informed by mental health. Obviously, trespassing is a general offense, but if the offender's behavior is a product of homelessness, and the homelessness is a product of substance abuse, then substance abuse is the underlying cause of the general behavior of trespassing. If the offender's homelessness is a result of a mental disorder, then the target need is mental health.

Of importance also are the distinctions between acquisitive offenses and immediate thrill-seeking crimes. The former can reveal a lot about an offender. At least the behaviors indicate that a good number of those individuals who engage in acquisitive behaviors are economically poor, economically unable to meet basic needs, or have a deviant behavior, such as substance abuse and gambling, which compels them to engage in such crimes. At the same time, the latter points more readily to mental health service needs. Indeed, it seems that many rational people would not find the act of hurting others thrilling or mentally pleasurable.

DISCUSSION QUESTIONS

1. List and discuss ways in which the Internet and phone technologies complicate the supervision of certain offenders.
2. Discuss some of the immediate gratification an offender gets from thrill-motivated offenses.
3. How much of the rise in adult arrest rates can be attributed to the rise in the number of females entering correctional institutions?
4. Does the continuous advancement in Internet and phone technologies negatively or positively affect the work of probation or parole officers? Explain.

REFERENCES

Akers, R. L., Sellers, C. S., & Jennings, W. G. (2017). *Criminological theories: Introduction, evaluation, and application* (7th ed.). Oxford University Press.

Bergal, J. (2010). *Hacktivists launch more cyberattacks against local, state governments.* PBS. https://www.pbs.org/newshour/nation/hacktivists-launch-cyberattacks-local-state-governments

Callie, H. B., & Ronald, L. S. (2013). Self-control, thrill seeking, and crime: Motivation matters. *Criminal Justice and Behavior, 40*(11), 1326–1348. https://doi.org/10.1177/0093854813485575

Carson, E. A., & Anderson, E. (2016). Prisoners in 2015. *Bulletin.* https://www.bjs.gov/content/pub/pdf/p15.pdf

DOJ. (2016). *PRO IP Act annual report FY 2015.* https://www.justice.gov/iptf/file/876191/download

FBI-UCR. (2017). *FBI releases 2016 crime statistics.* https://ucr.fbi.gov/crime-in-the-u.s/2016/crime-in-the-u.s.-2016

Kaeble, D., & Glaze, L. (2016a). Correctional populations in the United States, 2015. *Bulletin*, 1–4. https://www.bjs.gov/content/pub/pdf/cpus15.pdf

Minton, T. D., & Zeng, Z. (2016). Jail inmates in 2015. *Bulletin.* https://www.bjs.gov/content/pub/pdf/ji15.pdf

Puzzanchera, C., & Kang, W. (2017). *Easy access to FBI arrest statistics 1994–2014.* Office of Juvenile Justice and Delinquency Prevention. http://www.ojjdp.gov/ojstatbb/ezaucr/

Rantala, R. R. (2008). *Cybercrime against businesses, 2005. Special Report.* Bureau of Justice Statistics. https://www.bjs.gov/content/pub/pdf/cb05.pdf

Sentencing Project. (2017). Fact sheet: Trends in U.S. corrections. http://sentencingproject.org/wp-content/uploads/2016/01/Trends-in-US-Corrections.pdf

Truman, J. L., & Morgan, R. E. (2016). Criminal victimization, 2015. *Bulletin.* https://www.bjs.gov/content/pub/pdf/cv15.pdf

Walmsley, R. (2016). *World prison population list.* World Prison Brief. http://www.prisonstudies.org/world-prison-brief

SECTION III

Responding to Offending Behaviors

CHAPTER EIGHT

Competing Philosophies of Corrections

THE DRACONIAN POLICIES before, during, and after the Elizabethan era gave rise to the need for public policies to effectively protect society from criminal deeds and punish offenders for their offenses using humane and meaningful methods. That is, the correctional approaches being discussed in this chapter have emerged as a solution to past unjust, cruel, and unusual responses to criminality. The collective aims of these approaches are also to develop responses intolerant to inhumane and ineffective policies, such as branding, flogging, mutilating, and executing offenders for even minor offenses.

The main purpose of this chapter is to explain common philosophies that currently inform criminal justice correctional policies and practices. Specifically, retributive, procedural, restorative, and distributive justice are correctional philosophies that explain why some jurisdictions have capital punishment while others do not, why some states invest more in community corrections and others spend more on incarceration and less on community corrections, and why some people do not accept mental illness as a reason for criminality while others truly believe that certain mental illnesses can inform criminality. Ways in which retributive and procedural justice advance punishment while restorative justice and distributive justice emphasize treatment over punishment will also be discussed with the hope of demonstrating that correctional philosophies fall under three distinct criminological schools of thought—(1) classicalism, (2) neoclassicalism, and (3) positivism.

CONTEMPORARY AND COMPETING CORRECTIONAL PHILOSOPHIES

Investment in crime prevention and control is not a uniquely American practice; every country faces the challenges crime poses to public safety and, therefore, substantially invests in crime control and prevention programs. First, the best example of these efforts toward public safety is the fact that every country has law enforcement institutions charged with preventing and punishing criminal behavior. Second, every society creates and applies a level of fairness to prevent miscarriages of justice, whether intentional or unintentionally, while fighting crime. Third, public desire to control and to prevent crime and delinquency have existed throughout the history of modern human society, and certainly, the Elizabethan approaches are good examples.

Solutions to the problem of crime during the Elizabethan era provide a glimpse into the history of public responses to crime and punishment (Picard, 2016). Specifically, the belief during this period was that harsh and barbaric punishment could prevent and control crime. As a result, during the Elizabethan era (1558–1603), punishment was key. For example, some offenders were placed in pillories and compelled to stand with their heads and hands protruding through wooden plank holes. A crowd would then gather around the constrained offenders and throw objects at them while their heads and arms were trapped in the pillories. Interestingly also, although the public was not allowed to throw deadly objects at the restrained offenders, occasionally some people threw stones.

In some cases, offenders' ears were nailed to pillories. Others had their ears completely cut off as punishment. Some offenders were whipped until their backs were cut and covered in blood. Fornication and incest were punished by carrying the offender through the city in a cart while they wore a placard describing their offenses. The crimes of buggery, stealing, and robbery were punishable by death. Prisoners were burned, hanged, or disemboweled while still alive. Some condemned men had rocks piled on them, and some were left in dark cells where they were occasionally fed with foul water and stale bread until they died (Anderson, 2002, p. 295; Picard, 2016; Seiter, 2020).

Many of the policies that existed before, during, and after the Elizabethan era are not permissible today in the United States because such public policy responses to crimes would be viewed as violations of the Eighth Amendment's prohibition of cruel and unusual punishment. Some key Elizabethan concepts of punishment as crime prevention and control, however, remain at the core of most contemporary American correctional policies. In this regard, retributive, procedure, distributive, and restorative justice approaches collectively accept the notion that crime can be controlled and prevented. Differences, however, exist with regard to the methods that are employed to deliver certain correctional services, to incapacitate, to rehabilitate, and to punish offenders (Pence, 2000; Rawls, 2001; Solomon & Murphy, 2000; Wolff, 2006).

Procedural Justice

At its core, the procedural justice approach supports the belief that the criminal justice system serves justice by simply giving every offender or suspect adequate procedural rights and by complying with all the procedural practices in place to ensure fair criminal justice processing. This approach emphasizes the fair application of laws, policies, and procedures in ways that give accused persons fair chances in court and access to just and transparent criminal justice processing. Clearly, procedural justice advocates high respect for the fundamental equality of all humans and the equal treatment of all offenders in accordance with existing public laws. In this regard, decisions made at any stage of the criminal justice process must not fall outside the bounds of existing laws, policies, and procedures and must not compromise the need for individual liberty, at least as it relates to the subjection of persons to searches and seizures, trials, or punishment.

Procedural justice is mainly a corrective approach because its primary goal is not to prevent future criminal behavior but to administer the level of justice allowed by the law. Obviously, an argument can be made that the fair application of laws and procedures gives offenders a reason to have confidence in the criminal justice system and thus respect for and compliance with public laws. Although, in a way, such outcomes can prevent crimes, the core goal of procedural justice is not to prevent future criminal behaviors but to strictly apply the letter of the law with the hope that such respect for civil and human rights will warn future offenders that they too will suffer the full consequences of the law for the same behaviors. In other words, procedural justice does not advocate punishment or revenge but supports the belief that law is law and thus should be enforced or applied forcefully and objectively.

Studies do not, however, support the notion that a consistent and objective application of law across the board fosters public safety. Such conclusions obviously fail to take into account that access to procedural justice depends on many factors, such as societal views of the behavior, favorable jurors, fair media coverage of the particular crime, and access to competent attorneys (Meyer & Grant, 2003; Rhode, 2001, 2004). For example, there is evidence that, often, those who can afford to finance private attorneys get better justice than those who rely on public defenders (Gabbidon & Greene, 2005).

In practice, the American criminal justice system discriminates against certain offenders and suspects simply because of the type of offenses they are charged with or because of their personal social and biological characteristics (Meyer & Grant, 2003). For example, persons charged with terrorism, child molestation, rape, and hate crimes are more likely to receive unfair treatment than those who commit white-collar crimes, manslaughter, or resist arrest. Young Latino and African American men may not receive the same benefit of the doubt as do young white men when they are charged with gang-related crimes. In particular, racial bias leads jurors to convict black defendants more readily and to sentence them more harshly than white defendants, especially when the victims are white. In each of these cases, existing stereotypes, prejudices, and structural politics within the criminal justice system also lead to conclusions that are generally unfavorable to some offenders or accused persons (Bottoms et al., 2004; Gabbidon & Greene, 2005; Hymes et al., 1993; Lu, 2007; Umsted, 2014).

Retributive Justice

Americans live in fear of being harmed by unknown criminals because of the media, politicians, and people who believe that, generally, people commit crimes simply because of the pleasure they derive from the infliction of pain and suffering on innocent victims. Consequently, people are constantly reminded that criminal offenders are human enemies who should be viewed and treated as serious threats to public safety (Altheide, 2002). This fear of crime explains why children are told to not talk to strangers, people are warned against accepting rides from strangers or visiting the homes of strangers, and why many people carry pepper spray, firearms, or other forms of security arrangements or devices, even though most serious crimes, such as murder, rape, and child molestation, are overwhelmingly committed by family members, acquaintances, or people known to the victims. In the end, however, the fear of criminal victimization reinforces the grip of retributive justice policies on the American criminal justice system.

Retributive justice is the oldest and most commonly used response to criminal behaviors in the history of Western criminal justice systems (Akers et al., 2017; Williams & McShane, 2018). This correctional philosophy heavily relies on the belief that offenders weigh the benefits of crimes against the sanctions associated with such criminal behaviors before rationally and consciously deciding to engage in the criminal acts, consistent with the human desire for hedonistic or pleasure-seeking activities and for avoiding pain at all costs. Hence, the best way to discourage people from committing crimes is to attach severe sanctions to criminal behavior so that when people think about engaging in criminal acts, the fear of punishment will influence the cost-benefit analysis, rendering the pain or sanctions associated with a particular crime more powerful than the pleasure the criminal behavior may produce.

The retributive justice approach to crime obviously takes a zero-tolerance stance, with the belief that those who commit crimes must suffer the natural and statutory consequences of their behaviors. That is, "rational" decisions to engage in criminal activity should be rewarded with proportionate punishment that is capable of delivering both specific and general deterrence. Unfortunately, however, this assumption seems partly to explain why the retributive justice approach consistently fails to affect crime rates. Generally, people do not think about punishment when they are about to engage in criminal activities because punishment is strictly and legally meted out only to those who get caught. Instead, people concentrate on avoiding capture because logically only murderers who get caught are sentenced to death or life in prison, and only those speeders who get caught get traffic tickets. Also, only sex offenders who are caught are required to register as sex offenders. Those who avoid detection hardly suffer any consequences because they are viewed as "good citizens" with no criminal record. In fact, studies show that "76% of active criminals and 89% of the most violent criminals either perceive no risk of apprehension or are incognizant of the likely punishments for their crimes" (Anderson, 2002, p. 295).

The use of retributive justice in the United States also attracts other legitimate criticisms in regard to its effectiveness as a crime prevention and control approach. First, most offenders do not pose additional threats to society beyond the threats posed by the majority of so-called law-abiding citizens. Second, study after study has shown that the eye for an eye approach to crime does not work, nor did it work in the past. The clearest and most convincing evidence is in the United States, where retributive justice remains the main approach to crime control and where most criminal justice agencies divert vital public resources away from programs that target criminogenic risk factors to the infliction of punishment in the form of incarceration, death penalties and stricter supervision of pretrial releasees, probationers, and parolees. Yet despite the broad application of retributive policies, the United States continues to have high numbers of offenders in custody and high numbers of pretrial releasees, probationers, and parolees. In comparison to other developed countries, the United States also has the highest number of people with criminal histories and thus has a high number of people who have to deal with a number of post-detention civil and human rights restrictions, including restrictions on the right to vote, the right to live in or visit certain places, the right to work in certain industries, and the right to follow certain career paths.

Restorative Justice

The least popular, and at the same time an extremely important correctional philosophy or approach that deserves more attention than it is currently receiving, is the restorative justice approach to criminal behavior. This approach focuses on the restoration of cultural, socioeconomic, and moral conditions to the offender that existed prior to the occurrence of criminal offending behavior. The target, therefore, is to appeal to the humanity and sanity of both victims and offenders in the name of restoring a peaceful and acceptable communal relationship and environment. In other words, "The government should surrender its control over criminal matters to the victim, who is the actual sufferer of the offender's behavior. This process is believed to help offenders 'understand the harm caused by their actions'" (Siegel & Bartollas, 2016, p. 10).

Restorative justice views crime and delinquency as unfortunate acts against specific individuals and the community as a whole rather than against the state. For instance, a restorative justice system would view a case as *Peter v. John* rather than the *State of California v. John*. In the former, Peter is the victim, and John is the offender. In the latter, John is the offender, but the actual victim is missing, with the State of California acting on their behalf as the victim. The former is, therefore, better because restorative justice is mainly concerned with the mending of fences between the offender, the actual victim, and the community as a whole. The needs of victims, communities, and offenders are met through interventions that target the initial factors that informed the commission of the criminal behaviors. For example, if the offenders committed theft because of a lack of food, then the collective goal is to avoid future hunger and theft while at the same time holding the offender responsible and helping the victim recover from the act of victimization.

Restorative justice is both corrective and preventive. This approach prevents crimes by helping offenders develop empathy and teaching them about the consequences of their criminal behaviors. The process consists of the offenders taking responsibility for their criminal behaviors, confessing to wrongful acts against their victims, and asking for forgiveness. Victims voluntarily accept the offenders' confessions and forgive the offenders. The victims and the offenders then agree on how the offenders should make amends and reconcile with their victims and the community. The purpose of these steps is to correct the offenders' behaviors and at the same time to prevent future offending by the offenders. Indeed, each person that takes part in the reconciliation process learn about how a specific victimization impact victim, the community and the offender. That is the offenders, victims, and members of the community come out of the reconciliation or restorative process with a better understanding of the effects of the offending behaviors on others and on themselves. A restorative justice approach corrects and prevents crime by giving offenders opportunities to amend their relationships with victims and with their communities in lieu of punishment. Under this model, the victim is at the center of all the critical stages of criminal justice processing. It is expected that the experience will teach everyone, especially offenders, valuable life skills, such as conflict resolution, consequences of criminal behavior, and how to develop and express empathy for victims. Despite its therapeutic potential, restorative justice is criticized for allegedly failing to deliver specific and general deterrence messages to known and would-be offenders because of the lack of emphasis on punishment. This is, however, not a legitimate criticism because inherent in such criticism is the assumption that the alternative, punishment, meaningfully produces specific and general deterrence.

Distributive Justice

A long list of prohibited behaviors falls under the category of acquisitive crimes or crimes that are primarily motivated by a desire to acquire food, shelter, and other basic needs. It is, therefore, obvious that some relationships exist between criminal behaviors and living in poverty, in poor neighborhoods, in underfunded school districts, and in places without adequate social support or safety nets. In this respect, distributive justice practitioners view governments' failure to equitably distribute public resources as a partial cause of criminal behavior. In other words, the inequitable distribution of public wealth and other material goods in society can partly explain why certain criminal activities take place. Furthermore, the inequalities found in history and in public policy and institutions can inform certain types of crimes people commit to survive. Hence the just distribution of resources can weaken or minimize criminogenic risk factors associated with many high-risk behaviors.

Distributive justice is concerned "with the fair distribution of benefits and hardship, within a society" (Pence, 2000, p. 15; Wolff, 2006). In this regard, government has a duty to serve all citizens through the proper distribution of public resources, which is considered a crucial part of core government functions. The unequal distribution of public resources can also lead to social problems, such as drug use, abuse, and dependence, as well as gang-related crimes. For example, crimes and criminal victimization can be prevented if governments invest in the welfare of vulnerable populations, such as children, irrespective of racial, ethnic, economic, political, and social backgrounds.

The criticism against distributive justice is that the approach socializes criminal behavior because it allegedly rewards offenders for committing crimes against innocent victims. This claim is, however, not well-grounded because distributive justice is mainly concerned with the prevention of criminal victimization. For example, distributive justice calls for investment in schools, children, neighborhoods, poor families, and communities so as to prevent the occurrence of crimes. Even for those who are already in the criminal justice system, distributive justice mainly advocates for their access to resources that can help them avoid recidivism.

CLASSICAL, NEOCLASSICAL, AND POSITIVIST APPROACHES

Retributive, restorative, procedural, and distributive justice fall under three criminological schools of thought: (1) classicalism, (2) neoclassicalism, and (3) positivism. Classicalism draws more on retributive and procedural justice but passively on distributive or restorative. Neoclassicalism draws more on retributive and procedural justice and less on distributive and restorative justice because it sees the majority of criminal activities as products of rational calculations by the offender. Positivism draws mainly on distributive and restorative justice because it sees most offenses as products of a lack of access to critical resources and views criminal behaviors in general as matters that should be settled from the standpoint of helping both the victim and the offender recover from the harms associated with criminal behaviors. The proceeding discussions are, therefore, intended to provide an overview of these three criminological schools of thought. As shown in Table 8.1, each school of thought is unique but has certain characteristics in common with the others.

TABLE 8.1 *Core Differences of Criminological Schools of Thought*

	CLASSICALISM	NEOCLASSICALISM	POSITIVISM
Main Focus	Offenses	Offense and then offenders	Offenders and then offense
Causes of Crimes	Free will	Free will but takes into account age, history, and mental health	Biological, psychological and sociological conditions
Sources of Preventive Policies	Criminal laws and public sentiments	Criminal law and social research	Empirical and evidence-based practices
Response to Crimes	Punishment to effect specific and general deterrence	Punishment and treatment	Assessment and treatment

It is fair to say that each of the three criminological schools of thought has elements of punishment, crime prevention, and correction, as well as unique methods for correcting offenders' behaviors and preventing future acts of criminality. For example, neoclassicists approve of punishment as a deterrence but accept the role of therapeutic interventions where age, childhood history, or mental health are contributing factors. Positivists disapprove of punishment for the sake of inflicting pain and suffering and instead advance a method that uses therapy as a medium for holding offenders accountable as opposed to classicists who believe that the best method for preventing recidivism and stopping other potential offenders from engaging in specific criminal activities is a strict, timely, and objective application of sanctions.

Classical School of Criminology

Classicalism does not differentiate between individual offenders because classicists believe that all persons are (1) rational, (2) created equal, (3) interested in crime prevention in their respective communities, (4) endowed with the power to obey or violate societal norms, (5) likely to head toward pleasure and avoid pain, and (6) likely to be specifically and generally deterred when punishments are meted out fairly, promptly, objectively, and proportionately. Specifically, classicists believe that all humans are rational beings and created equal, with an equal stake in preventing crime or protecting society from harm but who rationally gravitate toward criminality because of the pleasure associated with crimes; therefore, the only way to deter criminal behavior is to punish offenders (Solomon & Murphy, 2000). Punishment serves three functions: (1) penalty for the criminal acts; (2) teaching an offender that criminal behavior is not, after all, a rational choice; and (3) deterring others with the fear of punishment were they to engage in similar behaviors.

The use of punishment as a deterrent has been around for centuries. For example, early versions of the Lex talionis policies, such as the eye for an eye approach to crimes, were extensively used for many categories of crimes, including petty crimes or misdemeanors. Carlson and Garrett (1999) described some of the sanctions and how they were carried out.

> Colonial America borrowed its judicial practices from England, where houses of confinement, or gaols, were used for short-term detention of law violators awaiting trial. In early England, confinement would have been considered too easy a punishment; the Anglo-Saxons sought revenge. Felons were killed, tortured, banished, transported away from their homeland and publicly humiliated. Corporal punishment was widely imposed, and the sanctions were extremely severe. Offenders were buried alive, beheaded, drowned, burned at the stake, boiled, stoned and otherwise mutilated in every imaginable way. All punishment was public, and even minor sanctions such as placement in the pillory were conducted in front of amused crowds. These sanctions were greatly valued and have contributed to the seeming bloodthirsty nature of revenge and retribution. (Carlson & Garrett, 1999, p. 8; 2006)

Classicalists identify two forms of deterrence: (1) specific and (2) general. The punishment of an offender serves as a specific deterrent because an offender is likely to avoid the same behavior in fear of suffering the same consequence. Punishment serves as a general deterrent because all potential offenders who are made aware of the pain inflicted on another will be generally deterred by the fear of receiving the same punishment.

Neoclassical School of Criminology

As the label indicates, neoclassicalism is an extension of classicism with a positivist angle. This criminological school of thought accepts the premise that criminal behaviors are products of free will; therefore, punishment can specifically and generally deter future criminality. Neoclassicists, however, also accept the conclusion that past criminal records, mental disorders, and age can collectively or individually explain certain criminal behaviors. It is the acceptance of age, criminal records, and mental disorders, in addition to rationality and hedonism, as having some form of causal relationship to criminality that distinguishes neoclassicalism from classicalism and that sets neoclassicalism apart from positivism—which recognizes a long list of criminogenic risk and needs factors, such as offenders' characteristics, family history, peer influence, academic achievement, and employment history (Anderson, 2002).

Neoclassicists believe in free will but also think that it can be corrupted by factors such as age and mental illness. These factors are capable of weakening the ability to engage in free will. Consequently, neoclassicists focus on both crimes and offenders but more so on crimes because punishment can regulate hedonistic tendencies and thus control crimes. For example, while neoclassicists share the belief that good—meaning strict—parenting can reduce the chance of future criminality, they also advocate for an aggressive criminal justice response if the parenting fails.

Positivism School of Criminology

Positivism informs the notion that different offenders need different treatment for different offenses because positivists believe that criminal behaviors stem from unique biological, psychological, or social pathological factors. Offenders must, therefore, be assessed and rehabilitated using policies and approaches that are empirically backed. Furthermore, since criminal behaviors are symptoms of many underlying factors, including mental, cultural, socioeconomic, political, and environmental conditions, responses to criminal behaviors must include a scientifically informed assessment and classification of each offender. The goal of risk and needs assessment is to explain each offender's behavior in terms of motivation and causation. This school of thought, therefore, focuses on offenders and not on crimes because most criminal behaviors are dictated by risk and protective factors. Those persons with more criminogenic risk and needs factors are also said to be at higher risk of committing crimes than those with lower risks and needs.

Solid public support for positivism emerged as an alternative to the classical approach to crimes in the 1970s, the period in which civil rights and feminist movements, along with social and behavioral scientists, began to get through to politicians and policy makers and encouraged them to embrace policies that could actually prevent and correct criminal behaviors using approaches that are humane, fair, and beneficial. In this critical period, particularly for the civil rights and feminist movements, people were concerned with criminal justice approaches that emphasized incarceration over treatment, and that was not working for, in particular, minority groups, including women and juveniles. Hence positivism banks on science, not criminal law, when responding to criminal behaviors. The use of risk assessment tools, as well as mitigating and aggravating factors, is important in this process because mitigating circumstances reduce the seriousness of an offense while aggravating circumstances increase the seriousness or risk of an offense, thus the need and desire for correctional services (Anderson, 2002).

CONCLUSION

The core purpose of each correctional philosophy and criminological school of thought is to address the issue of crime by minimizing or eradicating criminal offending behavior. While such goals exist with the understanding that no crimes can be completely wiped out in society, many serious crimes such as murder, rape, child molestation, terrorism, aggravated assault, and robbery, can be positively affected if public institutions adopt the correct clinical and legal approaches. In this regard, it is important to keep in mind that certain crimes require specific interventions. For example, a distributive justice approach and positivism can meaningfully affect theft, armed robbery, and other acquisitive offenses since such crimes are more common among people who are economically disempowered or who are in situations in which economic hardship motivates their offending behavior. Restorative justice can also be useful in criminal situations in which people already know each other and are bound to socialize again.

DISCUSSION QUESTIONS

1. Which American states or jurisdictions invest more in retributive justice?
2. Why do the U.S. federal government and some states continue to invest in capital punishment and incarceration while resisting distributive and restorative justice approaches to crime?
3. Why are many Americans afraid of being criminally victimized?
4. Which of the four correctional philosophies is best suited as a response to violent offenders, sex offenders, substance use or abuse offenders, or general offenders?
5. Why does the United States continue to have high rates of homicide despite its long history of imposing and carrying out capital punishment?

REFERENCES

Akers, R. L., Sellers, C. S., & Jennings, W. G. (2017). *Criminological theories: Introduction, evaluation, and application*. Oxford University Press.

Altheide, D. L. (2002). *Creating fear: News and the construction of crisis.* Taylor & Francis.

Anderson, D. A. (2002). The deterrence hypothesis and picking pockets at the pickpocket's hanging. *American Law and Economics Review*, *4*(2), 295–313.

Bottoms, B. L., Davis, S. L., & Epstein, M. A. (2004). Effects of victim and defendant race on jurors' decisions in child sexual abuse cases. *Journal of Applied Social Psychology*, *34*(1), 1–33. https://doi.org/10.1111/j.1559-1816.2004.tb02535.x

Carlson, P. M., & Garrett, J. S. (1999). *Prison and jail administration: Practice and theory* (1st ed.). Aspen Publishers, Inc.

Carlson, P. M., & Garrett, J. S. (2006). *Prison and jail administration: Practice and theory.* Jones & Bartlett Learning.

Gabbidon, S. L., & Greene, H. T. (2005). *Race, crime, and justice: A reader.* Routledge.

Hymes, R. W., Leinart, M., Rowe, S., & Rogers, W. (1993). Acquaintance rape: The effect of race of defendant and race of victim on white juror decisions. *Journal of Social Psychology*, *133*(5), 627–634. https://doi.org/10.1080/00224545.1993.9713917

Lu, L. D. (2007). Prosecutorial discretion and racial disparities in federal sentencing: Some views of former U.S. attorneys. *Federal Sentencing Reporter*, *19*(3), 192–201. https://doi.org/10.1525/fsr.2007.19.3.192

Meyer, J.A.F., & Grant, D. R. (2003). *The courts in our criminal justice system*. Prentice Hall.

Pence, G. (Ed.) (2000) *A dictionary of common philosophical terms*. McGraw-Hill Companies Inc.

Picard, L. (2016, March 15). *Crime and punishment in Elizabethan England*. British Library. Retrieved July 26, 2019, from https://www.bl.uk/shakespeare/articles/crime-and-punishment-in-elizabethan-england

Rawls, J. (2001). *Justice as fairness: A restatement*. Belknap Press of Harvard University Press.

Rhode, D. L. (2001). Access to justice. *Fordham Law Review*, *69*(5), 1785–1819.

Rhode, D. L. (2004). *Access to justice*. Oxford University Press.

Seiter, R. P. (2020). *Corrections: An introduction*. Pearson Education, Inc.

Siegel, L. J., & Bartollas, C. (2016). Cengage Learning.

Solomon, R. C., & Murphy, M. C. (2000). *What is justice? Classic and contemporary readings*. Oxford University Press.

Umsted, Z. A. (2014). Deterring racial bias in criminal justice through sentencing. *Iowa Law Review*, *100*(1), 431–453.

Williams, F. P., & McShane, M. D. (2018). *Criminological theory* (7th ed.). Pearson.

Wolff, J. (2006). *An introduction to political philosophy*. Oxford University Press.

CHAPTER NINE

Pretrial Service, Probation, and Parole Systems

PRETRIAL SERVICE, PROBATION, and parole officers are the true faces of community corrections. These officers are responsible for supervising some of the millions of offenders who are managed by one or more community corrections agencies and correctional facilities. For example, at year-end in 2017, there were 1,489,363 prisoners in state or federal correctional facilities, of which 1,306,305 were in state correctional facilities and 183,058 in federal penitentiaries (Bronson & Carson, 2019). In 2016, there were 1,506,757 prisoners in state and federal correctional institutions, of which 189,192 persons were under federal jurisdiction and 1,317,565 under state jurisdiction (Carson, 2018). Collectively, these numbers suggest that the number of persons in detention is actually declining.

The number of people who end up under community correctional supervision is higher than the number of detainees, and the differences continue to go up because of policy changes that favor community corrections over incarceration. For instance, on January 1, 2016, there were 4,586,900 adults under community supervision, of which 3,725,600 were on probation and 870,700 were on parole. At the end of that year, on December 31, there were an estimated 4,537,100 adults under community corrections supervision. In 2015, about 4,650,900 adults were under community corrections supervision, of which 3,789,800 were on probation and 870,500 were on parole (Kaeble, 2018). Of course, the differences between these data also suggest that the number of people under community corrections is going down. These changes can be attributed partly to the good therapeutic work community corrections agencies are doing, as well as the pressure of overcrowding in general on trial courts, defense attorneys, prosecutors, and correctional facilities that result in a high number of offenders being released from detention, allowed to plea-bargain, placed on probation, and being granted parole status (Cohen, 2012).

This chapter provides a brief historical overview of the community corrections system and specifically the history of pretrial release and probation and parole services' responses to criminality in the United States. This chapter also talks about the practice of assessing, classifying, and rehabilitating offenders outside the walls of prisons and jails. Probation is discussed most extensively because the story of probation is broadly the history of the American pretrial services, probation, parole, risk assessment, and classification, as well as the history of courts' reliance on investigative reports when choosing between incarceration and supervision under community corrections.

PRETRIAL SERVICES

The federal pretrial services system is active in more than 300 counties and in all federal districts. Every state has a pretrial services system in place to supervise tens of thousands of pretrial releasees (Mahoney et al., 2001). Pretrial service officers who work for those agencies serve "pretrial" defendants. The officers' main responsibilities are to help defendants who are released into the community before the conclusion of their criminal trials to return to court as required by trial courts and to refrain from committing additional crimes while on bail or on supervised release in the community. This arrangement did not, however, exist at the early stages of the American criminal justice system.

In the 17th and 18th centuries, pretrial release transactions were led by private individuals who were typically the defendants' friends, relatives, or employers. These individuals would post bail and assume responsibility for making sure that their bailed-out relatives, friends, or employees appeared at their next court hearings. Obviously, as the criminal justice population increased, so did the possibility of defendants failing to show up for court hearings, thus paving the way for the current commercial bondsman system. In this respect, the emergence of commercial bails bond agents did not end the ability of private third-person bailouts from friends or relatives, but the private surety system weakened as bail bond agents became the bridge to pretrial release: they would post the amount of the bail with the court and where necessary track down and compel offenders to appear on their scheduled dates and times.

BOX 9.1 MORE CRIMES MEAN MORE MONEY FOR BAIL AGENTS

Bail is a certain amount of money that is made legally accessible to the court to act as insurance that a defendant will appear at a subsequent court hearing. Bail amounts can run from a dollar to millions depending on the risk of the defendant escaping or committing crimes while on pretrial release. Unfortunately, however, the majority of offenders are too poor to afford high bails. As a result, defendants give a fraction of their bail amount plus collateral to bail bond agents. Once the agreement is made, the bail bond agents fill out a pre-prepared form that guarantees the full payment of the bail amount to the sheriff's office or the court if the defendant fails to appear at the next court hearing. Bail bond agents hold on to the collateral until the defendant is incarcerated or sentenced at the conclusion of the trial.

Bail bond agents operate with the expectation that the potential forfeiture of bail money and collateral will compel offenders to appear at future hearings.

Pretrial investigation reports, which are primarily concerned with whether an accused person will show up for future court dates or commit new offenses while being processed for current offenses, determine who is qualified for pretrial release and the type of conditions that should be imposed so as to reassure court attendance and a crime-free life.

In the late 19th century, the commercial bail system was the principal method in the United States to support pretrial releases (Mahoney et al., 2001, p. 7). This approach alone was, however, obviously not enough because the commercial bond system was only accessible by defendants who could raise enough money and who had the acceptable collateral to bond themselves out. Consequently, by the 1960s, the present pretrial release system, which emphasizes the release of defendants on their own recognizance, was already advancing.

This development led to congressional action, resulting in the creation of the current formal pretrial release-supervision system.

Congress enacted the Bail Reform Act in 1966 to mandate that defendants charged with noncapital offenses be released on either their own recognizance or without bail and, where necessary, released under pretrial service supervision (Cohen, 2012). The Bail Reform Act also addressed the process by which accused persons could be released prior to the conclusion of their trials. Indeed, the act was intended to make fairer any decisions about pretrial release or detention by requiring judicial officers to release defendants on the "least restrictive conditions that would ensure their appearance" at subsequent court dates.

The Bail Reform Act identified five factors to be taken into account when making pretrial release decisions: (1) the nature and circumstance of the offense, (2) the weight of evidence, (3) family ties, (4) employment history and potential, (5) financial resources, (6) character and mental condition, (7) length of time at current residence, (8) record of past convictions, and (9) past compliance with scheduled court proceedings. The goals of the act were reaffirmed in 1974 by the Speedy Trial Act, which created 10 pretrial service pilot programs in the federal court system that were "designed to provide judges with the information necessary to make conditional release decisions" (Mahoney et al., 2001). Specifically, Title II of the act authorized the director of the Administrative Office of the U.S. Courts to establish pretrial service agencies in 10 judicial districts. The act also authorized agencies to collect, verify, and report to the courts background information about defendants and to "recommend appropriate release conditions." In 1982, the Pretrial Services Act expanded pretrial services to all federal judicial districts, except the District of Columbia. The U.S. Probation and Pretrial Services System or the Office of Probation and Pretrial Services, a branch of the Administrative Office of the United States Courts, emerged out of these developments.

The U.S. Congress enacted the Bail Reform Act (1984), which granted judges the authority to look at the risk posed by each offender to the community when considering pretrial release orders since previously courts did not consider the specific danger and prospective criminal behavior of pretrial releasees. The Bail Reform Act of 1984 also reaffirmed the Bail Reform Act of 1966 and demanded that "at a detention hearing, the government is required by the act to prove by clear and convincing evidence that no condition of release would reasonably ensure that the defendant would appear for trial and not pose a risk to the community" (Cohen, 2012). This means that all offenders charged with noncapital offense are eligible for pretrial release unless there is evidence to show that such offenders will fail to appear at the next court hearing or commit crimes before the conclusion of the current criminal proceedings.

The call for a pretrial investigative report was extremely necessary. For example, according to testimony by federal trial courts, "Neither defense lawyers nor prosecutors were able to provide them [federal courts] with the requisite information for an informed bail decision" (Mahoney et al., 2001). One member of the judiciary, chairman of the Committee on the Administration of the Probation System of the Judicial Conference of the United States Gerald B. Tjoflat (11th Circuit), provided the following support for pretrial investigative reports at a congressional hearing:

> [T]he administration of justice is far better served when a magistrate or judge setting conditions of bail under the Bail Reform Act of 1966 has sufficient accurate and objective information regarding the defendant, his background, the offense and all other evidence

> that relates to the question of whether he will appear for trial. The system is far better served when the judge can make an informed decision, and pretrial services has made a major step in that direction. (Mahoney et al., 2001, p. 6; Tjoflat, 1982)

Pretrial service officers undertake the important tasks of investigating, analyzing, and reporting offenders' criminal, social, and biological histories. In addition, pretrial officers perform a wide range of other important tasks. In the following summary of the various purposes of pretrial release decisions and work, the American Bar Association captured some of the important duties of pretrial officers:

> The purposes of the pretrial release decision include providing due process to those accused of crime, maintaining the integrity of the judicial process by securing defendants for trial, and protecting victims, witnesses and the community from threat, danger or interference. The judge or judicial officer decides whether to release a defendant on personal recognizance or unsecured appearance bond, release a defendant on a condition or combination of conditions, temporarily detain a defendant, or detain a defendant according to procedures outlined in these Standards. The law favors the release of defendants pending adjudication of charges. Deprivation of liberty pending trial is harsh and oppressive, subjects defendants to economic and psychological hardship, interferes with their ability to defend themselves, and, in many instances, deprives their families of support. These Standards limit the circumstances under which pretrial detention may be authorized and provide procedural safeguards to govern pretrial detention proceedings. (ABA, 2019)

The tasks of pretrial officers include interviewing each person facing felony charges, gathering and verifying background information, creating reports for judges to aid them in making decisions about bail, and giving pretrial releasees access to existing community services. These pretrial service functions are necessary for many legal and therapeutic reasons. For example, the practice reduces overcrowding in jails and removes from detention innocent persons who do not pose significant threats to the public. After all, courts are more concerned about whether defendants will fail to return to court or if they will commit new offenses while on pretrial release status.

THE HISTORY OF PROBATION

The concept of plea bargaining, pretrial, probation, and even parole can be traced to the early history of criminal justice responses to crimes in the English system, which were anything but therapeutic. In this period, irrespective of whether a behavior was trivial or extreme, individual offenders were subjected to severe physical and psychological suffering, including flogging, torture, and execution. Obviously, none of the sanctions or responses were backed by empirical evidence or guided by the logical application of justice. For example, the English system's punishment of over 200 offenses with death cannot be justified using any therapeutic argument nor can it be defended as a just response to crime. In fact, in many ways, it was the desire to replace that unjust system that led criminal justice reformers and activists to push for more discretionary powers for judges so that they could make adjustments to sentences and make it possible for offenders to plea-bargain in exchange for leniency.

In the new system that emerged out of this reformation process, a plea for lenient interpretation of the law could be made to the court by offenders or others acting on their behalf. A defendant could also appeal to the Crown for pardon or mercy, and if a court determined that the offender was not a threat to society or that the offender could be rehabilitated outside of penal institutions, judges would issue alternative sentences similar to probation. Judges could reduce or increase jail time or exercise various forms of judicial reprieve, such as suspended sentences and temporary suspension of sentences based on the evaluation of each offenders' mitigating and aggravating factors. Even at the beginning of the 20th century, courts in the United States were still using methods such as suspended sentences for certain criminal behaviors, "laying the case on file," or "sentence deferred until further order of the Court" in response to criminal wrongdoing (Chappel, 1939, p. 708). The impetus for modern probation resulted from this history of judicial reprieves and, of course, the important work of John Augustus in the mid-19th century.

The history of probation cannot be told without the history of John Augustus, the father of American probation. Mr. Augustus was born in Massachusetts at the beginning of the 19th century (1829), where he lived as a successful businessman. Prior to volunteering with the courts, Augustus was a shoemaker in Boston and a member of the Washington Total Abstinence Society.

BOX 9.2 ABSTINENCE IS AN OLD ALLEGED SOLUTION TO UNWANTED BEHAVIOR

The Washington Total Abstinence Society could be best described as a religious Alcoholics Anonymous group. Members pledged to abstain from alcohol and to share what they knew about the harm alcohol abuse or dependence carried, as well as the benefits of abstaining from alcohol use. Members shared the belief that forgiveness and second chances went a long way in helping alcoholics live productive and alcohol-free lives. Members of the organization pledged the following:

> We whose names are annexed, desirous of forming a society for our mutual benefit, and to guard against a pernicious practice which is injurious to our health, standing, and families, do pledge ourselves as gentlemen that we will not drink any spirituous or malt liquors, wine or cider.

The movement took hold in the early part of the 19th century, and by 1829, there were about 1,000 societies with approximately 100,000 members. By 1834, there were 5,000 local societies and over a million members. Many of the chapters operated under different names, but they all shared the common belief that "total abstinence from all that can intoxicate" had a therapeutic function and, therefore, could put an end to the use and abuse of alcohol, which members of the Society believed were deviant acts (Maxwell, 1950).

To put his theory of rehabilitating offenders to the test, Augustus walked into a municipal courtroom in 1841 and bailed out a "common drunkard" who would become the first offender to receive "probation" or to be released to a third party for supervision on the promise to obey all laws, including special court orders, and to report back to the court about his progress. When the offender showed up in court for sentencing 3 weeks later in Augustus's company, he was sober and appeared to have completely changed in terms of his alcohol use and related behaviors. The experiment convinced Augustus to invest more in probation by convincing the courts that there was something meaningful about giving offenders second chances and about refraining from the strict application of the law in certain cases. For the remainder of his 17 years in his self-made probation officer career, Augustus would appear in court and offer to bail out defendants. After a period of supervising those offenders in the community, he would bring them back before the court with reports showing that each offender made significant progress in amending their thinking and behavior while out on bail under his supervision.

Throughout the period, Augustus used a well-established method that involved assessing offenders' ages, character, social influences, and other contributing factors to determine the likelihood of them successfully complying with conditions of pretrial release. Indeed, Augustus's methods represented the first-known efforts to gather biographical, social, criminal, and mental health histories to determine who was likely to benefit from therapeutic interventions. He kept records of his interactions with offenders and wrote reports to the courts. Augustus was so successful that by 1858, he had bailed out a total of 1,946 offenders, and during that period, the courts violated only 11 of the offenders for failing to comply with their conditions of supervised release. These methods and the practice of releasing offenders in the hope of rehabilitating them in the community under the supervision of community corrections officers marked the beginning of the modern American probation system.

The word *probation* itself comes from the Latin word *probationem* (nominative *probatio*), which translates into approval, assent, a proving, trial, inspection, or examination. In short, probation provides offenders with opportunities to prove themselves by showing the courts and the community that they are worthy of living in society. It is a process of examining offenders' behaviors and using methods that give offenders the chance to prove to the court that they can peacefully reside in society as law-abiding citizens.

John Augustus's efforts certainly informed the enactment of the first probation statute in Massachusetts and arguably the establishment of the first juvenile court in Illinois in 1899, as well as the widespread understanding that the circumstances that lead people to commit crimes differ from one person to another; therefore, the most useful responses to such behaviors differ (Abadinsky, 2012). Today, probation officers screen all offenders irrespective of pending charges, confirm or verify information provided by offenders, assess the risk of offenders' misconduct if released, write and present recommendations to the court based on risk-assessment results, conduct follow-up reviews, report on progress, supervise offenders, and submit reports to the appropriate authorities.

Congressional Response

The emergence of probation raised concerns among certain members of Congress who argued that granting discretionary powers to judges to allow or deny probation or to reduce sentences was unconstitutional because such power would give judges pardoning power that was only constitutionally available to the executive branch of the government. That is, "the power of a judge to place one on probation encroached upon the executive power to pardon," but the Supreme Court of the United States did not agree (Chappel, 1939). In one of the cases challenging the constitutionality of probation, the Court argued, "Probation was not sought to shorten the term. Probation is the attempted saving of a man who has taken one wrong step and whom the judge thinks to be a brand who can be plucked from the burning at the time of the imposition of the sentence" (*United States v. Murray*, 1928).

Earlier, in 1916, the U.S. Supreme Court ruled in Ex Parte United States that the "power of Congress to fix punishment for crime includes the power, by probation or other suitable legislation, to equip the courts in advance with such latitude of discretion as will enable them to vary and control the application of punishment to suit the exigencies of each case, in accord with obvious considerations of humanity and public wellbeing" (Ex Parte United States, 1916). Despite these rulings, however, it took the U.S. Congress almost another decade to enact the Probation Act of 1925 and establish the Federal Probation System. The act authorized the creation of a probation system in the federal courts and gave them the power to discretionarily suspend sentences or to place defendants on probation. The act also authorized courts to appoint one salaried probation officer and recruit voluntary probation officers, which in 1927 led to the country's first paid probation officer.

HISTORY OF PAROLE

The first legislation providing for the reduction of sentences for federal prisoners because of good behavior was enacted in 1867 (Fulwood, 2003). The most visible legislative action by Congress was in 1930 when the U.S. Congress created the National Parole Board and amended the Probation Act to authorize federal parole officers to supervise parolees. The practice of parole gained momentum throughout the Great Depression and World War II. By 1944, 48 states had created parole agencies to oversee parolees. Today, parole is a core branch of the criminal justice system in every American jurisdiction.

The purpose of parole is evident in the origin or meaning of the word *parole*, which is derived from the French word *parole* and translates into "word of honor." The modern use of parole as a formal response to offending behaviors is traceable to the 1840s' superintendent of the British penal colony in Australia, Alexander Maconochie, who also served as the governor of Norfolk Island. Maconochie had the belief that punishing offenders for past behaviors while training them for future law-abiding behaviors was a productive use of public resources. Evidently, he rejected determinate sentencing policies in favor of indeterminate or open-ended sentencing policies to give offenders opportunities to demonstrate their qualifications for leniency while in detention.

Indeterminate sentencing policies give judges a range of sentencing options, of which the most commonly used are the imposition of incarceration with the possibility of parole, flat probation with no institutional time, and sentences that allow for parole after the demonstration of good behavior in a correctional institution. Indeterminate sentencing policies, therefore, impose sentences without specific periods of time or release dates; rather, they give a range of time, such as "7 to 10 years" or "6 to 12 months"—meaning offenders must complete 7 years before they can qualify for parole or 6 months before offenders can be released on parole to complete the remaining 6 months under community supervision. The sentence generally states the period of incarceration in terms of "not less than" or "not more than" a certain prescribed duration of time.

Determinate or fixed sentencing policies deny judges the discretion to reduce or increase the length of an offender's sentence based on the crime. In many cases, statutes that demand determinate sentencing also rule out the option of probation for certain types of offenses. The policy dictates the sentencing options available to a judge for each criminal behavior, including the exact length of incarceration for each offense. The policy also limits judicial discretion by eliminating indeterminate sentencing and by not allowing parole because often prison terms must be served in full as stipulated by statute or presumptive sentencing guidelines.

Certain offenders, however, can still be released on parole for other reasons, such as overcrowding, good behavior, or good time credits. In some cases, the sentencing courts also issue split sentences that allow offenders to spend a certain amount of time behind bars and then be released into the community to serve the remainder of their time under supervision. In other words, a portion of the sentence is spent behind bars and the remainder of the sentence is spent in the community on parole or probation depending on the labeling system a state may use (Fulwood, 2003). It is because of the motivational effects of these policies to encourage good behavior that Maconochie advocated for and supported indeterminate sentencing policies as a response to serious criminal behaviors.

Maconochie became the governor of Norfolk Island in 1840. At the time, the island was home to convicts shipped there after committing severe violent crimes. Upon taking control of the island as governor, Maconochie instituted certain therapeutic policies designed to treat offenders with dignity—obviously, a therapeutic policy would not tolerate the infliction of pain and suffering for the sake of punishment. The policies were significantly advanced, but Maconochie's opponents did not allow them to fully develop and, consequently, his ideas were ignored after he left office. Luckily, however, his prison reform policies received a major boost during the time of Sir Walter Frederick Crofton, who chaired the board of directors of convict prisons for Ireland between 1854 and 1862.

Sir Walter was known for his prison reform policies, which were similar to the ones Alexander Maconochie introduced but failed to achieve. Indeed, Sir Walter also failed to make parole a national policy in the face of arguments that such policies were too lenient, but he expanded Governor Maconochie's philosophy by introducing a system that allowed convicts to earn points for good behavior. The point system had four stages for offenders to go through: (1) solitary, (2) interactive, (3) reformation, and (4) release stages (Abadinsky, 2012).

At the first stage, offenders were placed in solitary confinement for 9 months, the punishment phase, the period in which offenders paid their dues to society. In the second stage, offenders were moved into general population. Good behavior at the second stage qualified offenders to move to the third stage, where they were placed in a different institution, known today as a "halfway house," to demonstrate their reformation. The offenders who demonstrated a willingness to reform during this stage were moved to the fourth level where they were given tickets that allowed them to be conditionally released on parole to complete the remainder of their sentences under community supervision.

Parole means an offender has served part of his or her sentence honorably, is sufficiently rehabilitated, and poses little or no threat to public safety and thus can be discharged from the correctional institution to spend the rest of his or her sentence in the community. A decision to parole an offender is, therefore, a decision to grant that offender a conditional release prior to the expiration of the maximum term of the sentence imposed by the trial court. In the absence of parole, an offender must complete the entirety of the sentence in a correctional facility. However, the option of parole gives offenders the incentive to behave well while in detention because the possibility of being released serves as motivation for inmates to exhibit good behavior and to take advantage of available therapeutic programming.

Under both determinate and indeterminate sentencing policies, judges are required to consider offenders' aggravating and mitigating circumstances. Mitigating factors are favorable circumstances associated with an offender's behavior that a sentencing judge considers after an offender is found guilty, has entered a "no contest" plea, has been convicted by a jury, or has committed to a plea bargain. Aggravating factors are offenders' unfavorable circumstances that trial judges consider when sentencing offenders. Aggravating conditions are likely to increase the chances of incarceration and or to attract harsher sentences while offenders with more mitigating circumstances are likely to receive more lenient sentences, including probation. Offenders with more aggravating circumstances are likely to receive harsh punishments, including incarceration and even the death penalty. It is, therefore, reasonable to conclude that most pretrial releasees, probationers, and parolees are more likely to be low-risk offenders than those who do not qualify for these statuses.

REVOCATION OF PRETRIAL RELEASE, PROBATION, AND PAROLE STATUS

Obviously, in comparison to those who are incarcerated, the overwhelming number of offenders in community corrections are lower level offenders whose continuous presence in the community is vital for their social and economic survival. Offenders who receive pretrial release and probation status are also spared other negative effects of confinement, such as the loss of home, job, and property. Notwithstanding these good reasons in support of community corrections, from time to time, certain pretrial releasees, probationers, and parolees qualify for the revocation of their presence in the community. The process of revoking pretrial release, probation, and parole is, therefore, an important aspect of community corrections.

Clinically, probationers and parolees have similar needs, so both groups require similar supervision and services. Legally, each probationer and parolee could be violated for similar behaviors. In fact, in some cases, the community corrections status of pretrial releasees, probationers, and parolees can each be revoked for technical or new offense violations (Cohen, 2012). The latter refers to the commission of a new offense while on pretrial release, probation, or parole, and the former is a violation of community corrections status based on the breach of one or more conditions of pretrial release, probation, or parole. There are, however, significant differences between pretrial release, probation, and parole in terms of jurisdiction and the processes by which pretrial release, probation, and parole status are revoked.

It is important to note that prior to the 1960s, courts had a "hands-off" doctrine when it came to matters relating to corrections. The view then was that correctional matters were internal affairs that fell outside the control of the courts but within the expert control of jail and prison officials. In the 1960s and forward, this "hands-off" doctrine changed as courts became less "reluctant to intervene in the affairs of the correctional system," especially parole (Hanrahan, 1978, p. 160). Hence the U.S. Supreme Court has addressed a number of critical matters relating to the revocation of community corrections status with a particular emphasis on parole, which, unlike pretrial release and probation, is administratively managed and adjudicated by correctional authorities or parole boards. Much information can, however, be learned about pretrial release and probation from the discussion of parole revocation.

Legally, parole is a conditional release from confinement, and clinically, parole is designed to help prisoners reintegrate into society; therefore, parolees are under the jurisdiction of their correctional institutions and not the court in which they were tried and sentenced. This state of affairs also means that parole revocation hearings are presided over by one or more members of the parole board or an entity acting on behalf of the parole board or correctional institution.

Based on a preponderance of evidence, parole boards can revoke, reinstate, or modify parole status. In fact, a number of court cases have addressed critical aspects of parole revocation hearings. In *Menechino v. Oswald* (1970), for example, the Second Circuit ruled that parole revocation or the granting of parole status, as well as revocation proceedings, are therapeutic functions; therefore, they are not subject to the adversarial system that drives a criminal trial. In other words, parole release and revocation hearings are not fact-finding proceedings; therefore, offenders have no liberty interest because they are already imprisoned.

In *Greenholtz v. Inmates of the Nebraska Penal and Correctional Complex* (1979), the U.S. Supreme Court argued that offenders have no right to be released early but that states have the right to offer offenders the option of parole, and when parole is an option under state law, then a formal nonadversarial hearing is, of course, required to determine each offender's eligibility. In *Martinez v. California* (1980), the U.S. Supreme Court ruled that because parole boards act in a quasi-judicial capacity, the board grants parole officials immunity from tort claims. The immunity, however, is limited or not equivalent to the broad and total immunity, for example, that judges enjoy.

In 1998, the U.S. Supreme Court also ruled in *Pennsylvania Board of Probation and Parole v. Scott* (1998) that evidence seized by parole officers from parolees without a search warrant could be used at a parole violation hearing because parolees sign parole agreements consistent with the supervisory roles that exist between a parolee and parole officer. With regard to search and seizure, the Court ruled in *United States v. Knights* (2001) that the residence of a probationer can be searched based on reasonable suspicion because the need for rehabilitation and protection of society from offenders overrides the privacy needs of offenders.

The courts have also argued parole is an act of grace, not a right; therefore, parole can be given and taken at will. This position, however, fails to take into account that parolees earn parole through consistent hard work and good behavior over an extended period. That is, offenders actually earn their status through continuous demonstration of prosocial thinking and behavior. Besides, the criminal justice system also has a duty to show prisoners that the processes by which criminal and delinquent behavior are responded to are fair, and therefore, parole revocation and indeed consideration process must adhere to basic principles of fairness. In that regard, parole revocation must satisfy the basic constitutional due process requirement.

With regard to the process of revoking parole, the U.S. Supreme Court has ruled that at a minimum, parolees have the right to a personal inquiry by an impartial body at a reasonable place and time; the right to a written notice of any alleged violation; the right to be heard, to present witnesses, to confront witnesses, to challenge evidence and allegations; and the right to have an official finding of the hearing. The whole process of revocation of parole status must also be fundamentally just, the standard must be published, and the offenders must have access to the information and evidence used against them as the basis of denying status. Fairness also demands that unfavorable psychiatric, psychological, and medical reports, as well as unconfirmed reports used by the parole board to reach its decisions, must be made available to offenders (Abadinsky, 2012; Palmer, 2010).

In general, pretrial releasees, probationers, and parolees are allowed to testify and present witnesses, cross-examine parole or probation officers, and use legal representation.

Upon finding that a violation has occurred, the judge can revoke pretrial release or probation status and order the offender imprisoned, jailed, detained, or reinstated to community corrections status. The processes by which pretrial release and probation status can be revoked are, however, different with regard to who has jurisdiction and what factors trigger the revocation of status. For example, the revocation of pretrial release status is within the jurisdiction of each offender's respective trial court. Similarly, the revocation of probation falls under the jurisdiction of the court that tried or sentenced each offender. While the granting of pretrial release status is dictated by the extent to which an accused person is likely to appear at the next court hearing or to commit new offenses, the granting of probation is dictated by the type of crime committed, statutorily mandated sentences, offenders' criminogenic and needs scores, extralegal factors, and prosecutorial or public sentiment about an alleged offense.

CONCLUSION

The gradual development of pretrial, probation, and parole as a response to criminal behaviors is a testament to the fact that harsh punishments, such as incarceration or the infliction of physical pain, which have been practiced for centuries, are less effective than other responses in terms of the rehabilitation of offenders, costs, and public safety. In fact, it is partly the failure of punishment to rehabilitate that paved the way for the development of community corrections and the transformation of pretrial services, probation, and parole into major entities of contemporary criminal justice systems that exercise direct supervisory control over millions of offenders.

The slow progression to the current state of pretrial release, probation, and parole services also speaks to the fact that the science of managing offenders at all stages of the criminal justice process is complex and requires a well-developed knowledge base. These advancements also suggest that the development and delivery of therapeutic responses to crimes can only be sustained by a well-trained team of prosecutors, defense counselors, judges, and pretrial service, probation, and parole officers, as well as the public and, indeed, lawmakers.

DISCUSSION QUESTIONS

1. Of these groups, pretrial releasees, probationers, and parolees, which is more difficult to supervise?
2. Of these groups, pretrial releasees, probationers, and parolees, which pose the greatest threat to public safety in the community?
3. Should murderers who are sentenced to life have the opportunity to receive parole, subject to rehabilitation and changes in attitude and behavior?
4. How may pretrial release services therapeutically affect offenders' thinking and behavior?
5. How may probation or parole services therapeutically affect offenders' thinking and behavior?

REFERENCES

ABA. (2019). *Pretrial release.* https://www.americanbar.org/

Abadinsky, H. (2012). *Probation and parole: Theory and practice.* Pearson.

Bail Reform Act of 1966 (1966). Public Law 89-465-June 22, 1966. Retrieved from: https://www.govinfo.gov/content/pkg/STATUTE-80/pdf/STATUTE-80-Pg214.pdf#page=4

Bail Reform Act, 18 U.S.C. Section 3141 (1984).

Bronson, J., & Carson, E. A. (2019). Prisoners in 2017. *Bulletin.* https://www.bjs.gov/content/pub/pdf/p17.pdf

Carson, E. A. (2018). Prisoners 2016. *Bulletin.* https://www.bjs.gov/content/pub/pdf/p16.pdf

Chappel, R. A. (1939). Courts interpret the Federal Probation Act. *Journal of Criminal Law and Criminology, 29,* 708–717. https://scholarlycommons.law.northwestern.edu/cgi/viewcontent.cgi?article=2833&context=jclc

Cohen, T. H. (2012). Pretrial release and misconduct in federal district courts, 2008–2010. *Special Report.* https://www.bjs.gov/content/pub/pdf/prmfdc0810.pdf

Ex Parte United States, No. 242 U.S. 27 (1916).

Fulwood, I. (2003). *History of the federal parole system.* U.S. Department of Justice. https://www.justice.gov/sites/default/files/uspc/legacy/2009/10/07/history.pdf

Greenholtz v. Inmates of Nebraska Penal Complex, No. 78-201, 442 U.S. 1 (1979) (U.S. Supreme Court 1979).

Hanrahan, K. (1978). The impact of Morrissey and Gagnon on parole revocation proceedings. *Journal of Criminal Law and Criminology, 69*(2), 160–169. https://scholarlycommons.law.northwestern.edu/cgi/viewcontent.cgi?article=6066&context=jclc

Joseph Menechino v. Russell G. Oswald, No. 871, Docket 34665 (United States Court of Appeals, Second Circuit. 1970).

Kaeble, D. (2018). Probation and parole in the United States, 2016. *Bulletin.* https://www.bjs.gov/content/pub/pdf/ppus16.pdf

Mahoney, B., Beaudin, B. D., III, J. A. C., Ryan, D. B., & Hoffman, R. B. (2001). *Pretrial services programs: Responsibilities and potential.* National Institute of Justice, Issues and Practices. https://www.ncjrs.gov/pdffiles1/nij/181939.pdf

Martinez Et Al. v. California Et Al, No. 78-1268, 444 U.S. 277 (Supreme Court of United States 1980).

Maxwell, M. A. (1950). The Washingtonian movement. *Quarterly Journal of Studies on Alcohol, 11,* 410–452. https://www.google.com/search?q=trump&oq=trump&aqs=chrome..69i57j0j69i60l3j0.3871j0j7&sourceid=chrome&ie=UTF-8

Palmer, J. W. (2010). *Constitutional rights of prisoners* (9th ed.). Anderson Publishing.

Pennsylvania Board of Probation and Parole V. Scott, on Writ of Certiorari to the Supreme Court of Pennsylvania, Middle District No. 97-581 (Supreme Court of the United States 1998).

Tjoflat, G. B. (1982). *"Extend the operations of the pretrial services agencies"* [Testimony]. Hearings before the Subcommittee on Crime of the House Committee on the Judiciary, 97th Congress, 1st Session. Washington, DC, United States.

United States v. Knights, No. 00-1260, 534 U.S. 112 (United States Supreme Court 2001).

United States v. Murray, No. 275 U.S. 347 (1928).

CHAPTER TEN

Historical Background of Risk Assessment

THE HISTORY OF actuarial risk-assessment instruments can be broken down into four stages. At each level in the history of risk-assessment tools, a significant improvement is apparent in the way criminal justice professionals have assessed and classified offenders and how assessment results have informed the management and treatment of substance abuse, sex, violent, and general offenders, as well as those who exhibit mental health symptoms. At each stage, one can also see that the desire to improve methods of assessment and classification constantly produces structural and methodological changes in the field of risk and needs assessment and classification. The interests and practices aimed at improving the effectiveness of the process of assessing and classifying offenders and offending behaviors have been slowly pursued within the American criminal justice system for over a century and been sought after increasingly during the past 30 years. Consequently, different methods of assessment and classification are now available to criminal justice practitioners.

This chapter provides a brief overview of the history of risk-assessment and classification instruments that pretrial, probation, parole, and correctional officers use to assess and classify offenders' thinking, attitudes, behaviors, and social histories. Areas needing improvement are the structures and processes of administering risk and needs assessment tools, while some ideal features of holistic risk-assessment and classification tools are also briefly discussed as features that could make risk and needs assessment tools more functional. Specifically, the discussion covers the need to capture gender-specific needs and risks, as well as aggravating and mitigating factors in furtherance of the goal to achieve well-rounded assessment and classification results.

CRITICAL STAGES OF RISK-ASSESSMENT TOOLS DEVELOPMENT

In many ways, the history of risk-assessment instruments can be deduced from the history of the U.S. Federal Probation and Pretrial Services, which was set in motion by the U.S. Supreme Court's ruling in White & Supreme Court of the United States (1916). The defendant in this case pleaded guilty to several counts, including the embezzlement of public funds and making false entries in financial records. Accordingly, the defendant was entitled under the applicable statute to receive a minimum 5-year sentence of imprisonment. However, at the request of the defendant and against the objection of the U.S. district attorney, the trial court suspended the minimum 5-year sentence and ordered that the defendant maintain good behavior for 5 years. The U.S. federal government appealed the decision on the grounds that the permanent suspension of the sentence constituted a failure to enforce the 5-year sentence prescribed by Congress, and thus the order suspending the sentence was unconstitutional. The U.S. Supreme Court agreed.

The Court ruled that it is the U.S. Congress, and not the judicial branch of the government, that has the power to define crimes and prescribe sanctions for such crimes; therefore, the suspended sentence amounted to a refusal to impose a sentence prescribed by Congress; thus, the action was beyond the power of the courts (White & Supreme Court of the United States, 1916). The Supreme Court, however, recommended that Congress provide trial courts with suitable legislation that would give them some latitude of discretion to deal with the various cases that come before them. In response, Congress passed the Probation Act of 1925. This act established the federal probation system and gave judges the power to impose suspended sentences or place defendants on probation under terms and conditions appropriate within the view of the courts. The act further created the appointment of probation officers by trial courts to oversee compliance with conditions of release. During the same era, Congress created the National Parole Board and amended the Probation Act to authorize probation officers to supervise federal parolees.

Meanwhile, increases in the number of detainees in correctional facilities and the desire to reduce the cost of detaining people, especially those awaiting the conclusion of their trials, led to the enactment of the Speedy Trial Act of 1974. Title II of this congressional act limited pretrial service to 10 judicial districts to experiment with the effectiveness of pretrial service operations. Part of the act also authorized courts to establish pretrial service agencies and charged the agencies with the responsibility to prevent people who had been released into the community to await the conclusion of their trials from coming back into the system on new criminal charges (Speedy Trial Act, 1974). The success of the experiment resulted in the passage of the Pretrial Services Act of 1982. The statute, which was signed into law in 1982 by President Ronald Reagan, expanded the operation of pretrial services from 10 districts to every federal judicial district and, ultimately, paved the way for the recruitment of federal probation officers to oversee community supervision of defendants awaiting trial, as well as persons convicted and sentenced to probation.

The creation of pretrial services, probation, and parole at this point in the history of community corrections meant that court officials (pretrial services and probation) must interview defendants and review the files of each person charged with a crime. The obligation also meant that trial courts must investigate background information for each offender and provide final results for use as a basis for granting or not granting bail or probation, as well as for setting conditions of release. It also meant that pretrial defendants released into the community had to be supervised by pretrial service officers to ensure that they stayed out of trouble while awaiting the conclusion of their trials.

Obviously, these added responsibilities raised many critical questions, such as the following: How much restriction and supervision should a probationer or pretrial release person receive? In cases where courts have discretion, who should receive probation and who should not? How much probation should an accused person receive? Which offender is likely to comply with the conditions of release? Whose release conditions should include home confinement or curfew? Who qualifies for supervised or unsupervised release or probation? Who should be sentenced to prison or jail, and who should be placed on probation?

Which defendant poses a "serious risk" to society or is likely to flee justice, and which defendant does not pose such a threat? Which detainees ended up in minimum, medium, and maximum security housing or in solitary confinement. Who qualified for parole?

In addition to the many unanswered questions, agencies also had to ensure that offenders were treated in accordance with the 14th Amendment Equal Protection Clause, which mandates state agents to treat all offenders equally and protect detainees' interest in freedom from discrimination. In addition, criminal justice agencies had to respond to outcries from victims demanding justice, civil rights organizations' calls to respect the rights of all criminal defendants, and public demands that the government maintain high levels of accountability and transparency. Ultimately, these and other legitimate questions and important developments provided the moral and legal grounds necessary to bring about a standardized classification system.

Unfortunately, however, although the need for risk assessment became apparent in the early 1930s, it took nearly half a century for the current evidence-based risk-assessment tools to become standard instruments for use at all levels of the criminal justice system. It appears that part of the reason for the delay had to do with the prolonged time it took governments to recognize that devoting legislative resources to reducing incarceration rates required identifying and targeting the factors that push people toward criminal behaviors. In other words, up to the early 1980s, many of the criminal justice assessment and classification processes focused strictly on static risk factors without much consideration for needs and dynamic risk factors. Similarly, criminal justice practitioners had yet to understand how to manipulate criminogenic risk factors to affect positive change in thinking, attitudes, and behaviors.

The gradual development of contemporary risk-assessment instruments began in the 1920s, a period when Congress become more interested in issues pertaining to pretrial releases and probation. The first stage of the development of risk-assessment tools was characterized by the reliance on the professional intuition and opinions of criminal justice practitioners as the main basis for classifying offenders into categories and matching offending behavior with criminal justice sanctions. Since then, the criminal justice risk and needs assessment and classification methods have undergone many important changes. The following are highlights of some of the key changes.

First-Wave Assessments

The first official methods of subjecting offenders to different treatments based on individual differences, criminal history, and known facts about offenders started at the beginning of the 20th century. The process was entirely a matter of professional judgment in which criminal justice practitioners, mainly probation, jail, prison, parole, and clinical staff, such as psychologists, psychiatrists, and social workers, used their professional training and experiences to intuitively make judgments about who needed enhanced security and supervision (Bonta & Andrews, 2007). The actual process of assessing and classifying offenders at the time typically consisted of reviewing information gathered through unstructured and structured interactions with offenders; reports generated by arresting officers, pretrial services, corrections, probation, and parole officers; and reports created by other criminal justice agencies. The information would then be used to form intuitive opinions and make judgments about offenders' risk levels and the appropriate state responses to particular behaviors.

The use of professional opinions, however, meant that practitioners' recommendations and conclusions about who was a high- or low-risk offender often changed depending on each practitioners' knowledge and skill level and the context of their interactions with offenders. This intuitive classification system could not, however, withstand legal and empirical scrutiny because classifications were based on mere experiences and gut feelings with or without adequate empirical backing. Not surprisingly, the approach had no positive impact on recidivism rates. Obviously, since the goal of the criminal justice system was, and still is, to reduce recidivism, a reliable method had to be invented to separate low-risk offenders who required fewer services and less supervision from higher risk offenders who needed more services, including supervision. The move to get away from intuition-based assessment methods to a more scientifically standardized method did not, however, materialize until the early 1970s.

Second-Wave Assessments

The departure from the intuitive classification system that began in the late 1920s to a more empirical-based method of assessing and classifying offenders gained momentum when studies began to show that evidence-based, risk-assessment, and classification outcomes were far superior to the unguided assessment and classification results the intuitive judgment method produced (Johnson et al., 2011; Luallen et al., 2016). Thus the first wave of assessment and classification failed to produce reliable risk levels but did lead to the creation of risk-assessment tools in the mid-1970s (Bonta & Andrews, 2007).

The second wave of instruments was designed to estimate the probability of reoffending within a certain time frame after release into the community (Nafekh, 2002). Unlike the professional model, the actuarial risk-assessment approach uses statistical analysis to measure behavioral risk factors that empirical studies have shown to correlate with certain kinds of antisocial and prosocial behaviors. Each static risk factor, such as criminal history, was assigned a value, and the average or aggregate score was used to distinguish low-risk offenders from high-risk offenders based on who scored high and who scored low on the assessment scales. For instance, an offender with a total score of 7 to 9 was classified as high risk, one who scored 3 to 6 was designated as medium risk, and an offender who scored 0 to 2 was labeled as minimum risk (Hoffman et al., 1978).

The second wave of risk assessment instruments compelled practitioners to base decisions that affected offenders on empirical evidence. These instruments relied heavily on documented static risk factors. That is, the instruments measured primarily static risk factors, such as a history of arrest and convictions, history of substance abuse, unemployment, and past violent behaviors (Hoffman et al., 1978). Under this system, risk levels rarely changed because static factors rarely change, even when an offender makes the best effort to end offending behavior. If an offender scored high because of the number of his or her arrests, there was no way to reduce the risk level or have the arrest history discounted during future assessment. Therefore, the only change possible was an increase in risk for those who generated new histories, such as post-assessment and classification arrests.

Third-Wave Assessments

In the late 1970s and early 1980s, a series of studies showed that focusing on static risk factors with little regard for dynamic risks was not a viable way to predict offenders' overall risk of recidivism. For example, static factors alone do not measure changes in behavior over time because static factors by definition do not change. The assessment of both static factors and dynamic risk factors, such as thinking and attitudes, however, can better predict the likelihood of future reoffending over time. The third wave of risk assessment captured both static and dynamic risk factors.

Third-wave methods captured predictive dynamic factors, such as lack of interest in gainful employment or educational pursuits and association with negative friends. It is true that the status of not having a job in the past year can change in a week's time if the offender develops an interest in employment and manages to secure gainful employment. An offender can also go from having no high school diploma to having a high school equivalency diploma within a short period of time if that offender commits to the pursuit of education. These examples show that the addition of dynamic risk factors was a major advancement in criminal justice assessment and classification.

For the first time in half a century or so, criminal justice professionals were able to calculate offenders' risk levels, as well as form a good understating of how long it would take offenders to reduce existing risks and how difficult it would be to do so. The fact that the assessment of dynamic risk factors provided offenders with opportunities to mitigate their risk levels and allowed criminal justice practitioners to match certain behaviors to particular resources was significant for parole, probation, and correctional officers and staff. These developments, for instance, provided reasons for urging offenders with no high school diplomas to enroll in general education diploma programs with the hope of changing the risk of not graduating from high school into the protective factor of having acquired a high school equivalent education. The same was true for employment, angry outbursts, and substance abuse behaviors. Furthermore, the new changes made it possible to evaluate program effectiveness by simply comparing the percentage of offenders whose risk factors were mitigated or altered as a result of programming activities to those whose risk factors were aggravated after treatment intervention and those who did not participate in such programming activities.

Fourth-Wave Assessments

Despite the major advancements in the third wave of risk assessment tools, they failed to calculate needs levels. The fourth wave of risk assessment instruments, however, measured both static and dynamic risks, as well as needs and responsivity, which collectively helped identify the most appropriate interventions to minimize an offender's likelihood of recidivism, promote offenders' meaningful responses to treatment, and mitigate an offender's overall risk and needs level (Bonta & Andrews, 2007). The fourth wave of risk assessment instruments also assessed offenders' likelihood of benefiting from specific treatment interventions by looking at variables such as cognitive abilities, attitudes and beliefs, and offenders' motivation to change (Johnson et al., 2011). The fourth stage of the risk assessment process, therefore, involves three principles: (1) risk level, (2) type or needs, and (3) offender capacity level. This risk-needs-responsivity approach is designed to assess and predict the likelihood of committing new crimes, to identify specific risk factors that should be reduced or eliminated, and to match risk with appropriate treatment and services.

The risk principle refers to the assessment of static or unvarying risk factors, such as criminal history and age of first arrest, and the assessment of dynamic or modifiable risk factors, such as substance abuse behaviors, poor academic performance, and antisocial thoughts and attitudes. This approach demands that more resources be allocated for offenders with high needs and that fewer resources be devoted to those at low risk of engaging in criminal activities. The instruments assess needs levels by measuring the level of service that should be devoted to a specific risk factor associated with certain offending behaviors. That is, needs assessment identifies what ought to be learned, changed, and achieved and what resources should be made available to facilitate the acquisition of new knowledge, resources, and skills that directly enhance the offender's overall ability to avoid recidivism. Hence needs assessments look at factors that prevent an offender from being categorized at the level that this kind of assessment and classification would place them.

When needs are properly addressed, risk can be minimized, and the overall likelihood of an offender engaging in criminal activities decreases. However, when needs are left unaddressed, they can increase the chance of future criminal activities. The needs, therefore, determine how many resources each sex offender, violent offender, substance abuser, or general offender requires to live a crime-free life. That is, a high-risk offender who abuses controlled substances has needs that can be addressed with intensive substance abuse treatment. Needs assessment results dictate whether an offender accused of committing a sex crime needs specific sex offender treatment or if an offender charged with a violent crime would benefit from participation in anger management therapy. Similarly, the needs of an offender who is charged with burglarizing a home may turn out to be substance abuse therapy if assessment results show that the purpose of the criminal act was to finance a drug habit. An offender who becomes violent when under the influence of alcohol is also more likely to benefit from substance abuse treatment than anger management therapy. The need does not, however, predict which offender is likely to benefit from any of these interventions, and that shortcoming highlights the relevancy of responsivity.

The concept of responsivity also shows that an offender's readiness for learning new patterns of thinking and behavior to replace antisocial behaviors is very important and can be measured. The old tendencies can be improved if the time is taken to enhance the offender's motivation level, abilities, and strengths, as well as, most importantly, the offender's thinking and attitudes through cognitive behavioral manipulation and similar interventions. Furthermore, the measurement of responsivity answers questions about what can be done to prevent likely recidivism and whether an offender is ready for the challenges that come with achieving such change.

Responsivity is more appropriately understood in the context of learning because, as with most human behaviors, criminal activities are learned, and to break away from criminal behaviors means to learn new behaviors. In this regard, responsivity measures offenders' suitability for treatment and the effectiveness of treatments as they apply to particular offenders and their criminogenic needs. The measurement of responsivity, therefore, takes into account the likely effect of treatment interventions on the offender's cognition and social skills, learning style, and motivation to comply with treatment (Bonta & Andrews, 2007). Thus the assessment of responsivity is critical because changes in offenders' behaviors require changes in thinking and attitudes, and changes in thinking require cognitive adjustment, plus devotion and commitment to change.

In the end, the fourth stage of risk-assessment instruments is more reliable than the methods of the preceding three stages. Among many functions, current instruments help allocate resources, prioritize interventions, and target offenders' knowledge, attitudes, and interest in the furtherance of treatment. The instruments effectively distinguish between offenders who need intensive supervision and programming from those who need fewer interventions and offenders who can benefit from moderate or minimal institutional interventions and supervision from those who do not. This level of assessment and classification also allows criminal justice practitioners to capture mitigating and aggravating factors.

GENERAL WEAKNESSES

As a matter of general weakness, the current assessment and classification instruments still have room for growth. For example, research shows that most offenders have underlying mental health conditions, and most come from poor and high-risk environments and a wide range of social backgrounds. Individuals' unique circumstances inform their offending behaviors. Yet existing instruments fail to capture many of the underlying social and mental health conditions that aggravate the effects of other risk factors that inform antisocial thinking, attitudes, and behaviors. Hence, despite the visible efforts evidenced by the hundreds of risk-assessment and classification tools currently in use, one of the key weaknesses of existing assessment tools is that they fail to capture gender-specific risks and needs.

There is a good reason for assessment and classification tools to capture both factual information and the context of each piece of social and behavioral history, especially as they relate to gender-specific history. Although gender differences do not predict the likelihood of antisocial thinking, attitudes, and behaviors, there are certain gender-specific needs that are not captured by existing risk and needs assessment instruments, partly because the instruments currently in use were designed with male offenders in mind. Of course, up to the late 1980s, the number of women in the criminal justice system was very low. Also, compared to males, female prisoners are less likely to pose significant threats to institutional safety in the ways that male offenders do. Female offenders are also less likely to be viewed as threats to public safety. It is also not surprising that males dominate many categories of crimes, such as rape, sexual assault, murder, kidnapping, armed robbery, terrorism, and drug- and gang-related crimes.

Studies show that about 82% of female offenders who enter the criminal justice system do so for property, drug, and public disorder types of offenses. Today, however, the trend is slowly changing. All indicators show that the number of women committing crimes, getting arrested, and being jailed, imprisoned, and placed on probation or parole is increasing. In 2014 alone, there were nearly 1.2 million women under the control of the American correctional system (prisons 106,232, jails 109,100, probation 966,029, and parole 102,825) (Sentencing Project, 2016). The number of women in the criminal justice system is 8 times higher than it was in the 1980s. This represents an increase of over 700% from a total of 26,378 in 1980 to 215,332 in 2014 (Carson, 2015; Sentencing Project, 2016). Today, nearly every county's correctional facilities house female offenders (Swavola et al., 2016).

According to the Sentencing Project (2016), the profound change in the involvement of women in the criminal justice system is informed by stiffer drug sentencing and postconviction barriers that uniquely affect women. That is, mandatory and minimum sentencing guidelines and the so-called war on drugs are two of the key contributing factors—in addition to others—that push more and more women into the criminal justice system. This rapid increase demands that more attention be paid to the proper assessment of female offenders' needs to facilitate adequate protection and treatment of females. For instance, female offenders tend to have high needs that are not frequently associated with males. Female offenders overwhelmingly come from poor and low-income backgrounds. A high percentage of female offenders are also mothers who are extremely concerned for their children's welfare, have serious prevailing medical needs and or suffer from serious mental illnesses, have relevant histories of abusing drugs or alcohol, have experienced sexual and or partner violence, and have been victimized by someone charged with protecting them (McKeown, 2010; Sentencing Project, 2016).

Obviously, these sorts of histories can significantly influence the trajectory of needs levels, which has serious implications for corrections, probation, and parole officers because needs scores are closely correlated with risk scores. Furthermore, parole and probation officers are, at least in principle, primarily concerned with needs levels that dictate the degree and types of services an offender requires to become successful or to live a crime-free life (Swavola et al., 2016). For instance, studies show that males tend to score higher than females for violent history, early violent behavior, substance abuse, and negative or "I don't care" attitudes, but females score higher than males for personality disorders, impulsivity, and stress (McKeown, 2015). There are also reported differences in terms of history, especially with regard to the roles played by histories of being sexually or physically abused and the effects of substance abuse, parenthood, and past traumatic experiences, such as rape, on female offenders' interactions with the criminal justice system.

Most women who make contact with the criminal justice system do so because of nonviolent crimes, such as drugs, public disorder, and property crimes (Sentencing Project, 2016). However, most women in the criminal justice system come from troubled family backgrounds, have histories of sexual or physical abuse, and face harsh financial conditions. They also tend to exhibit more serious psychological problems than male offenders. Many have no solid employment histories, poor medical histories, inadequate education, histories of substance abuse, and are likely to have one or more children for whom they are the sole responsible party, financially and emotionally (Hanser, 2017). These unique characteristics mean female offenders require special attention. For example, the assessment of employment history does not favor young female offenders who are prevented from maintaining gainful employment because of pregnancy and the tedious hardships of caring for preschoolers. Fortunately, interest in enhancing existing risk-assessment tools to a level where they could adequately capture gender-specific needs and risk seems to be growing slowly (McKeown, 2010).

THE IDEAL INSTRUMENTS

Current assessment tools are far from comprehensive, and movement in the direction of perfection must include improvements in the ways tools are designed and administered. In this regard, a few basic steps are needed. First, the effectiveness of risk and needs assessment and classification instruments depends heavily on the accuracy of collateral data. Therefore, an ideal instrument would be one that measures the accuracy and reliability of information sources used to answer questions that appear on assessment and classification instruments.

Second, a good instrument requires satisfactory professional preparedness or a specific training process for the persons administering risk-assessment instruments to offenders. Third, instruments must be broad enough not to group offenders with unique backgrounds into common categories, such as sex offenders, substance abusers, violent offenders, or general offenders without regard for how individual backgrounds, such as socioeconomic, cultural, and mental health status, inform each offender's thinking and behavior. Fourth, future scales must include gender-specific items that capture the many important gender-specify needs.

Fifth, and last, the ideal instruments capture specific mitigating and aggravating circumstances and their effects on individual risk and needs levels. For instance, offenders whose behaviors are similar to the imaginary single mother who steals bread to feed her starving kids or the 18-year-old who sells drugs to help his mother pay utility bills and provide for his siblings can be distinguished from offenders who commit the crimes of theft and selling drugs to finance antisocial lifestyles. Of course, in both of these cases, crimes are committed, and as a result, risk factors exist. The crucial difference, however, is that assessment of the thought processes that generated the behaviors is vital for both needs and risk scores.

Clearly, the thinking processes that pushed the mother to steal bread and the 18-year-old to sell drugs are protective factors that minimize the aggregate weight of the risk factors associated with stealing and selling drugs. In these examples, the mitigating factors slightly dilute the effect of the two past criminal behaviors on future criminal behaviors. In the first example, the mother may be at risk because of the very circumstance that prompted the act of stealing, but her behavior shows that she cares about the well-being of her children; thus, the criminal history of stealing points toward a low risk of committing serious crimes that would land her in prison or separate her from her children. In the second example, the 18-year-old's involvement with drugs is high risk; therefore, the behavior ought to be viewed and scored with the understanding that the act exposes him to a wide range of risk factors, such as association with other high-risk offenders (drug sellers and users) who may reinforce his criminal thinking, attitudes, and behaviors, as well as aggravate the possibility of arrest. However, the thinking behind the behavior shows that the offender is strongly attached to his family and has regard for their welfare. Such a mindset is consoling because both social bond and social control theories argue that such care and state of mind are strong protective factors.

CONCLUSION

When dealing with human behaviors, the utmost caution and professional discretion must be exercised because each person is unique, and each behavior emerges out of and falls into a unique category. Assessment and classification results, like any social scientific results, must, therefore, be taken as a "likely" outcome and not an absolute prediction of when and what criminal behavior a particular offender will commit. With that in mind, contemporary risk and needs assessment scales are objective tools that work best when they are subjectively applied and scored. It is only with such subjectivity that the assessment process can fully account for the social constraints that shape the types and categories of criminal activities people engage in and how their conditions dictate the types of resources that will best serve their social, medical, mental health, and socioeconomic needs.

Attention to individual differences would also enhance the accuracy of risk and needs scores, especially for parolees and probationers whose successes often depend on the effectiveness of the services available to them. Often, the crimes for which people are arrested are symptoms of underlying problems that can be anything from drug abuse or addiction, anger problems, poverty, and history of abuse, to environmental conditions, antisocial peer association, antisocial thinking and attitudes, and psychological abnormality. The complex job of the risk-assessment tools and the criminal justice practitioners administering the scales is to pinpoint the source of the problem and the most appropriate response that will either minimize or eliminate the threat the risk factor poses to society and the offender.

DISCUSSION QUESTIONS

1. Which is more important, risk scores or needs scores, and why?
2. How much emphasis should be placed on an offender's responsivity level?
3. What are the key gender-specific risk factors that must be included in contemporary risk assessment scales to facilitate the full assessment of gender-specific needs?
4. Which specific individual differences or characteristics should be included in the calculation of offenders' needs levels?
5. What are some of the important contributions of personal and professional experiences to effective risk and needs assessment results?

REFERENCES

Bonta, J., & Andrews, D. A. (2007). *Risk-need-responsivity model for offender assessment and rehabilitation 2006–07.* Public Saftey Canada. http://www.pbpp.pa.gov/Information/Documents/Research/EBP7.pdf

Carson, E. A. (2015). Prisoners in 2014. *Bulletin.* http://www.bjs.gov/content/pub/pdf/p14.pdf

Hanser, R. D. (2017). *Introduction to corrections* (2nd ed.). Sage Publications.

Hoffman, P., Stone-Meierhoefer, B., & Beck, J. (1978). Salient factor score and releasee behavior: Three validation samples. *Law and Human Behavior, 2*(1), 47–62.

Johnson, J. L., Lowenkamp, C. T., VanBenschoten, S. W., & Robinson, C. R. (2011). The construction and validation of the federal post conviction risk assessment (PCRA). *Office of Probation & Pretrial Services, Administrative Office of the U.S. Court (Special Issue: Evidence-Based Practices in Action), 75*(2), 1–5.

Luallen, J., Radakrishnan, S., & Rhodes, W. (2016). The predictive validity of the post-conviction risk assessment among federal offenders. *Criminal Justice and Behavior, 43*(9), 1–17. https://doi.org/10.1177/0093854816650481

McKeown, A. (2010). Female offenders: Assessment of risk in forensic settings. *Aggression and Violent Behavior, 15*(6), 422–429. https://doi.org/http://dx.doi.org/10.1016/j.avb.2010.07.004

McKeown, A. (2010). Female offenders: Assessment of risk in forensic settings. *Aggression and Violent Behavior, 15*, 422–429. https://doi.org/0.1016/j.avb.2010.07.004

Nafekh, M. (2002). *The general statistical information of recidivism scale.* Research Branch Correctional Service of Canada. www.csc-scc.gc.ca/research/092/r126_e.pdf

Sentencing Project. (2016). *Incarcerated women and girls. Fact sheet: Incarcerated women and girls.* http://www.sentencingproject.org/wp-content/uploads/2016/02/Incarcerated-Women-and-Girls.pdf

Speedy Trial Act of 1974, 18 U.S.C.A. § 3161 et seq. (1974).

Swavola, E., Riley, K., & Subramanian, R. (2016). *Overlooked: Women and jails in an era of reform.* Vera Institute of Justice.

White, E.D., & Supreme Court of the United States. (1916). *U.S. reports: ex parte United States, 242 U.S. 27.* https://www.loc.gov/item/usrep242027/

CHAPTER ELEVEN

Logic of Risk, Needs, and Responsivity Assessment and Classification

PRETRIAL, PROBATION, CORRECTIONAL, and parole institutions in the United States, as well as courts that hear felony cases, use risk assessment instruments as guides to make the best possible decisions about a variety of critical criminal justice processes, including decisions about sentencing and security levels in correctional facilities and communities. Courts and pretrial officers use risk scores when setting bail, deciding to detain, and when contemplating other forms of sanctions and restrictions (Harris et al., 2015; Luong & Wormith, 2011; Nelson & Vincent, 2018).

Correctional facilities use risk-assessment results for a variety of decisions, including the decision to separate inmates who qualify for prison-based employment from those who do not; to determine prisoners' housing arrangements, such as placement in minimum security or maximum security prisons or cells; to identify inmate security needs and inmate visitation types; and to assess whether certain inmates qualify for a host of privileges, such as participation in group religious services or in particular treatment programs. Probation and parole officers also use the results of risk and needs assessments to inform the placement of offenders in treatment programs, to increase or decrease restrictions, and to subject offenders to certain conditions of probation and parole (Luong & Wormith, 2011; Nelson & Vincent, 2018).

The critical roles played by risk assessment raise the need to ask about factors weighed by risk-assessment instruments, how those factors are quantified, the limitations or shortcomings associated with the calculations, and, of course, what criminal justice practitioners do with the results of the risk-assessment process. This chapter answers these questions, as well as others concerning the operating logic that informs the use of risk-assessment and classification instruments, the manipulability of predictive factors, the limitations of assessing and classifying offenders, and the use of risk-assessment results to make decisions about what therapeutic intervention to design and implement and which offenders qualify for what intervention, privilege, or treatment.

TYPES OF PREDICTIVE FACTORS

The process of assessing risk and needs is informed by the idea that delinquent and criminal behaviors take place partly because of certain criminogenic risk and needs factors, while protective factors help people avoid criminal and delinquent behaviors.

That is, the existence of certain protective and risk factors can explain why people do or do not criminally offend. Risk, needs, and protective factors are identified through rigorous research activities informed by criminological theories and the desire to discover why people commit or do not commit crimes. In other words, the types and nature of information assessed by risk-assessment instruments are dictated by research results that link empirically identified factors to specific criminal or delinquent tendencies or activities (James, 2018).

Criminogenic Risk Factors

The use of the phrase *risk factor* is not limited to criminal justice practitioners or institutions. The phrase *risk factor* is widely used in the field of medicine and in other disciplines to describe existing threats and to talk about legal and therapeutic measures that must be taken to prevent unfortunate outcomes. The phrase *criminogenic risk factor* is, however, uniquely used by criminal justice practitioners to refer to personal, environmental, social, and mental health characteristics that have been researched and found to have the ability to influence specific future antisocial thoughts and behaviors or predict the probability of a person engaging in criminal or delinquent activities (Shader, 2001).

The list of known criminogenic risk factors identified by behavioral scientists is long. However, studies show that eight of those factors are core criminogenic risk factors: (1) antisocial behavior, (2) antisocial personality, (3) a history of antisocial cognition, (4) antisocial associates, (5) antisocial family history, (6) antisocial leisure activities, (7) poor school achievement, and (8) a history of controlled substance abuse (Bonta & Andrews, 2007; Shader, 2001). These factors, listed in Table 11.1, explain why most offenders engage in criminal activities, as well as why certain others do not engage in antisocial thinking and behavior (Bonta & Andrews, 2007; Grieger & Hosser, 2014; James, 2018; Lowenkamp et al., 2006; Shader, 2001; Wooditch et al., 2014). Consequently, at least one or more of these core criminogenic risk factors can be found in most risk assessment instruments currently in use by courts, correctional institutions, and pretrial probation, as well as parole agencies.

Beyond the core criminogenic risk, there is, however, a long list of other behavioral predictors or criminogenic risk factors with the documented potential to influence criminal and delinquent behaviors. For example, association with antisocial families, living in socially disorganized neighborhoods, and having a history of violent behavior have each been linked to specific antisocial behaviors. Specifically, antisocial family ties are risk factors for a variety of antisocial behaviors, such as domestic violence and substance abuse. Studies also show that a history of antisocial family ties leads to increased social problems, which, according to routine activity theory, increases the chances of committing crimes.

Living in socially disorganized neighborhoods also increases the chances of engaging in a multitude of criminal activities. In this respect, an increase in risk or criminal activities can be partly informed by the lack of a bond to the community, thus the absence of respect for the core communal prosocial norms, beliefs, and values. Studies have shown that criminal activities are more likely to occur in communities with a high concentration of high-risk persons, where potential victims are plentiful and there are not enough authority figures to supervise offenders or guard at-risk persons (Chung & Steinberg, 2006; Graif et al., 2014).

It is also worth noting that each of the core factors in Table 11.1 can produce more than one criminogenic risk factor. For example, poor employment history and financial hardship have been linked to poor educational achievement; hence, a deficient educational background and poor employment history can raise the chances of acquisitive crimes, such as shoplifting,

TABLE 11.1 *Core Criminogenic Risk Factors*

	CRIMINOGENIC RISK FACTORS	CRIMINOGENIC NEEDS
1.	*Antisocial Behaviors.* History of antisocial behaviors, including contact with the criminal justice system. Risk calculation focuses on the number of prior offenses and age at first arrest, detention, or criminal behaviors	The need to develop prosocial thinking and behavior and a history of prosocial behavior
2.	*Antisocial Personality.* History of acting impulsively and adventurously, pleasure seeking, restless aggression, and callous disregard for other human beings. Low self-control and high level of hostility	The need to eliminate or reduce hostility level, increase ability to improve self-control, reduce impulsivity and relentless aggression, and to replace poor problem-solving skills with good problem-solving skills
3.	*Antisocial Cognition.* History of antisocial attitudes, beliefs, and values and distorted thinking. Thinking styles supportive of antisocial behaviors, instant gratification, and rationalization of antisocial behavior	The need to reduce or eliminate antisocial thinking and behavior, develop prosocial thinking, attitudes, beliefs, and values. Need to stop justifying and minimizing antisocial behaviors
4.	*Antisocial Associates.* History of associating with peers who engage in antisocial thinking or who have antisocial attitudes, beliefs, values, and/or who use distorted thinking	The need to reduce association with antisocial peers and increase interactions with prosocial peers with prosocial attitudes, beliefs, values, and thinking
5.	*Family History.* History of poor relationships with family members. Interactions with members of the family who tolerate antisocial thinking and behavior	The need to increase ties to prosocial family members and develop prosocial relations with them
6.	*Educational Achievement.* History of poor academic performance, history of behavioral problems at school, and antisocial attitudes toward education in general	The need to develop prosocial attitudes toward education, improve academic performance, and eliminate antisocial behaviors at school
7.	*Leisure Activities.* Participation in antisocial, unstructured, or nonproductive activities during leisure time	The need to participate in prosocial, structured, or productive activities during free or leisure time
8.	*Substance Use, Abuse, and Dependence.* History of controlled substance use, abuse, or dependence	The need to progressively eliminate controlled substance use, abuse, and dependence

burglary, fraud, theft, and robbery. Similarly, a good example of how past antisocial behaviors inform future behaviors is a history of past violence, one of the most replicated and affirmed static risk factors that predict future violent behaviors (Rueve & Welton, 2008, p. 42). Similarly, the antisocial cognition domains can explain or predict all forms of antisocial thought patterns, including distorted or criminal thinking.

Criminogenic Needs Factors

The presence of criminogenic risk factors means the existence of criminogenic needs. Hence *criminogenic needs* refer to services and interventions needed to correct or mitigate the influence of specific criminogenic risk factors. The phrase is also used to describe specific thought patterns and behaviors that must be changed and the specific services and resources that must be obtained to make change possible and to prevent future criminal and delinquent behavior.

Since offenders with high-risk scores are likely to have high needs, pretrial, probation, and parole officers subject high-risk offenders to increased supervision and management.

Needs factors are specific to individual thought patterns, history, behaviors, and reality. For example, while the act of befriending antisocial peers is a criminogenic risk factor, and the corresponding criminogenic needs are to abandon such friends and to find prosocial friends, not every antisocial friend needs to be changed or abandoned simply because the friends are "bad." Clinically, only those antisocial associates who morally or actively support or influence antisocial behaviors are criminogenic risk peers, thus the criminogenic need to change such friends. If an offender's high-risk friends are not, in fact, direct enablers or contributors to an offender's at-risk behavior, or better yet, if the bad friends disapprove of an offender's antisocial behavior, then there is no criminogenic need to change friends. Such antisocial friends are protective factors.

Protective Factors

Inherent in the phrase *protective factors* is the understanding that every person has the potential to engage in criminal activities. However, those with more protective factors to mitigate the potential and compelling urge to commit crimes are less likely to give in to the urge to do so. Those persons with stronger protective factors and weaker risk factors are less likely to engage in criminal activities. That is, when protective factors interact with risk factors, there is an empirical assumption that the former can weaken the strength of the latter or eliminate the latter, thereby making it less likely for criminal activities to take place.

Protective factors include social, psychological, physical, and environmental determinants, behaviors and thought processes that studies show have the power to reduce a person's chances of participating in certain antisocial behaviors or that make it difficult to engage in lawbreaking behaviors. Protective factors are, therefore, individual characteristics that protect against the risk of committing crimes or engaging in criminal and delinquent behaviors. For example, educational achievements are protective factors that can mitigate the risk of financial difficulties and thus provide protection against acquisitive-type crimes, such as shoplifting and selling controlled substances. The assumption is that people with regular and lawful earnings are less likely to commit crimes because of financial hardship. Similarly, good social skills can protect against social conflicts, especially when a person is interacting with multiple people and personalities at work, in the community, and at home.

MANIPULABILITY OF PREDICTIVE FACTORS

The influence of criminogenic risk and needs factors on future delinquent or criminal thinking and behavior is generally dictated by an individual's overall risk level and the circumstances under which that person faces the choice of engaging in antisocial behavior. The effect of therapeutic interventions on each criminogenic risk or needs factor, however, depends on whether such a factor can be successfully manipulated or not. The phrases *dynamic risk and needs factors* and *static risk and needs factors* are, therefore, used to differentiate between changeable and nonchangeable factors. Distinctions between static and dynamic risk factors can help offenders focus on those issues that are likely to make a behavioral difference through therapeutic intervention. Such distinctions can also allow probation and parole officers to allocate appropriate resources to changeable critical factors, as well as to match the right offender with the right therapeutic intervention.

Static Factors

Certain criminogenic risk and needs factors are static factors that cannot be successfully manipulated to prevent future criminal behaviors and antisocial thinking. Static factors are constant, *static*, because no matter how much treatment a person receives and no matter how much the offenders may try their best to live a crime-free life, a prior antisocial history, such as a past arrest or probation or parole violation, does not change. Hence, criminal justice practitioners use the word to describe protective, risk, and need factors that cannot be therapeutically eliminated or changed, although in some instances, the effects of such factors on future antisocial thinking and behavior can be weakened or minimized using appropriate therapeutic interventions.

Examples of static risk factors include a history of prior detention and probation or parole violations. The assumption is that offenders with these histories have increased chances of future arrests and, therefore, are likely to violate future probation or parole. As static factors, some degree of these risks will always exist irrespective of cognitive and behavioral changes. Also, the existence of such a history means that the offender will likely deal with harsh collateral consequences of having a criminal history, such as loss or restriction of a professional license, restrictions on the types of jobs they can get and where they can live, and restrictions on who they can interact with and access to critically needed resources and services, as well as disqualification from receiving certain public assistance, including financial aid and welfare benefits. Collateral consequences of having a criminal history also include disqualification from holding public office or employment; disqualification from serving in the military; acquisition of benefits; restrictions on banking, commodity, and security transactions; receipt of federal benefits; and in the case of sex offenders, the requirement to comply with sex offender registration and notification.

Dynamic Factors

Most risk and protective factors are dynamic. As a result, the effect of dynamic factors on future criminal thinking and behavior can be minimized or eliminated through appropriate therapeutic manipulation. That is, reductions in dynamic risk factors reduce the likelihood of future antisocial behaviors. The amenability of dynamic risk factors can, however, be weakened when a dynamic risk factor is normalized or becomes more pronounced. For example, arriving late to work is a dynamic risk factor for getting fired. However, if arriving to work late happens more frequently, then the possibility of getting significantly increases. At the same time, the time and resources it takes to revise such risk increase significantly. Similarly, drug use is a dynamic risk factor, but if an offender feels mentally and physiologically compelled to use controlled substances frequently, then the possibility of a change becomes more challenging and less attainable.

RISK, NEEDS, AND RESPONSIVITY PRINCIPLES

Increasingly, criminal justice practitioners accept the view that the risk-needs-responsivity (RNR) approach to crime and delinquency prevention and control is the best way to assess and classify offenders as well as to reduce recidivism rates. It is, therefore, not surprising that a recent U.S. Congressional Research Service report acknowledged that the RNR model (Figure 11.1) has become the dominant paradigm in the field of risk and needs assessment (James, 2018, p. 4). Indeed, the RNR approach is commonly used by probation and parole departments, as well as custodial institutions, to supervise and manage defenders and conditions of probation and parole (Burrell, 2017).

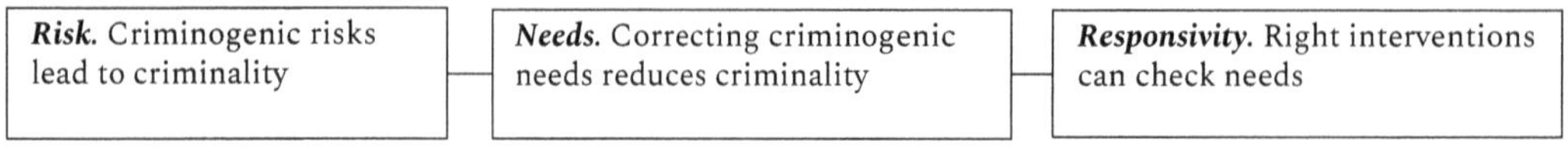

FIGURE 11.1 RNR Model

Some modern risk-assessment and classification tools are designed to capture criminogenic risk factors, needs factors, and offenders' likely responses to treatment. The push for risk, needs, and responsivity principles have much to do with the need to effectively reduce recidivism by preventing future acts of criminality or delinquency. It is, therefore, necessary to explain the distinctions between risk principles, needs principles, and responsivity principles, as well as how each of the three elements tries to correct past behaviors and to prevent future antisocial thinking and behavior.

Risk Principle

The principle of risk demands that risk be proportionate to services delivered to reduce the chance of future acts of criminality because studies show that the subjection of lower risk offenders to high-intensity supervision or programming can be an ineffective use of resources (Hanson et al., 2017). Thus courts and pretrial probation, correctional, and parole officers use risk factors associated with individual offenders, including their prior criminal records, the seriousness of current offenses, the offenders' use of physical violence, the harm suffered by victims, the risk offenders' actions pose to public safety, the offenders' mental health status, and the offenders' employment history and age as critical sources of criminogenic risk factors that predict offenders' likely future behaviors while under the control of the criminal justice system. The logic is that people with increased criminogenic risk factors are more likely to engage in criminal activities than those with fewer criminogenic risk factors. The risk principle further holds that treatment intervention as a response to crime and delinquency must target those criminogenic risk factors that are more closely and strongly related to individual antisocial thinking and behavior.

Obviously, it would be a waste of time and indeed public resources to subject an offender to treatment that has no logical relationship to the specific antisocial behaviors for which the offender is under criminal justice supervision. The placement of a low-risk offender in an intensive treatment program that is designed for high-risk offenders is also likely to produce undesirable results. Similarly, it is not helpful to compel someone who is profusely bleeding to learn how to prevent or stop a common cold and vice versa. In the same vein, placing someone with a minor shoulder cramp and no evidence of other serious medical conditions in an intensive care unit or placing low-risk offenders in programs that demand increased supervision and stringent conditions could be destructive. At the very least, such moves would put unnecessary pressure on offenders, thus increasing the chances of criminal and delinquent behaviors (Lowenkamp et al., 2006).

Needs Principle

The needs principle demands that treatment target the criminogenic needs that risk-assessment and classification processes identify as directly relating to an offender's past, current, and future delinquent or criminal thinking and behavior. In other words, treatment and behavioral interventions that seek to increase the likelihood of achieving better results with regard to recidivism must match the needs that are most closely associated with the offending behaviors.

The logic is that adherence to the needs principle can reduce the possibility of an offender being subjected to the wrong intervention. For example, subjecting a sex offender to a substance abuse treatment program or giving him or her controlled substance user services that are appropriate for those who are dependent on a substance is likely to produce opposite results. That is, interventions must match the criminogenic needs. Sex offender treatment is for sex offenders. Controlled substance abuse treatment is for controlled substance abusers. Child molester treatment is for child molesters, and violent sex offending treatment is for violent sex offenders.

Responsivity Principle

The responsivity principle argues that therapeutic interventions must fit the learning style of offenders and that interventions must take into account offenders' circumstances in terms of the conditions under which their behaviors occurred, the particulars of the behaviors, the physical ability of the offender to benefit from the program being offered, and "the relevant characteristics of the offender," including the offender's motivation level, preferred treatment intervention, personality, age, gender, ethnicity, and cultural background as they relate to the specific behavioral and treatment options (James, 2018). For instance, asking an offender to regularly attend a therapy session at a location that requires driving might not be helpful if that offender has no means of driving to the location. Similarly, asking an offender who only speaks Spanish to complete a program that requires reading and writing in English is not likely to produce desirable results.

The responsivity principle demands that therapeutic intervention and the practitioner delivering treatment services match the offender's personality, motivation level, learning style, and abilities. This approach holds that future criminal and delinquent behaviors can be reduced when treatments are tailored to each individual offender's motivation level, learning style, and ability to benefit from services when the intervention is provided by a qualified person and when the treatment is offered at the cognitive and physical levels of the offender in ways that are designed to reduce the targeted criminal and delinquent thinking and behavior (Wooditch et al., 2014).

The responsivity principle requires that low-risk offenders be separated from high-risk offenders and that low-risk offenders receive minimal services, while high-risk offenders should be given increased services. Offenders who are classified as high-risk should be appropriate for intensive probation or parole and thus should receive intensive social and psychological support to weaken the influence of the criminogenic risk and needs of their thinking and behavior (James, 2018, p. ii).

LIMITATIONS OF PREDICTABILITY

Criminogenic risk, needs, and protective factors are simply causal factors that predict relationships between thought patterns and behaviors and certain criminal or antisocial behaviors (Chung & Steinberg, 2006). Studies have shown that therapeutic programs that follow RNP principles are more likely to mitigate the risk of offenders' engaging in future antisocial thoughts and behaviors (Bonta & Andrews, 2007; James, 2018, p. 8). The use of the RNR approach in the planning and treatment of offenders' services can also maximize resources because such practices allow for the targeted use of public resources to achieve the best possible outcome. That said, the use of risk-assessment instruments, risk and needs scores, and classification levels to reduce the chances of future offending behaviors have certain limitations. First, a single risk factor rarely explains criminal behavior, criminal thinking, or antisocial activity. Rather, a risk only suggests a possible impact and the degree to which the impact is linked to other factors.

Second, the effect of each risk factor on future thinking and behavior can vary from one offender to another depending on individual levels of development; the individual's history, existing risks, and protective factors; mental health status; and existing resources and support that are at each offender's disposal. Indeed, the higher the number of risks associated with a person, the higher the chances of engaging in future delinquent or criminal behavior. Third, many thought patterns and behaviors share common risk factors; thus, one risk factor can explain or predict more than one thought pattern or behavior, including the offender's motivation level and personality as they relate to specific behavioral options (James, 2018).

Fourth, there is no single path to delinquency and criminality because behaviors are usually dictated by multiple risk factors, and most antisocial thinking and behavior share certain risk factors, although some are more impactful than others (Shader, 2008). For example, substance dependence is far more criminogenic than the risk factors associated with substance use. The former is more difficult to correct while the latter is relatively less difficult to correct. Fifth, each risk or protective factor affects a unique set of anti- and prosocial thoughts and behaviors. For example, while academic achievement is a protective factor against certain acquisitive offenses, such as shoplifting, burglary, and dealing in controlled substance sales, it does not protect against crimes such as child molestation, obstruction of justice, and many other nonacquisitive crimes.

RISK AND NEEDS LEVELS

The assignment of an offender to a risk level "should have an empirical basis and be aligned with a recognizable pattern of meaningful" and distinct characteristics (Hanson et al., 2017). Hence criminal justice practitioners use antisocial associates, antisocial behaviors, antisocial cognition, antisocial personality, family history, leisure activities, school and work potential, substance use or abuse, and other well-researched and confirmed risk and protective factors to calculate the criminogenic risk and needs levels of those who make contact with the criminal justice system. Criminal justice practitioners measure risk by assigning numerical values to each risk factor and using the average of the assigned values to calculate levels. Thus the higher the average scores, often on a scale of 4, 5, 10, or 12, the higher the risk level.

Risk scores and levels serve as core points of reference for determining bail, plea bargaining, sentencing, probation conditions, custodial security levels, and housing needs. Criminogenic risk and needs scores are also used to differentiate risk and needs levels among the same set of offenders. Specifically, the risk and needs score dictates which sex offender is high, medium, or low risk and which offender is a high-, medium-, or low-risk substance abuser. There is no universal level-label system; however, standardized labels are commonly used to describe the different levels of risk, needs, and offenders' responsivity.

The labels that most criminal justice practitioners commonly use are low, medium, and high risk and needs levels, or Levels I, II, III, and IV. Some jurisdictions, however, use five-layer systems (Levels I, II, III, IV, and V). Criminogenic risk and needs assessment results dictate who is low, medium, or high risk or which offenders are Level I, II, III, IV, or V violent offenders. Agencies also use these level-label systems to distinguish between low-risk and high-risk violent offenders and which sex offenders are more or less dangerous than other offenders.

Generally, the higher the risk level, the higher the bail, sentence, restrictive custodial housing arrangement, and restrictive probation and parole conditions. In other words, pretrial, correctional, probation, and parole officers also use risk levels to set supervisory restrictions for sex, violent, substance abuse, mental health–related, and general offenders (Nelson & Vincent, 2018). High-risk offenders receive more intensive treatment and services while medium-risk offenders receive medium-level intervention, and low-risk offenders receive minimal or even no intervention (James, 2018, p. ii).

Level I Offenders

The majority of adult and juvenile offenders are Level I offenders. Level I or minimum risk offenders generally have few, if any, criminogenic risks and needs. This level of offender tends to be remorseful, have strong protective factors that can reduce the chances of future acts of criminality, and have low chances of reoffending. Most offenders in this category end up on probation. Level I offenders are less likely to be subjected to stringent conditions and restrictions, such as house arrest, urine tests, and home visits by their pretrial, custodial, probation, and parole officers. Level I offenders are also more likely to comply with conditions of probation or parole, and at trial, they are more likely to be released on their own recognizance at all stages of the criminal justice process.

Level I offenders can be found in every behavioral domain, but the majority are general offenders, controlled substance users and abusers, and mental health–related offenders. Typically, Level I offenders make contact with the criminal justice system for crimes such as possession of drugs, DUI, contributing to the delinquency of a minor, statutory rape, shoplifting, and most white-collar crimes. Some offenders, such as child molesters, are classified as minimum risk in custodial settings but high risk in the community. The assumption is that the chance of a child molester recidivating while in a correctional setting is less likely because there are no children in the custodial setting. Under such conditions, it is illogical to classify a child molester as high risk. In the community, however, the same child molester is more likely to be classified above Level I because all pretrial releasees, probationers, and parolees have access to children, hence the high likelihood of recidivating.

Level II Offenders

A high number of offenders are Level II offenders. Offenders in this category generally have a few criminogenic risk factors and needs that moderately affect antisocial social behaviors in a way that the offenders are somewhat less likely to engage in future acts of criminality than a Level III offender but are more likely to do so in comparison to a Level I offender. Trial courts generally find this group of offenders less suitable for long-term incarceration and less suitable for release without bail. For probation and parole officers, Level II offenders are easier to manage or supervise and thus are more likely to have fewer supervisory restrictions and conditions. That is, Level II offenders are more likely to get lower bail but in comparison to Level I offenders, they are less likely to be released on their own recognizance. Offenders in this category can typically include people who commit crimes such as burglary and low-level domestic violence with minimal physical violence.

Level III Offenders

The offenders who are classified at Level III tend to have multiple criminogenic risk factors and needs that may include a history of violent crimes other than murder and some habitual antisocial behaviors, such as drug use, criminal street gang membership, and history of incarceration and/or not completing probation or parole. Unless otherwise stipulated by statute, Level III offenders are, therefore, more likely to be sentenced to jail or prison for shorter periods. Thus medium-level offenders' chances of recidivating, even after receiving treatment, is usually as low and as high as the chances of not reoffending. It is, therefore, difficult to match a specific offense to Level III-type offenders, although many sex offenders with some evidence of reoffending easily qualify as Level III offenders.

Level IV Offenders

Offenders who are classified at Level IV are generally considered threats to public and institutional safety because of their criminogenic risk and needs scores or statutory requirements of sanctions for their offenses. Level IV offenders typically have histories of serious antisocial thinking and behavior. Most Level IV offenders are also people with a history of committing heinous violent crimes against people, and they are more likely than Level III offenders to engage in criminal behaviors or activities while in custody or on probation or parole and thus can easily compromise institutional and public safety. Consequently, Level IV offenders are likely to receive prison or jail time at trial and more likely to receive stringent conditions of parole and custodial housing restrictions.

Level V Offenders

Offenders classified at Level V tend to have criminogenic risk factors and needs associated with each of the core sources of criminogenic and needs risk (behavioral history, family, education, employment, peers, drugs and alcohol, personality, and cognition) or at least one serious violent criminal action. The presence of multiple risk factors means the chances of the offender committing serious crimes if released into the community even under strong supervision are more likely (Hanson et al., 2017). This group of offenders is considered an extremely dangerous and serious threat to public safety. In custodial settings, Level V offenders are considered at high risk for escape, less likely to rehabilitate, and more likely to harm correctional staff, visitors, and other inmates; hence, they are typically housed in supermax cells or housing facilities. Level V offenders are typically death row inmates, people charged with terrorism, mass shooters, serial killers, and serial rapists. Trial courts usually set high bail or no bond for Level V offenders at all stages of the criminal justice process. The good news, however, is that Level V offenders account for a very small number of the prison and parole populations.

CONCLUSION

Offenders' risk and needs levels are determined by taking into account several factors about each offender and the nature of each offender's crimes, the offender's criminogenic risk scores and needs, and the statutorily prescribed sanctions for the offense that brought the offender into the criminal justice system. In institutional or correctional settings, the level represents the threat an offender poses to institutional security, their risk of escaping from custody, and the level of services therapeutically needed to control each offender's behavior within correctional institutions. In the end, however, the cumulative effect of multiple criminogenic risk and protective factors and the corresponding criminogenic risk and needs assessment scores inform final decisions.

DISCUSSION QUESTIONS

1. In terms of preventing future crimes or delinquent acts, which is more important and why, criminogenic risk, criminogenic needs, or offender's responsivity?
2. Which core criminogenic risk factor best explains sex offending behaviors among both adults and juveniles?
3. Compare and contrast the logic that drives the process of medical examination and the logic that explains the criminal justice risk-assessment and classification process.
4. Which core criminogenic risk factor explains violent offending behavior?
5. Which core criminogenic risk factor explains substance abuse-related offending behavior?

REFERENCES

Bonta, J., & Andrews, D. A. (2007). *Risk-need-responsivity model for offender assessment and rehabilitation 2007-06.* Public Saftey Canada. https://www.pbpp.pa.gov/Information/Documents/Research/EBP7.pdf

Burrell, W. D. (2017). Risk and needs assessment in probation and parole: The persistent gap between promise and practice. In F. S. Taxman (Ed.), *Handbook on risk and need assessment theory and practice* (1st ed.). Routledge.

Chung, H. L., & Steinberg, L. (2006). Relations between neighborhood factors, parenting behaviors, peer deviance, and delinquency among serious juvenile offenders. *Developmental Psychology, 42*(2), 319–331. https://doi.org/10.1037/0012-1649.42.2.319

Graif, C., Gladfelter, A. S., & Matthews, S. A. (2014). Urban poverty and neighborhood effects on crime: Incorporating spatial and network perspectives. *Sociology Compass, 8*(9), 1140–1155. https://doi.org/10.1111/soc4.12199

Grieger, L., & Hosser, D. (2014). Which risk factors are really predictive?: An analysis of Andrews and Bonta's central eight risk factors for recidivism in German youth correctional facility inmates. *Criminal Justice and Behavior, 41*(5), 613–634. https://doi.org/10.1177/0093854813511432

Hanson, R. K., Bourgon, G., McGrath, R. J., Kroner, D., D'Amora, D. A., Thomas, S. S., & Tavarez, L. P. (2017). *A five-level risk and needs system: Maximizing assessment results in corrections through the development of a common language.* The Council of State Governments Justice Center. http://saratso.org/pdf/A_Five_Level_Risk_and_Needs_System_Report.pdf

Harris, G. T., Lowenkamp, C. T., & Hilton, N. Z. (2015). Evidence for risk estimate precision: Implications for individual risk communication. *Behavioral Sciences & the Law, 33*(1), 111–127. https://doi.org/10.1002/bsl.2158

James, N. (2018). *Risk and needs assessment in the federal prison system.* Congressional Research Service. https://fas.org/sgp/crs/misc/R44087.pdf

Lowenkamp, C. T., Latessa, E. J., & Holsinger, A. M. (2006). The risk principle in action: What have we learned from 13,676 offenders and 97 correctional programs? *Crime & Delinquency, 52*(1), 77–93. https://doi.org/10.1177/0011128705281747

Luong, D., & Wormith, J. S. (2011). Applying risk/need assessment to probation practice and its impact on the recidivism of young offenders. *Criminal Justice and Behavior, 38*(12), 1177–1199. https://doi.org/10.1177/0093854811421596

Nelson, R. J., & Vincent, G. M. (2018). Matching services to criminogenic needs following comprehensive risk assessment implementation in juvenile probation. *Criminal Justice and Behavior, 45*(8), 1136–1153. https://doi.org/10.1177/0093854818780923

Rueve, M. E., & Welton, R. S. (2008). Violence and mental illness. *Psychiatry (Edgmont (Pa. : Township)), 5*(5), 34–48. https://www.ncbi.nlm.nih.gov/pubmed/19727251

Shader, M. (2001). *Risk factors for delinquency: An overview.* National Criminal Justice Reference Service. https://www.ncjrs.gov/pdffiles1/ojjdp/frd030127.pdf

Wooditch, A., Tang, L. L., & Taxman, F. S. (2014). Which criminogenic need changes are most important in promoting desistance from crime and substance use? *Criminal Justice and Behavior, 41*(3), 276–299. https://doi.org/10.1177/0093854813503543

CHAPTER TWELVE

Criminogenic Risk and Protective Factors

THE ASSESSMENT AND classification process of criminogenic risk and needs associated with most criminal behavior is partly informed by the desire to "keep low-risk cases low-risk and to bring high-risk down to low-risk" without interfering with offenders' existing strengths (Andrews & Dowden, 2007, p. 399). Indeed, rehabilitation is the primary goal of, particularly, probation and parole. To achieve this therapeutic goal, criminal justice practitioners must develop, at a minimum, a well-informed understanding of criminogenic risk and needs factors associated with most criminal and antisocial activities for which offenders find themselves under the supervision and management of criminal justice practitioners (Black et al., 2001).

Criminogenic risk factors are characteristics, variables, and hazards that make it more likely for an offender, rather than someone from the general population, to engage in antisocial behaviors (Hepburn & Griffin, 2004; Heyman & Smith Slep, 2001). This chapter, therefore, provides an overview of eight core criminogenic risk domains identified as factors that can inform future criminal thinking and behavior. More precisely, the discussion covers school and/or work, leisure and/or recreation, history of criminal behaviors, demonstrated antisocial personality, antisocial associates, antisocial cognition, substance abuse, and family and/or marital factors. Controlled substance use and abuse are treated as a stand-alone criminogenic risk domain because it is comparatively an unlawful behavior that can trigger many more criminal activities, including violent, sex, acquisitive, and white-collar crimes. Violent and sex offending behaviors are uniquely highlighted because they require special attention, as they do within police departments, correctional facilities, and pretrial, probation, and parole agencies.

ANTISOCIAL BEHAVIORS

Early and continuous involvement in criminal and antisocial behaviors increases the chances of future criminal and delinquent behaviors (Andrews & Dowden, 2007; Prins et al., 2015; Wooditch et al., 2014). Criminal or antisocial behavior covers every criminal law violation, and every criminal behavior is a red flag for future acts of criminality. Studies, however, show that a history of violent and/or sex offending behavior demands special attention and intervention because such behaviors affect victims and society more seriously than other criminal behaviors. As shown in Table 12.1, histories of violence and sexual offending behaviors also highly correlate with future offending behaviors. Consequently, police departments, courts, and pretrial service, probation, and parole agencies collectively treat violent and sex offenses more meticulously than other criminal behaviors.

TABLE 12.1 *Risks Associated With Criminal History*

RISK	SEX	SUB	VIO	GEN
Victim of past sexual abuse	*	*	*	*
Childhood history of physical abuse	*	*	*	*
Childhood history of emotional abuse	*	*	*	*
Childhood history of sexual abuse	*	*	*	*
Exposure to violent family conflicts	*	*	*	*
Antisocial beliefs and attitudes	*	*	*	*
Association with criminal peers		*	*	*
Gang membership or activities		*	*	*
History of sexually offending	*		*	
Coercive sexual fantasies	*		*	
Hostility toward women	*		*	
History of early aggressive behavior	*		*	
Controlled substance use and abuse		*		*
Lack of employment opportunities				*

The criminogenic risk factors listed in Table 12.1 show that violence, sex crimes, and general offending behavior share most criminogenic risk factors (Black et al., 2001). For example, people who have suffered sexual, physical, emotional, or psychological abuse have higher chances of committing sex, violent, substance abuse, and general offending behaviors than children who grow up without such histories. Similarly, people whose close family members tolerate violence or reward antisocial thoughts and attitudes supportive of controlled substance use also have an increased risk of controlled substance abuse-related behavior.

Sex Offenses

Histories of sexual offending behaviors are carefully and thoroughly assessed and addressed by criminal justice practitioners irrespective of whether an offender's current charges include a sex crime. Among other reasons that sex offenses receive such attention is in part the fact that damage caused to victims and society far exceeds other categories of crime. Indeed, offenses such as child molestation, rape, incest, and sexual abuse and assault can have a devastating psychological, physical, and social effect on victims (Black et al., 2001). Of course, there is not a single criminogenic risk factor that can independently and accurately predict the likelihood of future sexual or criminal offending behaviors. Rather, there are multiple criminogenic risk factors that make most sex offending behavior possible. Among such factors are those listed in Table 12.2, which can provide possible explanations for why most people commit sex crimes (Black et al., 2001; CSOM, 2008; Hepburn & Griffin, 2004).

TABLE 12.2 *Common Risk Factors for Sex Offending Behaviors*

1.	Physiological or biological reasons, such as sexual attraction to children
2.	Environmental and social settings that tolerate attitudes and beliefs associated with sexual offending behaviors
3.	Childhood exposure to inappropriate sexual behaviors, such as molestation, overt sexual acts, sexual violence, and physical, sexual, or emotional abuse
4.	History of prior sexually deviant behaviors
5.	Evidence of current deviant sexual fantasies

It is important to note that criminogenic risk factors affect offenders differently depending on their history and other factors, such as their physical, emotional, or cognitive circumstances. For instance, offenders who experience sexual abuse at an early age are more likely to be intensely affected than those without such a history. A history of deviant sexual behavior and fantasies, including those associated with bestiality, exhibitionism, frottage, pedophilia, pornography, rape, sadism, and voyeurism, increases the potential for future sex crimes. The environment also plays an important role in the development and continuation of offenders' behaviors. For example, the overwhelming majority, precisely 85% of sexual offending behaviors, are committed by family members or acquaintances. This finding means that since the majority of sex crimes take place in a setting socially conducive to such behaviors, the role played by families in the construction of the behavioral patterns people exhibit in life is critical.

Controlled Substances

All criminal behaviors, including possession of controlled substances, fall under criminal history. However, unlike violent and sex crimes, substance abuse-related behaviors are uniquely different in that the behavior can lead to many categories of criminal activities, including violent and sexual offending behaviors and white-collar and acquisitive crimes. Evidence also shows that many controlled substances can make certain users aggressive and angry. For example, certain stimulants, such as cocaine, crack, methamphetamine, and amphetamine, can induce paranoia and hallucinations to a point where users think that there are evil people trying to cause them harm, and in response to such unfounded fears, they may feel compelled to violently defend themselves against the perceived evils. Controlled substances in general also affect individuals' ability to satisfactorily fulfill their moral, legal, social, and cultural obligations (Bartol & Bartol, 2017). More importantly, controlled substances alter normal brain function to a point where a person becomes unable to exercise good judgment.

People who abuse alcohol and/or use other controlled substances are at high risk of engaging in criminal activity (Andrews & Dowden, 2007; Wooditch et al., 2014). At a minimum, those who use a controlled substance are good candidates for getting arrested for felonious possession of the controlled substance they commonly abuse. Also, the chance of getting arrested or having probation or parole revoked also increases with controlled substance use or abuse. Obviously, the effect of drugs on individuals' ability to prosocially think and behave when confronting a high-risk situation means that controlled substance abuse creates many opportunities for engaging in criminal and antisocial behaviors.

The most predictive risk factor for controlled substance use or addiction is experimentation with the controlled substance. Surely, every addiction begins with experimentation, although it is at the same time common for people, especially in their youth, to experiment with controlled substances. It is, however, deducible that although most people experiment with multiple controlled substances in their lives, not every experimentation leads to addiction. In fact, there are people who hate alcohol, marijuana, cocaine, and similar controlled substances the first time they experiment with them. As for those whose experiments progress to use, dependency, or addiction, studies show that one or more factors listed in Table 12.3 have played some role in that evolution (Mayo-Clinic, 2019; NIH, 2019).

TABLE 12.3 *Common Risk Factors for Controlled Substance Offending Behaviors*

1.	Having close friends who use controlled substances
2.	Having close family members who use controlled substances
3.	Having peers who use controlled substances
4.	Presence in areas where controlled substance use is tolerated
5.	History of being sexually abused during childhood
6.	History of being physically abused during childhood
7.	History of being emotionally abused during childhood
8.	Early exposure to controlled substance use
9.	Current history of chronic stress
10.	Inability or unwillingness to resist the use of controlled substances

With regard to when an experiment with a controlled substance becomes a serious problem for probation and parole agencies within the context of criminal behaviors, the factors listed in Table 12.3 have been identified as symptoms of controlled substance use that require evidence-based intervention to prevent future unwanted contact with the criminal justice system. In other words, experimentation becomes an issue for probation and parole officers, especially when assessing and classifying offenders, when one or more of the factors listed in Table 12.4 form part of the criminal or antisocial history (Mayo-Clinic, 2019; NIH, 2019).

The presence of any of the symptoms listed in Table 12.4 in the history of an offender suggests that there is a controlled substance use problem. That is, the more these signs are present in an offender's history, the higher the chances for that offender to use controlled substances in the future. The presence of such evidence also suggests that controlled substance-related behavioral problems require evidence-based interventions. In order words, people who report spending time procuring, using, and recovering from drug use are at increased risk of abusing controlled substances and thus are at an elevated risk of future criminality or making unwanted contact with the criminal justice system.

Violent Behavior

Offenders with a history of violent crime are treated with a certain level of seriousness by all branches of the criminal justice system, including the police, the courts, and pretrial service, probation, and parole agencies. Each of these agencies aggressively responds to violent

TABLE 12.4 *Common Symptoms of Substance Use Problems*

1.	Feeling mentally and physiologically pressured to use controlled substances
2.	Continuous elevation of the amount needed to get a desired level of intoxication
3.	Making specific efforts to keep a continuous supply of a controlled substance
4.	Spending money on controlled substances above one's financial means
5.	Failure to meet obligations, including work and school because of controlled substance use
6.	Cutting back on social or recreational activities because of controlled substance use
7.	Use of controlled substances despite being aware of their negative effects
8.	Committing crimes to support controlled substance use
9.	Increasingly spending time on the procurement and use of a controlled substance
10.	Experiencing withdrawal symptoms when attempting to stop substance use
11.	Unable to socially function without controlled substance use
12.	Evidence of poor judgment, learning, and decision making because of substance use

criminal behaviors, especially violence against children, women, and older and disabled persons. The goal for every probation and parole agency is, therefore, to lessen the likelihood of violent victimization by people who are under their supervision and management. Table 12.5 shows factors linked to violent behavior, and although these factors do not directly cause violence, they increase the likelihood of individuals perpetrating violence in the future (CDC, 2019; Farrington, 1997).

TABLE 12.5 *Common Factors That Increase the Chances of Future Violence*

1.	Belonging to groups that condone violence
2.	Lengthy history of aggression or past violent behavior
3.	History of angry outbursts
4.	Interest in weapons or explosives
5.	Habit of making violent threats when angry
6.	Cruelty to animals
7.	Fire setting
8.	Mere access to guns or other weapons
9.	History of family violence
10.	History of weapon possession or use by family
11.	Involvement with street gangs
12.	History of being abused as a child
13.	History of being violently victimized
14.	History of early aggressive behavior
15.	History of high emotional distress
16.	Antisocial beliefs and attitudes in favor of violence
17.	Presence in socially disorganized neighborhoods

Violence is an inappropriate expression of anger and frustration, and certain factors increase the tendency for violence. For example, possession of guns or other lethal weapons during an emotionally distressed state of mind obviously heightens the chances of violence. Similarly, being in possession of guns and other lethal weapons while under the influence of controlled substances, which weakens an individual's ability to reason well, can increase the likelihood of such weapons being used to inflict self-harm. When these conditions are fused with economic hardship and lack of needed resources in general, a sense of hopelessness can ultimately lead to violence.

The information in Table 12.5 shows that a combination of individual characteristics and history, relationships, and community and societal factors can increase the chances of future violence. Precisely, violence can be influenced by family members, peers, environments, cultures, and sociological factors. Environments with available guns and drugs and a culture of violence tend to produce increased rates of violence. Mental illnesses or disorders can also inhibit individuals' ability to make good decisions, including the decision to refrain from violent acts. Indeed, individuals with mental illnesses are not comparatively at greater risk of committing crimes than law-abiding citizens; however, when certain mental illnesses are left unaddressed, serious self-abusive behaviors or violence against self or others can result (CDC, 2019; Farrington, 1997).

General Behaviors

An overwhelming number of criminal behaviors on the books are not violent, sexual, or controlled substance-related but white-collar, acquisitive, and thrill-seeking types of crimes that fall under the general category of offenses. It is, therefore, not surprising that most adults and, indeed, older youth have at least some history of committing one or more white-collar, acquisitive, and/or thrill-seeking offenses. Common examples of general offenses include driving without a license, tax evasion, shoplifting, perjury, tampering with evidence, obstructing justice, simple theft, and financial fraud (Wooditch et al., 2014). The likelihood of committing any of these general offenses increases when one or more of the risk factors listed in Table 12.6 form part of an offender's criminal history.

TABLE 12.6 *Common Risk Factors for General Offending Behaviors*

1.	Tolerance of sexual offending behaviors within a family
2.	Poor economic standing and opportunities
3.	Frequent changes in home address
4.	Membership in an antisocial peer group supportive of crime
5.	Family history of substance use
6.	Poor social cognition and skills
7.	Few ties to prosocial institutions, such as school and family
8.	High levels of emotional distress

Each of these factors can influence future criminal behavior. For example, substance abuse is common in environments where such behaviors are tolerated. People whose families glorify or accept substance use are at greater risk of using controlled substances than people whose families disapprove of such behaviors. An increased level of stress can increase the desire for controlled substances to cope with the stress or the sources of discomfort. Also important is association with people who use controlled substances or who socially reward such behaviors. Indeed, people with such relationships can be led by their friends to develop favorable views of controlled substances and can be pressured to use them. Poor economic standing and scarce opportunities are other factors that can increase the chances of, particularly, acquisitive crimes.

With respect to the history of violence, sex crimes, and abuse of controlled substances, the degree to which a behavioral pattern deviates from other behaviors in the same behavioral category can make a difference in the level of impact such behavior may have on future offending behaviors. Obviously, the length of the history, the number of times the behavior occurred, the degree to which the behaviors match or deviate from other behaviors in the same behavioral category, and the age at which the behaviors occurred can each affect the overall impact on future behavior. The general rule is that the shorter the history, the fewer the number of behaviors, the less intensive the behaviors and the age appropriateness at the time of the behaviors, the weaker the overall impact of the histories on future behaviors. The longer the history of victimization, the higher the likelihood of future offending behaviors. The shorter the history of past behaviors, the lesser the impact of such histories on future criminal activities. The more intense the behavior, in terms of the degree of criminality, the higher the chances of future criminality.

EMPLOYMENT AND EDUCATIONAL HISTORY

Low academic performance or achievement and lack of satisfactory school and work histories increase the potential for future criminal behaviors, particularly acquisitive crimes that are primarily influenced by the motivation to acquire financial and material resources (Andrews & Dowden, 2007; Wooditch et al., 2014). In this regard, an argument can be made that unemployment can result from a lack of employment opportunities (Melick, 2003). For the purpose of criminogenic risk assessment, the focus is on individual offenders' ability to secure and maintain legitimate employment and to lawfully support themselves with the money they earn from legal employment using existing opportunities and resources.

Studies show that unemployment significantly affects the rate of property crimes, such as burglary and auto theft, and violent crimes, such as robbery and assault (Raphael & Winter-Ebmer, 2001). In this regard, the factors listed in Table 12.7 can reduce an individual's chances of securing a job or maintaining gainful employment and thus can elevate the chances of future acts of criminality. The logic is that as economic hardship increases, so does the desire to seek illegal means of sustenance. For example, although there is no universal definition of hardship, crimes such as prostitution, illicit drug sales, robbery, and burglary are generally motivated by some form of financial hardship.

TABLE 12.7 *Education and Unemployment Risk Factors*

1.	No lawful means of income
2.	Lack of job opportunities because of occupational unpreparedness
3.	Lack of appropriate training or education for employment
4.	Unwillingness to secure lawful employment
5.	History of failing to keep gainful employment

A substantial body of literature views the lack of employment and education as critical criminogenic risk factors and supports the conclusion that unemployment and/or lack of appropriate education or training can increase the chances of acquisitive crimes (Bennett & Ouazad, 2016). The relationships between crime and employment and between crime and education obviously exist because education increases an individual's capacity to competitively secure and maintain gainful employment. That is, the more educated or trained an offender, the higher the chance of securing and maintaining gainful employment. It is worth remembering that the absence of lawful means of income does not necessarily mean that an individual's desire for what money can buy ceases to exist.

INDIVIDUAL CHARACTERISTICS

Studies have shown that people who adventurously seek pleasure and exhibit weak self-control, who are restlessly aggressive, and/or who are callously offensive experience a higher risk of recidivism and of engaging in criminal activities (Andrews & Dowden, 2007; Valdivia et al., 2014; Wooditch et al., 2014). Certainly, offenders with these sorts of characteristics can benefit from interventions designed to help offenders develop problem-solving skills, skills required for self-management, and, for some offenders, training in anger management and coping skills. The factors listed in Table 12.8 have been identified as risks that can influence acts of criminality (Farrington & Jolliffe, 2015; O'Riordan & O'Connell, 2014; Valdivia et al., 2014).

TABLE 12.8 *Core Factors Associated With Individual Characteristics*

1.	Evidence of being adventurous and preoccupied with seeking pleasure
2.	Evidence of weak self-control, especially when tempted to engage in criminal activity
3.	Evidence of restless aggression toward people, property, or animals
4.	Evidence of lack of sympathy and empathy and shows of callousness
5.	Evidence of inability to get along with others and being disagreeable
6.	Evidence of extroversion and lack of conscientiousness and emotional instability

Obviously, in life, people are required to get along with others, to say no to criminal and antisocial behaviors, and to not be driven mainly by adventurous pleasure-seeking activities. Offenders with antisocial personalities, however, find it hard to conform to social norms because of their unwillingness or lack of desire to get along with others and to say no when necessary. Offenders in this category also tend to display aggressiveness and show coldheartedness toward the suffering of others. The effect of factors such as peer influence and personality traits can also be influenced by offenders' ages at the time of the prohibited behaviors or at the time of the risk and needs assessment and classification process—the older the offenders, the weaker the effect on them (Monahan et al., 2009; Valdivia et al., 2014).

ANTISOCIAL PEERS

Offenders who associate with or who have friends who associate with people who participate in criminal practices or who have friends who tolerate or reward criminal thinking, behavior, and tendencies and lack prosocial support for prosocial behavior are at elevated risk of future criminal activities (Andrews & Dowden, 2007; Wooditch et al., 2014). Indeed, beyond the impact of family on future behaviors, peers are sources of influence for many criminal and antisocial behaviors. It should, however, be noted that studies show that the impact of peers on antisocial and criminal behaviors significantly drops after age 20 because as individuals mature socially and cognitively, they become resistant to peer pleasure and more prepared to fully comprehend the effect of their friends on their behaviors (Monahan et al., 2009). Table 12.9 lists core antisocial peer-related factors that can increase future acts of criminality.

TABLE 12.9 *Core Factors Associated Antisocial Peers*

1.	Offender has friends who pressure him or her to engage in criminal and antisocial behaviors
2.	Offender has friends who socially reward antisocial and criminal behaviors
3.	Offender has friends known as criminal or deviant, evidenced by their behaviors
4.	Offender commits crimes in the presence of peers who approve of such behaviors
5.	Offender's friends hold antisocial attitudes and beliefs toward authority, public laws, rules, and norms

While most friendships are not criminogenic risk factors but protective factors, sometimes the negativity of friends becomes a way to predict the thinking and behavior of those who are close to such people. Risk-assessment and classification processes, therefore, assess the number of friends an offender has and the characteristics, thinking, attitudes, and behaviors of those friends in an attempt to gauge the extent to which an offender is likely to engage in specific antisocial and criminal behaviors. The conclusion is that the more criminal and antisocial an offender, the higher the chances of that offender engaging in prohibited acts.

FAMILY DYNAMICS

Family environments that tolerate or reward antisocial behavior, including physical violence and conflict, are good sources of criminal and antisocial behaviors. Hence, ties to unhealthy family environments can increase an individual's overall risk of participating in criminal activity (Andrews & Dowden, 2007; Wooditch et al., 2014). Of course, what constitutes an "unhealthy" family can differ from one cultural environment to another, but in this context, an unhealthy family is one that has the characteristics listed in Table 12.10. Studies show that these factors can inform many categories of offenses and social problems that increase the chances of making unwanted contact with law enforcement agencies.

TABLE 12.10 *Common Factors Associated With Family Dynamics*

1.	History of family members collectively tolerating physical, sexual, and psychological violence
2.	Family history of condoning the use of or actually using controlled substances
3.	Family history of participating in criminal organizations, such as gangs
4.	Family history of domestic violence
5.	Family history of participating in intrafamilial physical, sexual, and psychological abuse of another family member

The process of assessing and classifying criminogenic risk factors focuses mainly on how members of a family treat each other; the overall level of tolerance for antisocial behaviors in general; the extent to which a family exercises respect for public norms, rules, laws, and public authority; members' attitudes and beliefs toward core prosocial factors, such as academic achievement and gainful employment; individual or collective histories of controlled substance use; violence; and sexual offending behaviors. Of course, the most predictive factors are controlled substance use or abuse and a history of intrafamilial physical, psychological, and sexual abuse (Heyman & Smith Slep, 2001; Wooditch et al., 2014). A negative family history is one where members of a particular family approve of prohibited acts and enable or socially reward each other's participation in criminal and antisocial activities.

MENTAL HEALTH AND CRIMINAL THINKING

People who suffer from acute mental illnesses are more likely to be victimized by so-called normal people and are less likely to victimize others. Indeed, individual attitudes and beliefs and rationalization of and support for criminal and other antisocial behaviors and thinking, as well as the frequent and uncontrollable display of emotion, such as anger and resentment, are criminogenic risk factors that inform future criminal and antisocial thinking and behavior (Andrews & Dowden, 2007; Wooditch et al., 2014). Studies have also found that offenders who frequently display cognitive distortion or criminal thinking like those listed in Table 12.11 are at increased risk of engaging in criminal activity (Bucklen & Zajac, 2009; Wooditch et al., 2014). The list of behaviors labeled criminal thinking, distorted thinking, or thinking errors is lengthy, but the criminal thinking listed in Table 12.11 shows the criminal thinking most commonly used by offenders during treatment and during times when they may be faced with the consequences of their behaviors.

The reason behind most criminal thinking is the unwillingness to accept responsibility for wrong deeds in fear of the consequences. That said, it is important to note that the use of criminal thinking is more common among sex and violent offenders. For instance, sex offenders are known for blaming their victims for wearing tight outfits, exposing their bodies, being in rooms alone with them, not resisting their approaches, or teasing in a provocative way. Violent offenders also use criminal thinking to legitimize their violent tendencies and behaviors. Violent offenders blame their victims and minimize their own behaviors.

Although mental illness itself is not a known criminogenic risk factor—people with mental illness are more likely to be victimized by others—there are three symptoms that must be taken into account when assessing and classifying offenders, especially within correctional institutions: (1) a history of hearing voices or being given commands to engage in criminal, violent, or any antisocial behavior; (2) suicidal ideation or having the urge or plan to commit suicide; (3) homicidal ideations or having the desire or plan to kill another person; and (4) having access to lethal weapons.

FREE TIME

Leisure periods are times of day or periods in a week when people are free to engage in activities of their choice because they have no external commitments. Studies show that those

TABLE 12.11 *Common Criminal Thinking Offenders Use*

1. *Blaming.* One of the direct penalties for criminal activity is suffering the consequences attached to a prohibited behavior. Hence offenders avoid consequences by using the cognitive tactic of placing blame on another person, often the victim, with the hope of escaping the consequences of their behaviors. Indeed, there is no legitimate excuse, legally speaking, for criminal behavior. It is important for the offender to accept responsibility if treatment is the ultimate goal.
2. *Entitlement.* This sort of criminal thinking is a common example of distorted thinking used by offenders. Entitlement means an offender feels permitted to engage in a prohibited act. Spousal and date rape can be influenced by the belief that the offender has a right to victimize the victim. Offenders who espouse entitlement believe that they have a right to services, people, and property.
3. *Justification.* Most offenders realize the wrongfulness of their actions after the fact. Hence, to escape responsibility, they may try to make their behaviors look normal by justifying their actions. In this case, offenders try to explain the "correctness" of their prohibited behaviors by arguing that they acted correctly in the first place. For example, a violent offender may argue that they acted in self-defense. In this example, the offender is not denying the behavior but is arguing that the behavior was justifiable.
4. *Fronting.* Offenders use this sort of criminal thinking to argue that their thoughts and behaviors are so proper that they could not have committed the prohibited act. The goal here is to convince their probation or parole officers that they are not responsible for the prohibited acts; therefore, they should not be subjected to the consequences prescribed for their criminal or antisocial behavior.
5. *Minimization.* One of the tricks offenders play is to make a terrible criminal behavior look not so terrible. For example, child molesters may argue that they did not do anything that will cause their victims to bleed, or they did not penetrate their child victims. A violent offender may argue that they did not hit their victim with a hammer; it was only a light blow to the stomach. What offenders in these examples fail to realize is that during a conflict, hitting another person in any way is an act of violence and that a child molestation is a child molestation. The key indicators of minimization are "not a big deal," "only," and "just," such as, "I don't use hard drugs; I only use soft drugs like marijuana, not every day, but only on weekends."
6. *Uniqueness.* Offenders may use the criminal thinking "uniqueness" to convince their probation or parole officers that they are uniquely different from other offenders, and so they should not be treated the same way as other offenders.
7. *Mind reading.* Another way offenders try to avoid taking responsibility for their behaviors is by arguing that they did what they did because their victims wanted them to, although the victims did not actually say so. For example, a sex offender may argue that the victim did not physically fight them off or stop them; therefore, the victim must have wanted the victimization. Of course, this thought is distorted—simply put, not physically resisting does not mean that the victim wants to be victimized. Here the offender is jumping to conclusions about another person's feelings and thinking.
8. *Confusion.* Offenders play dumb or claim to be confused after realizing that they have engaged in a prohibited act. They pretend that they did not know at the time that their behavior was prohibited or that they were confused. The problem is that when confused, the proper behavior is to ask for clarification. Of course, these offenders are trying to exploit the notion that when someone acts in a state of confusion, they should not be held accountable.
9. *Victim Stance.* The criminal thinking known as the victim stance is often used when offenders are asked to complete certain tasks as a consequence of their prohibited behavior. However, instead of acting as ordered, offenders present themselves as victims of circumstance; that is, despite their efforts, everything continues to work against them. A victim stance statement may sound like "no matter how much I spend on fixing my car, it always breaks down on Monday, the day I am supposed to attend counseling."

who engage in productive or structured activities, such as playing sports, reading, performing domestic tasks, spending time in socially healthy environments, or engaging in positive activities, during their free time are less likely to engage in criminal activities compared to those who spend their free time in socially unhealthy environments, such as places where illicit drugs or gambling are common. The risk also increases for offenders who joyride or aimlessly spend time at unstructured places and gatherings. Table 12.12 contains common free time–related risk factors that predict future acts of criminality, especially for sex and violent offenders (Andrews & Dowden, 2007; Wooditch et al., 2014).

TABLE 12.12 *Common Factors Associated With Free Time*

1.	Offender has a history of aimlessly cruising around
2.	Offender engages in unstructured activities during free time
3.	Offender has a history of frequenting unstructured environments where criminal activities are common
4.	Offender engages in criminal activities during free time
5.	Offender engages in antisocial activities during free time

The farther away from home the behavior occurs, the higher the impact on future behavior. That is, unstructured activities that take place within the immediate vicinity of the offender's place of residence may not be as impactful as those that occur in places that have more vulnerable victims, more people from different social backgrounds, and a range of criminogenic risk and needs factors (Messner & Blau, 1987). Obviously, victims who are strangers to an offender are more vulnerable to serious acts of violence than someone who is known to an offender. Also, unstructured activities outside the home create opportunities to get in contact with people who may have similar free time–related criminogenic risk factors.

CONCLUSION

It is worth noting that many risk factors are more predictive for youthful offenders than adults. For example, criminal history is more predictive for adults who know better and have more evil intent than juvenile offenders, many of whom are without the proper guidance or just exploring behaviors or playing unwisely as children usually do. However, in both cases, whether involving an adult or juvenile, each criminogenic risk domain can affect an individual's thinking and behavior differently depending on many personal characteristics and factors. For example, the impact of each criminogenic risk factor can be weakened or enhanced by other factors like an offender's culture, socioeconomic standing, environmental conditions, and attitudes and beliefs.

Given the fact that the strength of an offender's criminogenic and protective factors can be weakened or strengthened by individual circumstances, it is important for criminal justice practitioners to go beyond the mere history of criminal and antisocial behavior, befriending or associating with antisocial persons, belonging to a dysfunctional family, having poor academic performance or work ethic, having unstructured use of free time, engaging in controlled substance use and abuse, and thinking in antisocial ways. For each of these domains, individual history, culture, mental status, socioeconomic standing, and the circumstances that prompted and facilitated the development of such histories should be taken into account when conducting a risk and needs assessment. Indeed, even in situations where such background information exists, criminal justice practitioners should consider the totality of an offender's history, thinking, and behavior.

DISCUSSION QUESTIONS

1. Comparatively, which of these domains has the most impact on future criminal thinking and behavior?
2. Comparatively, which domain has the least impact on future criminal thinking and behavior?
3. Are the criminogenic risk factors presented in this chapter universal or limited to Western societies, such as the United Kingdom, Australia, Canada, and, particularly, the United States?
4. Do at-risk peers affect each other's antisocial thinking and behavior differently in different cultural settings? Why or why not?
5. Is the use of criminal thinking in the context of violent and sex crimes different from the use of criminal thinking in the context of general offenses or controlled substance use or abuse? If yes or no, why?

REFERENCES

Andrews, D. A., & Dowden, C. (2007). The risk-need-responsivity model of assessment and human service in prevention and corrections: Crime-prevention jurisprudence. *Canadian Journal of Criminology & Criminal Justice*, *49*(4), 439–464. https://doi.org/10.3138/cjccj.49.4.439

Bartol, C. R., & Bartol, A. M. (2017). *Criminal behavior: A psychological approach* (11th ed.). Pearson.

Bennett, P. & Ouazad, A. (2016). The relationship between job displacement and crime. Vox. https://voxeu.org/article/relationship-between-job-displacement-and-crime

Black, D. A., Heyman, R. E., & Smith Slep, A. M. (2001). Risk factors for child sexual abuse. *Aggression and Violent Behavior*, *6*(2), 203–229. https://doi.org/https://doi.org/10.1016/S1359-1789(00)00023-9

Bucklen, K. B., & Zajac, G. (2009). But some of them don't come back (to prison!): Resource deprivation and thinking errors as determinants of parole success and failure. *The Prison Journal*, *89*(3), 239–264. https://doi.org/10.1177/0032885509339504

CDC. (2019). *Violence prevention, 2019.* https://www.cdc.gov/violenceprevention/youthviolence/riskprotectivefactors.html

CSOM. (2008). *Fact sheet: What you need to know about sex offenders.* https://www.csom.org/pubs/needtoknow_fs.pdf

Farrington, D. P. (1997). Early prediction of violent and non-violent youthful offending. *European Journal on Criminal Policy and Research*, 5(2), 51–66. https://doi.org/10.1007/bf02677607

Farrington, D. P., & Jolliffe, D. (2015). Personality and crime. In J. D. Wright (Ed.), *International encyclopedia of the social & behavioral sciences* (2nd ed., pp. 774–779). Elsevier.

Hepburn, J. R., & Griffin, M. L. (2004). *An analysis of risk factors contributing to the recidivism of sex offenders on probation* [Report submitted to the U.S. Department of Justice]. https://www.ncjrs.gov/pdffiles1/nij/grants/203905.pdf

Heyman, R. E., & Smith Slep, A. M. (2001). Risk factors for family violence: Introduction to the special series. *Aggression and Violent Behavior, 6*(2), 115–119. https://doi.org/https://doi.org/10.1016/S1359-1789(00)00020-3

Mayo-Clinic. (2019). *Drug addiction (substance use disorder).* Retrieved August 18, 2019, from https://www.mayoclinic.org/diseases-conditions/drug-addiction/symptoms-causes/syc-20365112

Melick, M. D. (2003). The relationship between crime and unemployment. *The Park Place Economist, 11*(1), 30–36.

Messner, S. F., & Blau, J. R. (1987). Routine leisure activities and rates of crime: A macro-level analysis. *Social Forces, 65*(4), 1035–1052. https://doi.org//10.2307/2579022

Monahan, K. C., Steinberg, L., & Cauffman, E. (2009). Affiliation with antisocial peers, susceptibility to peer influence, and antisocial behavior during the transition to adulthood. *Developmental Psychology, 45*(6), 1520–1530. https://doi.org/10.1037/a0017417

NIH. (2019, June 2018). *Understanding drug use and addiction.* Retrieved August 18, 2019, from https://www.drugabuse.gov/publications/drugfacts/understanding-drug-use-addiction

O'Riordan, C., & O'Connell, M. (2014). Predicting adult involvement in crime: Personality measures are significant, socio-economic measures are not. *Personality and Individual Differences, 68*, 98–101. https://doi.org/https://doi.org/10.1016/j.paid.2014.04.010

Prins, S. J., Skeem, J. L., Mauro, C., & Link, B. G. (2015). Criminogenic factors, psychotic symptoms, and incident arrests among people with serious mental illnesses under intensive outpatient treatment. *Law and Human Behavior, 39*(2), 177–188. https://doi.org/10.1037/lhb0000104

Raphael, S., & Winter-Ebmer, R. (2001). Identifying the effect of unemployment on crime. *Journal of Law & Economics, 44*(1), 259–283.

Valdivia, M., Nguyen, T., Arbach, K., & Andrés-Pueyo, A. (2014). Personality, age, and antisocial peers: Relationships with violent and non-violent crimes. *Personality and Individual Differences, 60*, S39. https://doi.org/https://doi.org/10.1016/j.paid.2013.07.101

Wooditch, A., Tang, L. L., & Taxman, F. S. (2014). Which criminogenic need changes are most important in promoting desistance from crime and substance use? *Criminal Justice and Behavior, 41*(3), 276–299. https://doi.org/10.1177/0093854813503543

CHAPTER THIRTEEN

Risk-Assessment Tools

ASSESSMENT SIMPLY MEANS the examination of something to gain more understanding and appreciation of that thing. Classification refers to the placement of things into various categories using specific patterns of measurement, which in this case are generally assessment tools or instruments. The need for risk-assessment tools has long been prompted by the desire to provide protection, security, treatment, and respect for individual civil rights. Consequently, plenty of risk-assessment tools currently in circulation measure the tendency of an individual to engage in sexual, substance abuse, violent, and/or general offending behaviors. Given that most institutions use at least one or more unique tools for a specific offender population or category, estimates show that the number of different risk-assessment instruments in circulation runs from 120 to 400 (GIFR 2016; McKeown 2015; Singh et al. 2011).

Despite the high number of risk-assessment instruments in circulation, not a single tool can accurately predict every sexual, violent, substance abuse, or general offender's risk of recidivism. A one-size-fits-all assessment tool would be useless because people come from different backgrounds. While each offender is different, each behavior also occurs within a unique social and situational context. What is more, each institution demanding the assessment and classification has a unique institutional goal and objective, and each criminal justice professional conducting the assessment and classification has a unique point of reference.

Despite the diverse backgrounds of offenders, risk-assessment tools commonly assess offenders' psychosocial and behavioral histories and current social and psychological statuses, thinking, attitudes, and behaviors. This chapter, therefore, provides an overview of assessment instruments commonly used by correctional facilities, pretrial services, probation and parole agencies, and criminal justice practitioners at various levels to assess and classify offenders. The various items or statements contained in assessment and classification tools seek critical information used to make decisions about the appropriateness of institutional housing conditions and the treatment and management of offenders within correctional facilities and in the community. The items or statements in each exhibit are samples of some of the common items found in typical criminal justice assessment and classification tools.

SCORING ASSESSMENT TOOLS

Insurance companies take a keen interest in correctly predicting the likelihood of their clients' filling insurance claims. Companies assess and classify their potential clients by calculating values assigned to known risks, such as a recent history of speeding, DUI, and living in areas where auto theft is common. So when insurance companies say that a driver is at risk, they mean the driver is at risk of causing an accident or filing an insurance claim. Similarly, American criminal justice systems have a special interest in predicting which offenders are likely to successfully participate in pretrial and presentencing programs, complete probation or parole, partake in specialized programing or treatment within correctional institutions, or comply with general rules. Thus when criminal justice practitioners say an offender is at risk, it means the person is either at risk of breaking existing laws or of causing harm to themselves or another person. Such predictions are generally informed by observable behavioral patterns that have been recorded or that are being observed.

To assess risk levels, developers of risk assessment instruments group the behaviors recognized by research, theory, and existing law as risk factors into categories—namely, those of behaviors belonging to sex offenders, violent offenders, substance abusers, mental health offenders, and general offenders. Each item in each category is assigned a specific value that generally ranges from 0 to 3, 0 to 6, or 0 to 9. Total values for all items in a category are computed and used to place offenders in one of three risk or needs categories: minimum, medium, and high or Level 1, Level 2, and Level 3, depending on the agency conducting the assessment.

In the proceeding illustrations, items are scored from 0 to 8. The average score for each individual's category—general, mental health, sex, substance abuse, or violent offender—is used to place offenders in one of the following categories of risk: 0 = low-low, 1 = low, 2 = low-high, 3 = low-medium, 4 = medium, 5 = medium-high, 6 = low-high, 7 = high, and 8 = high-high. A "no" answer to any item equals a 0 score for that item, and a "yes" answer to any statement gets a score of 1 to 8 depending on the seriousness of the facts informing the "yes" response. A yes to certain statements automatically elevates the offender's risk score for that item to the maximum score of 8. The average score for each domain determines the risk level for that category.

Exhibits 13.1, 13.2, 13.3, 13.4, 13.5, and 13.6 illustrate the kinds and types of risk-assessment scales in use within most criminal justice systems in terms of how they are scored by criminal justice practitioners in the areas of corrections, pretrial, probation, and parole. Risk levels can swiftly move up and down from low to high or from high to low if a change in behavioral history occurs. Such changes may include new charges, the commission of new crimes, or a significant change in thinking, attitude, and behavior. Even the commission of victimless crimes and behaviors, such as substance abuse, suicidal behavior, and prostitution, can increase risk levels if they become a part of an offender's behavioral profile after initial assessment and classification. Crimes against other persons, property, and animals also increase risk levels.

Typically, when scoring the likelihood of recidivism for a particular category of behavior, scores between 1 and 8 should be informed by the type and severity of the sexual, violent, substance, or general behavior, as well as the kind and severity of the type of risk and needs. For example, if the answer to a statement about whether the offender has abused drugs three or fewer times a week in the last two months is a "yes," the corresponding score must be the maximum score possible (8) for hard drugs like cocaine or methamphetamine. The score should, however, be below midrange (1–4) if the drug is marijuana and the frequency of use is occasional and not every day or week. If local law treats marijuana possession as a felony, then the score should be in the midrange (4–6). Indeed, whether or not the harm associated with marijuana use outweighs the harm linked to other federal schedule I drugs, such as heroin, LSD, or methamphetamines, the consequences for possession of recreational quantities of marijuana are less severe since most jurisdictions do not prosecute marijuana possession and many treat the act as a misdemeanor offense or have already legalized marijuana for recreational use.

Consequently, the level of mitigating and aggravating factors associated with a "yes" response to a statement may be discretionarily used to increase or decrease risk and needs levels within the same level. For instance, if the average score for substance abuse is 1.5, the risk assessor can discretionarily move the score to a low-high (2) or backward to a low (1). Justification for the adjustment should, however, cite the presence of one or more relevant predictive factors known for mitigating the effects of the calculated risk on the offender's future thinking, attitudes, and behaviors as they relate to future recidivism. A typical offender in this case would be someone who, at the time of classification, appears genuinely serious about ending their substance abuse habits.

PREDICTIVE FACTORS

Offenders who end up in the criminal justice system come from diverse cultural, socioeconomic, educational, ethnic, mental health, religious, and behavioral backgrounds. However, not every unique piece of information associated with an offender can be reliably used to predict that offender's thinking, attitudes, and behaviors. For this reason, risk-assessment tools solicit specific pieces of information categorized as static or dynamic risk and protective factors that have predictive values (i.e., the potential to predict the risk of recidivism for a particular category of criminal or criminogenic behavior). Criminal justice practitioners, therefore, look to three sources of information for identifying, assessing, and classifying known static and dynamic factors that predict at-risk behaviors and tendencies: (1) prevailing laws, (2) social and behavioral sciences' research findings, (3) and criminological and sociological theories.

Prevailing law dictates which offender is a sex offender, violent offender, substance abuser, or a person who does not fit into any of these categories. In some jurisdictions, prevailing law defines risk levels for certain categories of behavior, such as sex offending behavior, in terms of their threat to the public. Criminological and sociological theories play the important role of helping to identify specific predictive variables in an offender's psychosocial history, thinking, attitudes, and actions that ought to be calculated to predict risk levels. Social and behavioral sciences' research, especially that relating to sexual, violent, substance abuse behaviors and mental health, explains the context within which the thinking developed, attitudes formed, and antisocial behaviors occurred, as well as how social and cognitive conditions of offenders contribute to criminogenic thinking, attitudes, and behaviors.

Violent Offender Assessment

Generally speaking, aggressive behaviors are not necessarily violent, and violent acts do not always equal aggressive behaviors. More specifically, aggression refers to assertive behaviors characterized by the overt use of verbal or nonverbal physical threat, intimidation, or force. Violent behaviors are more destructive than most aggressive behaviors, as they involve the use of physical force aimed at causing bodily pain and suffering to a person or animal or destruction of property. In this case, yelling at someone is an aggressive act, while punching a person, animal or property is an act of violence. It is, however, the case that aggressive behaviors tend to increase the possibility of violent acts because both behaviors are associated with anger, and anger is a symptom of emotional inducement. Exhibit 13.1 shows factors that are used to predict individual future violent behaviors.

EXHIBIT 13.1 COMMON PREDICTIVE FACTORS FOR VIOLENT BEHAVIORS

	Predictive Items		0 to 8
1.	Offender has committed one or more violent crimes		
2.	Offender shows an excessive level of anxiety during stressful situations		
3.	Offender shows overt and intense displays of sudden frustration		
4.	Offender frequently displays anger		
5.	Offender has committed one or more violent crimes in the past		
6.	Offender reacts with inappropriate force in ordinary situations		
7.	Offender frequently uses intimidation in stressful situations		
8.	Offender strikes objects or furniture when feeling frustrated or angry		
9.	Offender is involved with firearms or weapons		
10.	Offender exhibits homicidal ideation		
11.	Offender minimizes violent behaviors		
12.	Offender blames violent behaviors on victims or others		
13.	Offender did not show any significant anxiety *before* violent behaviors		
14.	Offender did not show any significant anxiety *during* violent behaviors		
15.	Offender did not show any significant anxiety *after* violent behaviors		
16.	Offender does not show remorse for violent behaviors		
17.	Offender does not have a realistic plan to correct violent behaviors		
18.	Offender is not motivated to alter violent behaviors		
*Score 8 for "yes" to item 1, and for all other items, score "0" for a "no" and 1 to 8 for "yes" answers. Do not compute items that have no answers.		Total	
		Average	

In the context of classification, a violent offender is (1) a person who is charged with or convicted of one or more offenses that are legally designated as violent acts, (2) a person who uses deadly force or engages in behaviors that could cause serious bodily harm to someone during the commission of one or more crimes, or (3) a person who attempts to use firearms or weapons, physical threats, or force against a person or property in the commission of crimes. Typically, kidnapping, aggravated assault, murder, unlawful imprisonment, physical intimidation, sexual and nonsexual assault, robbery, carjacking, criminal damage, arson, attempted murder, and similar acts of violence directed at another person, animal, or object are examples of violent crimes. The nature of the violent act, the age of the parties involved, and the offender's propensity to recommit the indexed offense are some factors that inform risk levels.

Sex Offender Behaviors

A sex offender is a person who engages in unwanted, deviant, or illegal sex acts or behaviors (Exhibit 13.2). The sexual act can be physical, such as rape or sexual assault, or it can be nonphysical, such as possession of child pornography. A sexual act may involve a person, animal, object, or one's self. A sex offender is also a person who is charged or convicted of engaging in a prohibited sexual act. It is, however, important to note that a legal designation of sex offender does not always translate into a clinical designation of sex offender or in the offender needing treatment. For instance, in at least 13 states, a person arrested for public urination commits a sex offense (HRW 2007). That is, if a person is caught in some state discreetly urinating on a tire in an open mall parking lot, that person becomes legally a sex offender, but clinically, they may not be a sex offender. Similarly, if a person decides to walk the streets naked in protest of something like the legislation of the human body, that person may be charged with public indecency, thus making them a sex offender. However, again, that person may not likely be a clinical sex offender unless their actions are motivated by the need to derive sexual pleasure.

In many jurisdictions, prohibited sexual behaviors include sexual conduct with a minor, sexual assault, molestation of a child, rape, incest, indecent exposure, public sexual indecency, and production, distribution, or possession of child pornography—including sexting—that involves obscene photos of a person under the age of 18. In many jurisdictions, sexual acts such as bestiality and unsolicited voyeurism also constitute sex crimes. Sexual deviance includes behaviors that are regarded as abnormal by a majority of the public. Many such behaviors are also illegal and include uninvited exhibitionism, unsolicited frottage, unwanted lewd communication, participation in bestiality, unwelcomed sadism, uninvited voyeurism, commission of necrophilia acts, exhibition of pedophilia behaviors, and evidence of deviant fantasies or arousal to deviant stimuli.

State and federal laws provide for the classification of sex offenders based on the risk of sexually reoffending or the degree of danger to the public. The risk level generally runs from low (Level 1) to high (Levels 3 or 4), or from minimum to high. Those with low risk are classified as Level 1 or minimum-level offenders. Those with moderate levels of dangerousness are classified as Level 2 or medium-risk offenders. Offenders who pose a high degree of danger to the public and who are likely to reoffend are labeled Level 3 or high-risk offenders. Levels are used to determine the level of restriction and supervision each offender should receive while under the jurisdiction of the criminal justice system.

Collectively, the duration of each sexual offense, the number of sexual acts, the types of sexual activities, the number of people whom the offender sexually abused, the age difference between the offender and the victim, and the nature of sexual aggression used by the offender form the basis for predicting future sexual offending behaviors. The key sources of theoretical guidelines are differential association and the theories of social learning, bonding, and social control. These theories postulate that criminal behaviors are learned

EXHIBIT 13.2 SEXUAL OFFENDING BEHAVIORS

	Predictive Items	0 to 8
1.	Offender has committed one or more sexual offenses	
2.	Offender gets sexually aroused by deviant sexual images or acts	
3.	Offender has attempted/completed more than two deviant sexual acts	
4.	Offender has used violence to commit at least one deviant sexual act	
5.	Offender started sexually offending at a young age—before age 18	
6.	Offender is three or more years older than the victim	
7.	Offender has a history of physically hurting animals	
8.	Offender has a history of sexually abusing animals	
9.	Offender has a history of intentional fire setting	
10.	Offender uses elaborate planning to groom victims	
11.	Offender uses elaborate methods to conceal sexual offending behaviors	
12.	Offender blames sexual behaviors on victim or others	
13.	Offender did not show significant anxiety immediately *before* sexual behaviors	
14.	Offender did not show significant anxiety *during* sexual behaviors	
15.	Offender did not show significant anxiety *after* sexual behaviors	
16.	Offender does not show remorse for sexual offending behaviors	
17.	Offender does not have a realistic plan to correct behaviors	
18.	Offender is not motivated to alter sexual offending behaviors	
Score 8 for "yes" to item 1, and for all other items, score "0" for a "no" and 1 to 8 for "yes" answers. Do not compute items that have no answer.	**Total**	
	Average	

behaviors, and those whose behaviors are not controlled by prosocial institutions, such as work, school, family, other civic organizations, or engagements are at greater risk of engaging in criminal behaviors.

Sex offenders come from all backgrounds, both male and female, young and old and from all educational, economic, social, cultural, ethnic, and political backgrounds. Notwithstanding those facts, studies show that an estimated 1 in every 5 girls and 1 in every 7 boys have suffered sexual victimization, and most documented sex offenders are males (Finkelhor 1994). It is, therefore, logical to assume that most offenders in this category are male.

Substance Abuse

Offenders with substance abuse needs are overrepresented in correctional facilities and in parole, pretrial services, and probation departments. These offenders are generally people who use one or more controlled or prohibited drugs and narcotics that can cause sedation or intense feelings of elation. The list of commonly abused drugs is long and typically includes heroin, opium, codeine, cocaine, amphetamines, mushrooms, phencyclidine, cannabis or hashish, alcohol and other hallucinogens, inhalants, opioids, sedatives, and stimulants.

Quite often, substance abuse behaviors (Exhibit 13.3) start with experimental use in which the offender tries a particular drug in the company of peers. Gradually, the person progresses to a stage where the drug renders them unable to meet common life demands without being under the influence. At this stage, an offender's physical condition may show evidence of deterioration. The offender may exhibit the inability to maintain healthy interpersonal and professional relationships and may show the tendency to engage in criminal activities to finance the drug habit. At this point, offenders may also have more people in their social circles with similar drug abuse lifestyles and social and economic difficulties. Normal life obligations, such as work and school, become contingent upon the presence of drugs in the body, and drug use becomes normalized.

Substance abuse behavior is a risk factor for many valid reasons. First, the behavior impairs abusers' ability to engage in consequential thinking. Second, drugs in general are very expensive, and since tolerance levels for any particular drug tend to increase, even those who are financially sound ultimately have difficulty supporting their drug habits. Third, while substance use itself may not qualify as a criminal act in many instances, the possession, distribution, purchase, and sale of drugs are illegal; therefore, substance abuse increases an offender's chances of getting arrested, charged, and prosecuted for drug-related offenses. Other risks associated with substance abuse that are often overlooked by offenders are the long-lasting social and legal consequences. Substance abuse forces abusers into a new world where they are compelled to make new "friends" who can morally and sometimes financially support and reinforce their substance abuse habits. Substance abuse also increases the chance of unemployment and financial burden and pushes offenders into a sub-society in which poverty, crime, and poor health are normalized.

Given the effects of drugs, risk-assessment instruments assess the length of time that an offender has abused certain illicit drugs, the quantity that is regularly consumed, the desire to reduce or quit the use of drugs, the amount of time that is spent on procuring substances, and the relationship between substance abuse and criminal activities. Risk-assessment instruments also capture how the substance abuse behaviors affect the offender's ability to secure and maintain gainful employment, produce satisfactory schoolwork, and maintain relationships with family members and prosocial friends, as well as how drug abuse influences other social commitments, such as bill paying. Some institutions, and indeed all institutions, should also look at the effects of substance abuse on the offender's physical and mental health, including the offender's participation in dangerous undertakings, such as driving while under the influence of a controlled substance.

There are many controlled substances in circulation, and each drug tends to affect the minds of abusers with regard to feeling and impairment in different ways. In terms of consequences, however, all drug use increases the chances of arrest and prosecution, as well as medical and mental health problems. The case has long been made that drug and alcohol abuse also lead to kidney, liver, neurological, cardiovascular, and mental health diseases and illness. In addition, the unsupervised use of controlled substances can result in addiction, aggressiveness, hallucinations, impaired judgment, impulsivity, and paranoia. Drug use that involves the sharing of needles can also significantly increase the contraction of infectious diseases, such as HIV and hepatitis. Heroin, LSD, methamphetamine, and cocaine all have a

EXHIBIT 13.3 SUBSTANCE ABUSE

	Predictive Items	0 to 8
1.	Offender has been charged with drug abuse-related offenses	
2.	Offender currently uses marijuana	
3.	Offender currently uses cocaine, acid, or similar controlled substances	
4.	Offender currently abuses prescription drugs	
5.	Offender currently abuses alcohol or other drugs	
6.	Offender has committed crimes to support substance abuse habit	
7.	Offender has committed crimes while under the influence of substance	
8.	Offender does not show adequate anxiety *before* substance abuse behaviors	
9.	Offender did not show adequate anxiety during substance abuse behaviors	
10.	Offender did not show adequate anxiety after substance abuse behaviors	
11.	Offender currently has no remorse about the substance abuse behavior	
12.	Offender does not have a realistic and achievable plan to correct behaviors	
13.	Offender is not motivated to change substance abuse behaviors	
14.	Offender has had at least one blackout as a result of substance abuse	
15.	Offender felt sick when they stopped abusing one or more substances	
16.	Offender's family member or friend has complained about the offender's drug use	
17.	Offender's family member has sought substance abuse help for him or her	
18.	Offender unsuccessfully attended at least one substance abuse treatment program	
Score 8 for "yes" to item 1, and for all other items, score "0" for a "no" and 1 to 8 for "yes" answers. Do not compute items that have no answer	**Total**	
	Average	

high potential to create severe psychological and physical dependence, and thus their effects on offenders tend to be greater than those of, say, valium or, as some may argue, marijuana.

General Offending Behaviors

A long list of offenses, such as property and white-collar crimes, fall into the category of general crimes (Exhibit 13.4) because the crimes are not sexual, violent, or substance abusing in nature. Some common crimes in this category include blackmail, corruption, credit card fraud, embezzlement, impersonation, insurance fraud, larceny or theft, tax evasion, and welfare fraud. These and similar crimes do not generate a need for substance abuse treatment, sex offender therapy, or intervention for anger problems and violent tendencies. They have, however, the same predictive values as sex and violent offending or substance abuse behaviors.

If a general criminal behavior is motivated by the desire to support specialized behaviors, such as drug abuse, then the need for specialized intervention, including substance abuse treatment, may arise. The connection between general crimes and specialized criminal behaviors, such as sex and violence, may be more apparent in the area of substance abuse, where certain types of general criminal behaviors are informed by specialized needs to obtain

EXHIBIT 13.4 GENERAL OFFENDING BEHAVIORS

	Predictive Items		0 to 8
1.	Offender has been arrested for nonsexual, substance, or violent behaviors		
2.	Offender currently commits nonviolent, sexual, or drug crimes		
3.	Offender cannot easily secure employment		
4.	Offender does not currently have a job		
5.	Offender blames criminal behaviors on others		
6.	Offender does not show significant anxiety *before* offending behaviors		
7.	Offender does not show significant anxiety *during* offending behaviors		
8.	Offender does not show significant remorse *after* offending behaviors		
9.	Offender does not currently show remorse for illegal behaviors		
10.	Offender does not have a realistic plan to correct offender behaviors		
11.	Offender is not motivated to alter offending behaviors		
Score 8 for "yes" to item 1, and for all other items, score "0" for a "no" and 1 to 8 for "yes" answer. Do not compute items that have no answer		Total	
		Average	

controlled substances. In such circumstances, the intervention must target the specialized behavior that influenced the general crime. That is, if a substance abuser engages in forgery, thefts, financial fraud, and similar criminal activities to finance a drug habit, then the behaviors speak more to risks associated with substance abuse because the main source of motives, drives, attitudes, and rationalizations for the general criminal behaviors is the substance abuse.

Mental Health Assessment

The overwhelming number of people with serious mental illness (Exhibit 13.5) are not violent people, sex offenders, or substance abusers. For instance, Peterson et al. (2014) and their colleagues analyzed 429 crimes committed by 143 offenders with three major types of mental illness. Their results show that although many people who enter the criminal justice system have one or more mental health diagnoses, the relationship between an offender's psychiatric symptoms and their criminal behaviors are very weak, and the percentage of cases where direct relationships existed tends to be very small. Specifically, they found that only 4% of crimes were related directly to psychosis, 3% were related to depression, and 10% were informed by bipolar disorder, including impulsivity. The findings in this and other studies suggest that although many of the criminal behaviors for which offenders made contact with the criminal justice system were informed by risk factors other than mental illness, certain acute mental illnesses can predict some criminal behaviors (Sestoft, 2006).

Of course, having a mental health disorder is more of a disability or an illness than a crime or an offense. However, risk-assessment tools capture mental health disorders because in some cases, they have the potential to contribute to criminal, delinquent, or self-abusive behaviors. The prediction tends to be stronger in cases where the offender is also a substance abuser. Mental health assessments, therefore, calculate the degree to which a mental condition may provoke or lead to crime or self-abusive behaviors, as well as the level of resources or intervention needed to minimize the potential effects of offenders' mental health disorders.

EXHIBIT 13.5 MENTAL ILLNESS

	Predictive Items		0 to 8
1.	Offender has attempted suicide in the past		
2.	Offender engages in self-abusive behavior, such as cutting		
3.	Offender currently has suicidal ideation		
4.	Offender is not motivated to stop self-abusive behaviors		
5.	Offender refuses to take psychotropic medication as prescribed		
6.	Offender was prescribed psychotropic medication		
7.	Offender hears voices that command them		
8.	Offender thinks they have no mental health needs		
Score 8 for "yes" to item 1, 2, 3, and for all other items, score "0" for a "no" and 1 to 8 for "yes" answers.		Total	
		Average	

As a result of the connection between criminal behaviors and mental illness, criminal justice professionals must acquire skills for identifying offenders who qualify for mental health diversion or mental health referral. Mental health diversion programs consist of both inpatient and outpatient treatment to which mental health practitioners refer the following offenders:

- those at high risk of reoffending because of mental illness,
- those who are incapable of forming the evil intention required for most criminal offenses, and
- those who are not able to understand the wrongfulness and consequences of their behaviors because of mental illness.

Mental health referral is the connection of an offender with an appropriate mental health professional for further assessment for mental health needs. Referrals give the offender an opportunity to access mental health services, including community-based treatment and rehabilitation, as an alternative to incarceration.

Mental health status generates many risk factors. First of all, mental health disorders place offenders with mental health needs at great risk of violent victimization by other people. Second, mental conditions increase the chance of self-abusive behaviors, including the tendency to engage in behaviors such as self-cutting or attempting or committing suicide. Third, although the relationship is weak, a few mental health conditions, such as depression, bipolar disorder, and psychosis, can increase the chance of future offending behaviors (Sestoft 2006). Luckily, however, much progress has been made in the field of psychiatry, as a result, many mental illnesses can now be controlled with medication.

Secured Custody Classification

There is no stage in the criminal justice process where risk scores are so critically important than during the incarceration stage. Jail and prison environments experience constant inflow and outflow of inmates from every criminal, psychological, and social background. They house low-risk inmates, such as petty thieves and drunk drivers, as well as super-high-risk inmates, including murderers, armed robbers, and terrorists. Prisons and jails receive young and old, criminal gang members and civil servants, including former law enforcement personnel turned criminal offenders. Thus, given the volatility of prison and jail environments, all incoming offenders are routinely subjected to comprehensive risk-assessment processes.

Prison and jail classification uses a comprehensive classification system that relies on objective criteria based on offenders' behavioral history, including their history of using weapons to commit crimes, prior history of escape, severity of current charges, and prison or jail time to be served. In doing so, jails and prisons use some combination of the items listed in Exhibit 13.6. The results of the assessment are used to determine the appropriateness of the types of housing for each inmate and are designed to match offenders with the right security, protection, and supervision.

EXHIBIT 13.6 CUSTODIAN CLASSIFICATION

	Predictive Items	0 to 8
1.	Offender is charged with violent crime*	
2.	Offender is charged with attempted escape or with escape*	
3.	Offender has a history of attempted escape or conviction of escape*	
4.	Offender is a member of a security threat group*	
5.	Offender is charged with a crime that carries a maximum of death or life imprisonment	
6.	Offender currently has high bail or "no bond" status	
7.	Offender is charged with a felony	
8.	Offender is a member of a criminal street gang	
*Score "0" for a "no," 8 for "yes" to item 1 to 4, and for all other items, score 4 to 8 for "yes" answers. Do not compute items that have no answers.	Total	
	Average	

Assessed risk scores are used to place offenders in one of five housing categories: (1) minimum, (2) medium, (3) maximum, (4) supermax, and (5) administrative segregation. Minimum facilities or housing units hold people who pose a minimum threat to other inmates, correctional staff, and visitors; who are charged with nonviolent offenses; who have been ordered to post low bail; or who have no history of prior imprisonment, escape, attempted escape, or assault against law enforcement. Medium-risk offenders are people who are being held for violent crimes other than crimes that carry a maximum life or death sentence; inmates with histories of prior imprisonment, escape or attempted escape, or assaults against law enforcement personnel; and inmates who are members of criminal street gangs.

Maximum security housing or units hold offenders who are members of security threat groups or who have committed serious violent crimes, excluding crimes that carry a death sentence or life imprisonment. Security threat groups are prison gangs, such as the Aryan Brotherhood and Mexican Mafia, that present as inherent threats to the safety of any prison or jail official, other inmates, visitors, or facility property (Skarbek, 2012; Winterdyk & Ruddell 2010).

Supermax jails or prisons hold death row inmates and offenders who are convicted of murder, who are serving life sentences, or who pose extreme threats to the safety of other prisoners, staff, and visitors. Administrative segregation units hold inmates who may not necessarily pose a significant threat to the smooth running of correctional facilities but whose lives would be in danger if they were placed in the general population. Typical administrative segregation inmates are incarcerated corrections and police officers, child molesters or rapists, and high-profile offenders, including vulnerable celebrities. Irrespective of their risk scores, these categories of inmates are generally at high risk of being murdered or seriously assaulted by other inmates; thus, segregating them is the best administrative way of providing those offenders with the adequate protection they need.

CONCLUSION

Criminal justice practitioners use risk assessment as a basis for making decisions regarding sentencing, as well as for calculating how to protect the community from future victimization by offenders through the determination of supervision and management levels and how to make treatment decisions that are designed to eliminate or minimize offenders' chances of recidivism. Hence risk scores are used at all levels of the criminal justice system, including the court, correctional facilities, local law enforcement agencies, pretrial services, and probation and parole.

Trial judges use risk scores, among other factors, to make decisions about special conditions and restrictions, such as sex offender registration and qualification for probation and other community services. Courts also use risk scores when making decisions about continuous detention, bail, and sentencing, including the granting of probation. Correctional agencies use risk levels as a guide when making decisions about the level of supervision an inmate may require to ensure the safety of other detainees, staff, and visitors at a correctional facility. Probation and parole departments also use risk scores as a basis for specialized conditions of probation and parole, including curfews, residences, and allowable work environments. These agencies also use risk scores as the basis for all critical decisions regarding offenders' progression through the criminal justice system and to ascertain offenders' suitability for treatment (McKeown 2015). In addition, risk scores are the primary sources of measuring offenders' progress in treatment and for minimizing offenders' risks of recidivism.

DISCUSSION QUESTIONS

1. Which predictive items must be included in behavioral assessment scales for substance abuse, sex, or violent offenders?
2. What are the key differences between secured custody classification, community corrections classification, and legal classification?
3. The mindset of an offender at the time of an offense, during an offense, and after an offense is a critical key piece of information for risk and needs assessment and classification. Why?
4. Which category of offenders needs more help to prevent relapses: violent offenders, sex offenders, substance abusers, or general offenders?

REFERENCES

Finkelhor, D. (1994). Current information on the scope and nature of child sexual abuse. *The Future of Children*, *4*(2), 31–53.

GIFR. (2016). *Global institute of forensic research.* Retrieved September 30, 2016, from https://www.gifrinc.com/

HRW. (2007). *US: Sex offender laws may do more harm than good.* https://www.hrw.org/news/2007/09/11/us-sex-offender-laws-may-do-more-harm-good

McKeown, A. (2015). Female offenders: Assessment of risk in forensic settings. *Aggression and Violent Behavior*, *15*, 422–429.

Peterson, J. K., J. Skeem, Kennealy, P., Bray, B., & Zvonkovic, A. (2014). How often and how consistently do symptoms directly precede criminal behavior among offenders with mental illness? *Law and Human Behavior*, *38*(5), 439–449.

Sestoft, D. (2006). Crime and mental illness: It is time to take action. *World Psychiatry*, *5*(2), 95–95.

Singh, J. P., M. Grann, & Fazel, S. (2011). A comparative study of violence risk assessment tools: A systematic review and metaregression analysis of 68 studies involving 25,980 participants. *Clinical Psychology Review*, *31*, 499–513.

Skarbek, D. (2012). Prison gangs, norms, and organizations. *Journal of Economic Behavior & Organization*, *82*(1), 96–109.

Winterdyk, J., & Ruddell, R. (2010). Managing prison gangs: Results from a survey of U.S. prison systems. *Journal of Criminal Justice*, *38*(4), 730–736.

CHAPTER FOURTEEN

Ethical Obligations

IN MANY INSTANCES, a criminal justice staff working with adult offenders is like a rat working with a snake—one erroneous move can be costly, and at all times, the rat has to be on guard. Almost on a regular basis, correctional staff must also be on guard when dealing even with offenders who are kind, helpful, and respectful, as well as those who commit themselves to making correctional staff member's lives miserable. Naturally, correctional staff may find certain offenders more likable than other offenders. Some offenders have distasteful criminal histories, such as sex and violent crimes, and some have serious mental health conditions that some correctional staff may find difficult to serve. At the same time, correctional staff members are required to treat each offender with respect and without bias or favoritism.

Correctional agencies and facilities recognize that the temptation to accept gifts, to falsify or cover up material facts, to favor or serve certain offenders better than others, to participate in inappropriate relationships with current or ex-offenders, and to serve family members, friends, relatives, and acquaintances better than others increases the chances of unethical behavior. Therefore, correctional agencies and facilities require that criminal justice professionals behave in ways consistent with their legal and professional obligations and expectations. Correctional staff must operate strictly within the scope of organizational mandates, which are derived primarily from the U.S. Constitution and other federal and state laws, plus institutional policies and procedures, as well as other applicable codes of conduct that regulate correctional officers' behavior, especially in areas where there are no explicit rules or guidelines regarding what is right or wrong. Unfortunately, the contexts in which the need for discretionary action arises frequently vary, especially for pretrial, detention, probation, and parole officers.

Factors that increase the potential for serious ethical violations include professional ethical obligations, individual socialization, need for accuracy in reports, ability to recognize and correct for stereotypes and prejudicial practices, and competing values, views, and beliefs (Douglas et al., 2017), all of which make the issue of ethical violation very important for criminal justice professionals. In this regard, this chapter touches on some of the most common ethical codes of conduct and challenges that are associated with criminal justice professionals' interactions with offenders. Specifically discussed are codes of ethics that regulate the behaviors of pretrial, probation, and parole officers, as well as clinical staffs, which include medical and psychological teams. Of particular focus are ethical duties and existing codes of ethics that are at the core of the successful performance of correctional functions, as well as how compliance with such rules enhances therapeutic efforts and protects the interests of offenders, as well as the correctional staff members and the institutions they serve.

CODE OF CONDUCT FOR CRIMINAL JUSTICE PROFESSIONALS

There is no such thing as a general code of conduct. For many reasons, it would be improper to cluster all correctional or professional groups under a single code of conduct. In the case of correctional functions, each offender and each correctional staff member's function is unique with unique sets of ethical challenges. What is possible is the grouping of correctional codes of ethics under certain common headings: pretrial, detention, probation, and parole officers' codes of conduct, including codes of ethics applicable to clinical staff and police/detention officers. The codes of ethics applicable to these correctional staff collectively demand integrity, honesty, impartiality, professionalism, and adherence to the rule of law, as well as the treatment of service recipients with dedication and respect.

Police Officers and Sheriffs' Deputies

Legally speaking, the job of police officers focuses on protecting lives and property. In the event of a breach of peace, police officers and sheriffs' deputies are mainly duty bound to gather the necessary information and evidence so the courts can determine the most appropriate criminal justice response. In reality, however, police officers and sheriffs' deputies do serve as correctional officers during the brief period they spend with suspects in their custody; hence, they are subject to the same code of ethics that regulates correctional staffs' interactions with offenders. At least constitutionally, detainees are prisoners, and thus they are subject to the same constitutional protections.

The fact that most people who encounter the criminal justice system do so through contact with police officers and sheriffs' deputies means that these officers have to navigate multiple ethical challenges on a regular basis. Indeed, no matter how brief the contact might be, during the period that such suspects spend in police care, police officers or sheriffs' deputies do perform some sort of correctional supervision that is subjected to the Law Enforcement Code of Ethics; agency rules, policies, and procedures; and, of course, existing federal and state laws.

In general, the code of ethics for police officers demands ethical behavior from officers. For example, the code of ethics listed in Box 14.1 urges police officers to serve their communities and to protect lives and property with integrity, honesty, and respect for the constitutional rights of all persons to liberty, equality, justice, and dignity. Further, the Police Officer Code of Ethics specifically asks officers to display honesty in thought and deed, to maintain confidentiality, and to courteously and appropriately enforce the law without fear, favor, or malice while keeping in mind that the badge they wear symbolizes public trust in the officers' ability to faithfully and professionally discharge the duties and responsibilities of law enforcement officers.

BOX 14.1 POLICE OFFICER CODE OF ETHICS

As a law enforcement officer, my fundamental duty is to serve the community; to safeguard lives and property; to protect the innocent against deception, the weak against oppression or intimidation and the peaceful against violence or disorder; and to respect the constitutional rights of all to liberty, equality and justice.

I will keep my private life unsullied as an example to all and will behave in a manner that does not bring discredit to me or to my agency. I will maintain courageous calm in the face of danger, scorn or ridicule; develop self-restraint; and be constantly mindful of the welfare of others. Honest in thought and deed both in my personal and official life, I will be exemplary in obeying the law and the regulations of my department. Whatever I see or hear of a confidential nature or that is confided to me in my official capacity will be kept ever secret unless revelation is necessary in the performance of my duty.

I will never act officiously or permit personal feelings, prejudices, political beliefs, aspirations, animosities or friendships to influence my decisions. With no compromise for crime and with relentless prosecution of criminals, I will enforce the law courteously and appropriately without fear or favor, malice or ill will, never employing unnecessary force or violence and never accepting gratuities.

I recognize the badge of my office as a symbol of public faith, and I accept it as a public trust to be held so long as I am true to the ethics of police service. I will never engage in acts of corruption or bribery, nor will I condone such acts by other police officers. I will cooperate with all legally authorized agencies and their representatives in the pursuit of justice.

I know that I alone am responsible for my own standard of professional performance and will take every reasonable opportunity to enhance and improve my level of knowledge and competence.

I will constantly strive to achieve these objectives and ideals, dedicating myself before God to my chosen profession ... law enforcement (IACP, 2018).

The International Association of Chiefs of Police's (IACP) Law Enforcement Code of Ethics, adopted at the 64th Annual IACP Conference and Exposition in October 1957, provides a good summary of the ethical commitments that law enforcement agencies and their employees make to offenders, victims, and the public. In addition to the Police Officer Code of Ethics, police officers and sheriffs' deputies are bound by the Law Enforcement Oath of Honor. The oath echoes the values and expectations captured in the Police Officer Code of Ethics. The brief text reads, "On my honor, I will never betray my badge, my integrity, my character or the public trust. I will always have the courage to hold myself and others accountable for our actions. I will always uphold the constitution, my community, and the agency I serve." As is evident, at the very core of the oath is the commitment to uphold all the rights and privileges accorded by the U.S. Constitution to individuals who involuntarily contact the correctional system. The oath also recognizes the ethical need for police and sheriffs' deputies to serve with integrity their communities, agencies, and the people with whom they come into contact.

Pretrial Service and Probation Officers

Upon the determination that probable cause exists to support a claim of criminal wrongdoing by an arresting agency—that is, that the facts and circumstances surrounding a case can lead a reasonably cautious person to believe that an accused person is guilty of a particular crime—the accused may be assigned a pretrial service officer. The most important task of a pretrial service officer is, therefore, the initial collection of pertinent information about the suspect facing allegations of serious criminal wrongdoing and the assessment and classification of each suspect's compliance with specific pretrial court orders, including special and general conditions that assist a trial court in supervising a suspect while awaiting the conclusion of a criminal trial.

Pretrial service officers frequently use risk-assessment scales to determine the risk posed by a defendant of failing to return to court or being arrested for a new crime and the level of supervision desired for a pretrial release. To achieve these goals, pretrial service officers conduct pretrial service investigations, interview defendants, and collect other relevant information to confirm or dismiss certain information already held, as well as to determine the defendant's likelihood of appearing or not appearing in court and where necessary to identify conditions that the court must impose to guarantee the appearance of the suspect at future proceedings. Obviously, the effective pursuit of these goals often generates an important ethical question about whether the defendants should be given access to the sources of information that, especially, adversely affect the recommendations and decisions of the pretrial service officers.

Pretrial service officers work for officers of the trial courts (judges and prosecutors) and with suspects who have not been tried or convicted or in some cases or jurisdictions who have been convicted but not yet sentenced. In other words, the pretrial officers may supervise suspects until they are acquitted, or their charges are dismissed, or until they are placed on probation, sentenced, or begin to serve their sentences. As a result, pretrial service officers are concerned with just a few matters: the likelihood of a defendant being arrested for a new crime, the threat posed to society if the suspect were to be released prior to the conclusion of their trial or sentencing, or the likelihood of the suspect not showing up for the next court proceeding.

BOX 14.2 FEDERAL PROBATION AND PRETRIAL OFFICERS ASSOCIATION (FPPOA) CODE OF ETHICS

As a federal probation/pretrial services officer,

I am dedicated to rendering professional service to the courts, the parole authorities and the community at large in effecting the social adjustment of the offender and assuring the compliance of defendants with their legal responsibilities.

I will conduct my personal life with decorum, will neither accept nor grant favors in connection with my office, and will put loyalty to moral principles above personal consideration.

I will uphold the law with dignity and with complete awareness of the prestige and stature of the judicial system of which I am a part. I will be ever cognizant of my responsibility to the community which I serve.

I will strive to be objective in the performance of my duties, respect the inalienable rights of all persons, appreciate the inherent worth of the individual, and inviolate those confidences which can be reposed in me.

I will cooperate with my fellow workers and related agencies and will continually attempt to improve my professional standards through the seeking of knowledge and understanding.

I recognize my office as a symbol of public faith and i accept it as a public trust to be held as long as I am true to the ethics of the federal probation and pretrial services system. I will constantly strive to achieve these objectives and ideals, dedicating myself to my chosen profession

Source: *Federal Probation and Pretrial Officers Association. (2018). Code of Ethics. www.fppoa.org/page/code-ethics*

To better predict any of the outcomes, the pretrial service officers must examine each offender's social history, including financial standing, marital status, residential history, and employment history and potential. Based on the information collected, pretrial service officers make recommendations to trial judges regarding matters relating to bail and legal representation—the states pay for the defense of those who cannot afford an attorney by assigning to them appropriate public defenders. In some cases, recommendations are made to funnel cases to diversion programs designed to remove defendants from the traditional criminal justice track into treatment programs that address the behaviors that brought defendants to the criminal justice system.

Detention Officers

Of all the people who serve the criminal justice system, detention officers face the most ethically challenging interactions with those who have involuntarily contacted the criminal justice system. Indeed, detention officers interact with offenders under some of the most intense conditions. In addition, detention officers spend most of their time at work dealing with offenders in a confined environment. Given the increased opportunity for unethical behavior, detention officers are guided by federal and state laws, the American Correctional Association's Correctional (ACA) Code of Ethics, and individual agencies' policies and procedures.

ACA, founded in 1870, is a nonprofit or nongovernmental trade association. The ACA Code of Ethics, listed in Box 14.3, was adopted by the Board of Governors and Delegate Assembly in August 1994. The association accredits over 900 prisons, jails, and community residential centers (halfway houses) within and outside the United States. Since its formation, the ACA has played a crucial role in prison reform within the United States.

BOX 14.3 ACA CODE OF ETHICS

The **American Correctional Association** expects of its members unfailing honesty, respect for the dignity and individuality of human beings and a commitment to professional and compassionate service. To this end, we subscribe to the following principles.

Members shall respect and protect the civil and legal rights of all individuals.

Members shall treat every professional situation with concern for the welfare of the individuals involved and with no intent to personal gain.

Members shall maintain relationships with colleagues to promote mutual respect within the profession and improve the quality of service.

Members shall make public criticism of their colleagues or their agencies only when warranted, verifiable, and constructive.

Members shall respect the importance of all disciplines within the criminal justice system and work to improve cooperation with each segment.

"American Correctional Association Code of Ethics," http://www.aca.org/ACA_Prod_IMIS/ACA_Member/About_Us/Code_of_Ethics/ACA_Member/AboutUs/Code_of_Ethics.aspx?hkey=61577ed2-c0c3-4529-bc01-36a248f79eba.

Members shall honor the public's right to information and share information with the public to the extent permitted by law subject to individuals' right to privacy.

Members shall respect and protect the right of the public to be safeguarded from criminal activity.

Members shall refrain from using their positions to secure personal privileges or advantages.

Members shall refrain from allowing personal interest to impair objectivity in the performance of duty while acting in an official capacity.

Members shall refrain from entering into any formal or informal activity or agreement which presents a conflict of interest or is inconsistent with the conscientious performance of duties.

Members shall refrain from accepting any gifts, services, or favors that is or appears to be improper or implies an obligation inconsistent with the free and objective exercise of professional duties.

Members shall clearly differentiate between personal views/statements and views/statements/positions made on behalf of the agency or Association.

Members shall report to appropriate authorities any corrupt or unethical behaviors in which there is sufficient evidence to justify review.

Members shall refrain from discriminating against any individual because of race, gender, creed, national origin, religious affiliation, age, disability, or any other type of prohibited discrimination.

Members shall preserve the integrity of private information; they shall refrain from seeking information on individuals beyond that which is necessary to implement responsibilities and perform their duties; members shall refrain from revealing nonpublic information unless expressly authorized to do so.

Members shall make all appointments, promotions, and dismissals in accordance with established civil service rules, applicable contract agreements, and individual merit, rather than furtherance of personal interests.

Members shall respect, promote, and contribute to a work place that is safe, healthy, and free of harassment in any form (ACA, 2018).

ACA's Code of Ethics demands that detention officers, among other functions, promote ethics within the justice profession and demonstrate responsible and humane correctional policies and practices (ACA, 2018). Further, the ACA also "expects of its members unfailing honesty, [and] respect for the dignity and individuality of human beings" (ACA, 2018) and thus holds that correctional officers subscribe to the principles advanced in its code of ethics.

Detention officers' duties and operations are also regulated by a long list of court rulings and institutional policies. For instance, the U.S. Supreme Court and other federal and state courts have addressed many aspects of detention officers' interactions with detainees (Palmer, 2010). More specifically, courts have ruled that detention serves the purpose of "punishment"—that is, that the mere detention of a person is a serious form of punishment. Therefore, the offender should not be subjected to additional punishment unless such punishment is warranted by a new law or policy violation. Also, offenders retain all of their civil and human rights when in detention, jail, or prison and only the exercise of such civil and human rights that threaten legitimate penological operations or correctional duties—the duty to prevent escape, maintain security within the correctional institutions, and rehabilitate—can be lawfully restricted. For instance, use of force is only allowed to maintain safety and security, to prevent escape from detention, or to facilitate treatment. Even so, the use of such force must be progressive or incremental from the least intrusive, such as a verbal warning or command, to the most intrusive, such as the use of deadly force.

In the event that a correctional staff member must restrict or deprive detainees of certain protected rights, such actions must be warranted by a legitimate and compelling state interest or function—matters that are directly related to the prevention of escape, the maintenance of the safety of all persons within the correctional institution, or the promotion and deliverance of treatment or rehabilitation. In situations where the law, policy, or procedure fails to provide a precise course of action, correctional staff must use their discretion in ways that strongly favor the greater good (*Hudson v. McMillian*, 1992; Palmer, 2010). Indeed, violation of any of these guidelines qualifies as an ethical violation.

Probation and Parole Officers

Detention is never permanent—every offender who enters a correctional facility is bound to reenter the free world either dead, as a probationer or parolee, or as a free person having been released. Those who end up on parole or probation are supervised by either probation or parole officers who are tasked with a variety of therapeutic and legal responsibilities. This also means that probation and parole officers are guarded by certain codes of ethics similar to the codes of ethics that regulate detention officers. The key principles that drive probation or parole officers' interactions with detainees can be cued from the American Probation and Parole Association (APPA) Code of Ethics listed in Box 14.4.

BOX 14.4 APPA CODE OF ETHICS

I will render professional service to the justice system and the community at large in effecting the social adjustment of the offender.

I will uphold the law with dignity, displaying an awareness of my responsibility to offenders while recognizing the right of the public to be safeguarded from criminal activity.

I will strive to be objective in the performance of my duties, recognizing the inalienable right of all persons, appreciating the inherent worth of the individual, and respecting those confidences which can be reposed in me.

I will conduct my personal life with decorum, neither accepting nor granting favors in connection with my office.

I will cooperate with my co-workers and related agencies and will continually strive to improve my professional competence through the seeking and sharing of knowledge and understanding.

I will distinguish clearly, in public, between my statements and actions as an individual and as a representative of my profession.

I will encourage policy, procedures and personnel practices, which will enable others to conduct themselves in accordance with the values, goals and objectives of the American Probation and Parole Association.

I recognize my office as a symbol of public faith and I accept it as a public trust to be held as long as I am true to the ethics of the American Probation and Parole Association.

I will constantly strive to achieve these objectives and ideals, dedicating myself to my chosen profession (APPA, 2018).

The APPA requires that probation and parole officers render professional services and uphold with dignity all state and federal laws and institutional policies and procedures. The code of ethics for probation and parole officers also requires officers to exercise respect for the worth of the individuals they serve and with whom they interact, as well as to demonstrate professional competence at all times (APPA, 2018).

FPPOA also has a code of ethics, shown in Box 14.2. The content of the document is also similar to that of the APPA. For example, the FPPOA compels probation and pretrial officers to render professional services to the courts; to remain faithful and dedicated to the moral principles enshrined in the code of ethics; to show respect for law, policies, and procedures; and to serve the criminal justice system with dignity (FPPOA, 2018).

Clinical Staff

Police, detention, probation, and parole officers are the faces of the criminal justice system. However, at the very core of any correctional intervention are clinical staff who play pivotal roles in the assessment, classification, and treatment of offenders. There are, therefore, a wide range of clinical staff members who interact with offenders as part of the rehabilitation process. Key members of this group are qualified medical and mental health practitioners, typically consisting of institutional psychologists and psychiatric and medical staff. Obviously, as licensed medical and mental health practitioners, clinical staff are guided in their decisions and behaviors by their individual professional codes of ethics, state and federal laws, applicable correctional codes of ethics, and institutional policies and procedures.

Clinical staff members perform a variety of tasks, including counseling, administration of behavioral modification programs, and assessment and classification of risk and needs, such as academic, mental and medical needs. In addition, clinical staff provide therapeutic consultations and administer and monitor psychotropic and other medication (Convention on the Rights of the Child, 1990). Clinical staff members also advise all other correctional staff and third parties who contract services to criminal offenders. In a therapeutically oriented correctional institution, clinical staff also identify offenders whose main problem areas are substance abuse, mental illness, or violent or sexual offending behaviors. Specifically, criminal justice clinicians administer special diagnostic assessment tools, synthesize and screen assessment results, and continuously assess criminogenic risk and protective factors so as to offer offenders aid for successful modification of unwanted behavior. This long list of critical duties suggests that correctional clinical staff must deal with a wide range of ethical issues.

DEALING WITH AND PREVENTING CORE ETHICAL ISSUES

Irrespective of the agency or criminal justice occupational classification, there are certain ethical issues that most criminal justice professionals regularly encounter in the course of every normal 8-hour shift. Ethical issues associated with report writing, off-duty behavior, conflict of interest, use of force, reportable behavior, need and right to know, professional training and professional authority, and other matters are commonly encountered by every correctional officer.

One could, however, minimize the consequential harm that flows from social and professional interactions. In this respect, the ethical issues relevant to correctional and law enforcement and clinical functions can be grouped under distinct themes, such as ethical questions associated with writing reports, use of force, dealing with conflicts of interest, diversity issues, when to report or not to report new behaviors, living prosocial lives off duty, dealing with work-related matters while off duty, and revealing damaging or consequential information to those who may or may not have a need or right to know. Also critical are the acquisition of adequate professional training and maintenance of well-disciplined interpersonal boundaries when interacting with suspects, offenders, or anyone with whom contact is made during the course of one's professional function.

Need and Right to Know

Correctional staff members have access to many sources of information, such as the National Crime Information Center (NCIC) database, which contains private information on individuals within and outside the criminal justice system. The NCIC database was launched on January 27, 1967, and currently serves as an electronic clearinghouse of crime data. Law enforcement and correctional staff can access the database from anywhere at any time. In 2015, the database processed an average of 13 million transactions per day. The database contains information about stolen articles, such as boats, guns, license plates, and vehicles. It also contains information about people, such as those on supervised release, sex offenders, foreign fugitives, immigration violators, missing persons, persons under protection orders, unidentified persons, gangs, known or appropriately suspected terrorists, wanted persons, identity theft cases, and known violent persons. The database also holds national information about the physical description of people, including height, weight, race, eye color, gender, and aliases.

States can access the NCIC database via their state criminal history information system. The California Law Enforcement Telecommunications System, for instance, is run by the California Department of Justice. Local law enforcement agencies can make inquiries into the system on a need-to-know and a right-to-know basis. The California Law Enforcement Telecommunications System similarly contains criminal history and law enforcement–related information, including warrants, restraining or protective orders, supervised release, missing and unidentified persons, Department of Motor Vehicles information, and information contained in the FBI NCIC database.

Besides the NCIC database and related state databases, correctional officers also have access to offenders' court and social files, which contain a wide range of information, including assessment reports, criminal histories, and other personal information. The obvious question, therefore, is who has a need and right to know specific information concerning an offender? Certainly, there is a distinction between a right and a need to know a particular piece of information about an offender. That is, although correctional staff members have the right to access offenders' criminal histories, the need to access such information for the sole purpose of entertainment or in search of a motive to mistreat an offender is unethical. In the same vein, a transportation officer has both the right and need to look up a detainee's escape history when trying to establish that risk during the transportation of the offender from one location to another. The same officer does not, however, have a need to access the same record just for fun, although they may have a right to access such information.

Ethics of Report Writing

Generally, what offenders tell their clinicians and other correctional staff members who are charged with rehabilitating them is confidential, and thus the disclosure to a third party would violate such confidentially unless the disclosure of such information is intended to prevent significant future harm to the offender or others—under such conditions, the information may be disclosed but, of course, subject to clinical and correctional judgment (NIAAA, 2015). The ACA, for instance, demands that its members "preserve the integrity of private information" and "refrain from seeking information on individuals beyond that which is necessary to implement responsibilities and perform their duties," as well as "refrain from revealing nonpublic information unless expressly authorized to do so" (ACA, 2018). The problem, however, is when revealing information goes beyond what is necessary.

Indeed, one of the critical functions of any pretrial, probation, or parole officer is the responsibility of gathering information about suspects or offenders, assessing such information, and using conclusions drawn from this process as a basis for decisions that directly or indirectly affect offenders or suspects. The process of completing each report, no matter how brief, is, therefore, critical and raises a number of important questions, principally around the accuracy of the information upon which the officer relied, the soundness of the decisions and recommendations that flowed from such information, and the possibility of misrepresenting all or part of the information, as well disclosing something that is harmful but not necessarily useful for assessment and classification or the deliverance of treatment.

The collection of data, assessment of information, and classification of suspects or offenders are, in fact, similar to the process of conducting social science research, and thus many of the ethical rules that apply to the collection and analysis of data and the development of results and conclusions are similar to what pretrial, probation, and parole officers, as well as clinical staff, have to undergo. As with social science research that involves human subjects (Chambliss & Schutt, 2016; Maxfied & Babbie, 2009), at a minimum, the process should not cause intentional harm to offenders. Consequently, the offenders should be clearly informed about what they are participating in and the level of anonymity or confidentiality they can expect; the benefit of what they are compelled or coaxed to engage in must also outweigh the potential harm associated with such a process. These conditions must be maintained for each offender unless they are voluntarily and explicitly waived by a defendant, and as much as possible, each offender's participation in such a process should be voluntary.

Off-Duty Ethical Issues

In many occupations, life after work is a private matter. Indeed, painters, mechanics, nurses, and many other professionals can work as strippers or at a massage parlor during off-duty hours and also befriend anyone they want, unless, of course, they are employed by the criminal justice system. In addition, it is okay for former or current mechanics or painters to run into old or current clients and say something about their relationship with such clients in the presence of a third person. The expectation is not, however, the same for criminal justice practitioners, whose ethical guidelines demand specific actions in even some of the simplest off-duty social encounters, such as meeting ex-probationers or parolees in a public space, because such encounters would create the possibility of revealing offenders' protected information.

Every criminal justice employee, in particular police officers and sheriffs' deputies, as well as pretrial, probation and parole officers, is continuously on some sort of "intensive probation" at all times, including while on and off duty, and must avoid any participation in unethical behavior. Consequently, participation in certain prohibited or questionable acts, such as the commission of new offenses, frequenting places known for criminal activity, or testing positive for any controlled substance while on or off duty can easily lead to termination of employment.

It should be noted that the likelihood of someone adversely using a detainee's criminal history is always greater during even a simple social encounter, such as running into an ex-offender. Therefore, the possibility of violating offenders' or suspects' privacy always exists, notwithstanding the fact that correctional staff also have moral and legal duties, as well as professional mandates to respect and preserve the right of offenders to privacy and due process.

One of the main areas of concern relating to off-duty behavior is the ethicality of accessing, sharing, or transmitting an offender's protected information. Without a doubt, anonymity and confidentiality can be violated by an officer who initiates verbal contact with an ex-detainee, probationer, or parolee while off duty in front of one or more people because such action has the potential to make that individual's criminal history public. Since the criminal history of an individual is a private matter and thus should be disclosed only when there is a legitimate need to do so, walking up to an ex-detainee and saying, "You look much better in civilian clothes than a prison uniform," or "How is life off probation or parole?" or "Come here and say hello to your probation officer" is unethical. First of all, none of these actions is legitimately related to the correctional officer's official functions. Second, in each of these cases, the correctional officers' behaviors violate the privacy rights of the offender. Indeed, anyone who hears such statements is likely to conclude that the person has a criminal history. Furthermore, although such persons may have a right to know, they may not necessarily have a legitimate need to know the information.

Conflict of Interest

Conflict of interest is one of many inevitable consequences of being a public servant, and the ethical challenge it creates is more pronounced than other ethical dilemmas in the criminal justice system. Regularly, criminal justice professionals come into contact with offenders they personally dislike for a variety of reasons, including the behaviors for which offenders contact the criminal justice system or the behaviors offenders exhibit in correctional facilities. Given the high number of people who involuntarily contact the criminal justice system, the chances of having one or more family members, relatives, friends, or acquaintances under the supervision of one or more criminal justice processes is likely. Unfortunately, however, every time a conflict of interest emerges, the likelihood of an unethical action or decision increases significantly.

Conflict of interest, in the context of this chapter, refers to a situation where the personal interest of an individual is in direct conflict with that person's official and professional duties and responsibilities. For example, a conflict of interest arises when a probation or parole officer who hates people accused of child molestation is charged with making recommendations about a child molester going to jail or receiving probation or parole. Normally, such a task would be routine; however, a conflict of interest exists the moment the officer learns that if the offender is placed on probation, he will be staying a few houses down the street from the parole or probation officer's children. That is, the officer is caught between making the most accurate assessment of what is better for the offender, their family, and society as a whole and the need to keep their own children away from a convicted child molester who the officer fears will sexually victimize again. Of course, in situations like this, it is unethical to send the offender to jail purely to protect the officer's children.

As in most unethical situations, when an official action is motivated by personal gain, unethical behaviors are likely. Also, once a conflict of interest is formed, the chances of unethical behaviors increase in part because the officer's interest (needs, beliefs, wishes) has the potential to cloud their judgment. The best way, therefore, to address conflict of interest is to avoid the conflict altogether or prevent the conflict from fully forming. Prevention of unethical behavior resulting from a conflict of interest is possible by taking preventive actions, such as informing one's immediate line of supervision and refraining from acting as the key decision maker in matters that create conflicts of interest. Certainly, such steps can mitigate the chances of unethical behavior in certain cases.

Diversity and Equal Treatment

True fairness, equality, and justice cannot be obtained without respect for cultural, ethnic, religious, and gender differences. The U.S. Constitution prohibits the unequal treatment of people by any public employee. This means that certain differences, such as religion, nationality, ethnicity, race, gender, age, and sexual orientation, are legally protected against discrimination. Most societies would also agree that discrimination against a person because of their gender, race, ethnicity, nationality, religion, medical condition, or sexual orientation harms others and thus such behavior is unethical.

Many of the ethical issues arising out of a diverse context can, however, be mitigated by intentionally and actively celebrating diversity, including shared values, traditions, languages, norms, and customs. These can be accomplished by strongly supporting conclusions that people of one gender, racial, ethnic, national, and religion are not more likely to engage in any of the common crimes, such as robbery, murder, or theft, than the people who identify with another gender or racial, national, ethnic, or religious group.

Use of Force

The use of force is briefly discussed under "detention officer" because apart from police officers, detention officers use more force in their interactions with offenders than probation and parole officers. That said, probation, pretrial, and parole officers do use force in the normal performance of their official duties. For instance, the use of force might be necessary to prevent further victimization or to facilitate rehabilitation. Furthermore, the power to detain, which in itself constitutes a use of force, is one of the core duties of a probation or parole officer. The possession of this power means that the use of force is, however, a serious ethical matter.

The main concern about unethical behavior is focused on when to use force, to what degree, and to what purpose. Of course, as for most ethical questions, there is no universal answer. The existence of anything close is the constitutional standard that demands that when confronted with the need to use force, an officer must use the least punitive, restrictive, or intrusive means of force necessary. That is, the use of force must be progressive or incremental, from the least intrusive, such as a verbal warning or command, to the most intrusive, such as the use of deadly force (*Hudson v. McMillian*, 1992; Palmer 2010).

Evidently, this policy leaves room for discretion regarding when to use force, how much force to use, and which form of force to use in response to certain behaviors. The use of force may be necessary based on a reasonable perception of the officer responding to the unwanted behaviors to enforce criminal justice goals or policies, including prison rules and regulations. The use of force, however, becomes unethical when it is informed by the "malicious infliction of pain" (*Whitley v. Albers*, 1986) or "used maliciously and sadistically to cause pain" *Hudson v. McMillian* (1992).

Reportable Information

A probation officer has just been assigned an offender who is charged with possession of a controlled substance and has been placed on probation. Obviously, one of the specialized conditions is that the offender not possess or use any controlled substance without proper documentation or prescription. During the initial intake meeting or interview, the offender is asked to be honest about behaviors and intentions when interacting with any correctional staff. Specifically, the offender is told to speak about his offending behaviors without being asked. Three weeks later, the offender confesses that he has not been honest all along.

The ethical dilemma is that the offender confesses to being in possession of marijuana and cocaine for personal use. Indeed, as in this example, one of the common ethical issues confronted by correctional staff, especially probation and parole officers, is what to report for the purpose of sanctions and what to withhold for the purpose of rehabilitation. In this example, on the one hand, the offender just confessed that he is currently committing a felony by being in possession of controlled substances. On the other hand, the admission suggests that the offender is responding well to interventions. Any attempt to prosecute the crime he just admitted to would likely prevent future disclosure of such behaviors and, of course, make other offenders unwilling to report such wrongdoings to their probation, pretrial, or parole officers. There are a few known behaviors, such as the intention to harm others or engage in self-abusive behaviors, including suicide, self-mutilation, or anorexia, that must be reported for obvious reasons.

MITIGATION OF ETHICAL CHALLENGES

Total avoidance or prevention of ethical challenges is impossible, but many ethical challenges can be mitigated through the maintenance of personal boundaries, adherence to professionalism, acquisition of appropriate professional training, and taking steps to minimize unethical behaviors during social interactions with offenders and maintaining appropriate interpersonal boundaries. The lack of certain professional training and interpersonal boundaries may not be unethical, but this has the potential to increase the risk of unethical behaviors, such as sexual exploitation and acts of favoritism. Fortunately, these risks can be mitigated.

Professional Training and Scope

Criminal justice agencies devote a great deal of time and resources to the training of their staff prior to the commencement of employment and during each officer's tenure. The gist of the training revolves around ethical matters and is designed to help officers perform their duties more effectively. Those preemployment and in-service trainings reinforce the need to report only factual information and not to intentionally misrepresent any information, to use discretion wisely, to work within the scope of the prescribed authority, to maintain self-control at all times regardless of provocation to do otherwise, and to show respect and care for all people without regard to race, skin color, age, religion, national origin, sexual orientation, gender, or disability.

Competency requires that correctional staff possess at least the minimum necessary skills and knowledge for conducting accurate assessment and classification of risk and needs, as well as the administration of treatment interventions. Fortunately, correctional institutions and agencies heavily invest in preemployment and post-employment training in addition to the fact that correctional agencies and institutions go a long way to select the best available candidates for employment. It is only through such efforts that correctional officers can be saved from many forms of unethical, incompetent, and illegal practices.

Interpersonal Interactions and Boundaries

Anyone with knowledge about staff-offender interactions in correctional institutions would readily admit that one of the most frequent ethical problems arises out of interpersonal boundary violations. For example, every detention facility has to deal with issues involving staff members' sexual relationships with offenders and other ethical violations that are closely associated with interpersonal boundary violations. Problematic interpersonal boundaries are unique to the relationship that exists between an offender and a staff member—these are interactions that take place outside the narrow scope of professional duties.

Personal relationships are guided by the same ethical codes of conduct that regulate official interactions. Certainly, there are policies and procedures, as well as in-service trainings, in institutions that address interpersonal interactions with offenders, with the desire to prevent boundary violations. The most common ethical problems that arise out of interpersonal interactions are sexual interactions between offenders and staff, overidentification with offenders or their issues (i.e., being blind to offenders' actions), horseplay, and social interactions between staff and offenders with sexual overtones. Fortunately, however, unethical behaviors arising out of interpersonal social interactions can be minimized by avoiding or reducing certain predictors, such as being too close with an offender.

Certainly, the possibility of unethical behaviors resulting from interpersonal interaction can be greatly reduced if an officer avoids giving an offender access to personal letters or photos, granting special requests or engaging in acts of favoritism, spending unexplainable amounts of time with certain offenders, and being overly concerned about offenders. In a correctional setting, steps can also be taken to avoid many potential harms by not working with certain offenders in secluded areas and not taking inmates out of their cells at unusual times. Also, avoiding bringing in food or soda for offenders and not allowing offenders to address correctional staff by their first names can minimize the potential for harm. At a general level, avoiding sexualized communication; maintaining a courteous and professional demeanor at all times; refraining from any exploitation of the relationship or emotional, financial, or physical abuse of offenders; and avoiding verbal or physical altercations will minimize the chance of interpersonal boundary violations.

CONSEQUENCES OF VIOLATING ETHICAL CONDUCT

Agencies are vicariously liable, in many cases, for their employees' unethical behaviors, such as sexual misconduct with offenders, excessive use of force, and discriminatory practices. Consequently, institutions and agencies treat unethical behaviors seriously. Thus at an individual level, the cost of unethical behavior ranges from verbal or written reprimands to suspension with or without pay, demotion, dismissal, and other serious outcomes, including criminal prosecution. Notwithstanding these common consequences, one of the most consequential results of ethical violations is the possibility of producing victims. At the very least, every ethical violation is committed against a person. Furthermore, unethical behaviors generate legal and financial burdens for correctional agencies and institutions because any response to ethical violations can be both costly and time-consuming. The good news, however, is that the recognition of ethical dilemmas and respect for privacy, confidentiality, and anonymity can mitigate the potential occurrence of unethical behaviors.

CONCLUSION

At every level of the criminal justice process, opportunities arise for ethical violations. To make matters worse, there is no one answer for how to deal with any of the ethical issues highlighted in this chapter; although the universal ethical rule, cause no harm, applies to every situation, the phrase does not correct for every ethical dilemma or challenge. In fact, it is almost impossible to not cause "any" harm because there are identifiable or even quantifiable harms associated with most tasks and decisions undertaken by correctional staff and clinicians (Sokol, 2013).

Every ethical situation poses a unique challenge for criminal justice staff because each situation that gives rise to ethical questions is unique. Furthermore, the variation and frequency of ethical challenges and dilemmas also mean that correctional duties are performed under intense conditions of indecision and ethical ambiguity. The uncertainty that this reality creates is, however, helpful because it keeps correctional staff members alert and thus responsive to the ethical needs of offenders and the public interest by making sure that offenders are professionally treated and their privacy and concerns for protection from unethical violations are respected.

It should be remembered that offenders who deal with the criminal justice system, especially detainees, are a vulnerable population. Second, the concentration of power and resources in the hands of correctional staff members makes it highly likely that officers will commit unethical acts against offenders. Hence discussions about ethical guidelines are in essence discussions about what correctional staff can ethically do or not do. Being alert and responsive to ethical guidelines, laws, and challenges is crucial for the adequate performance of correctional functions, both within and outside correctional institutions.

DISCUSSION QUESTIONS

1. Which ethical challenges and or ethical issues are most serious in terms of impact?
2. What other factors, beyond those highlighted in this chapter under report writing, make writing reports a serious ethical challenge?
3. To what extent can one argue that any violation of penal law is an unethical behavior?
4. What are some of the most severe consequences for offenders and correctional staff members resulting from major unethical privacy violations?

REFERENCES

ACA. (2018). *The American Correctional Association code of ethics.* Retrieved May 3, 2018, from http://www.aca.org/ACA_Prod_IMIS/ACA_Member/Home/ACA_Member/Home.aspx

APPA. (2018). *The American Probation and Parole Association (APPA) code of ethics.* Retrieved May 5, 2018, from https://www.fppoa.org/page/code-ethics

Chambliss, D. F., & Schutt, R. K. (2016). *Making sense of the social world: Methods of investigation.* SAGE Publications.

Convention on the Rights of the Child. (1990). *Resolution 44/25 of 20 November 1989.*

Douglas, T., J. Pugh, Singh, I., Savulescu, J., & Fazel, S. (2017). Risk assessment tools in criminal justice and forensic psychiatry: The need for better data. *European Psychiatry, 42*, 134–137.

FPPOA. (2018). *Federal Probation and Pretrial Officers Association.* Retrieved May 5, 2018, from https://www.fppoa.org/

Hudson v. McMillian, 503 U.S. 1 (1992).

IACP. (2018). *The International Association of Chiefs of Police or IACP's law enforcement code of ethics.* Retrieved May 4, 2018, from http://www.theiacp.org/codeofethics

Maxfied, M. G., & Babbie, E. (2009). *Basic of research methods for criminal justice and criminology.* Cenage Learning.

NIAAA. (2015). *Alcohol screening and brief intervention for youth: A practitioner's guide.* https://www.niaaa.nih.gov/sites/default/files/youth-guide.pdf

Palmer, J. W. (2010). *Constitutional rights of prisoners.* Mathew Bender and Company.

Sokol, D. K. (2013). Ethics man: "First do no harm" revisited: Following the dictum means balancing moral principles. *BMJ: British Medical Journal, 347*(7932), 23–23.

SECTION IV

Classification of Offenses and Offenders

CHAPTER FIFTEEN

Judicial Classification

LEGAL VARIABLES ARE primarily created by and derived from a set of public laws that include the U.S. Constitution, penal statutes, court orders, judicial precedents, public opinion, and contemporary public policy responses to criminal behaviors. This procedure is similar to the 7th-century Anglo-Saxon Law of Aethelberht of Kent, which created a legal classification that calculated risk and sanctions based on the gravity of the offense, the status of victims, and the offender's social position and class (Jones, 1998). Under the law at the time, crimes against so-called noblemen were considered more serious than crimes against commoners, freedmen, and slaves. Sanctions for such crimes differed in severity also, with offenders who committed crimes against noblemen receiving more severe consequences (Kalhous & Meringolo, 2012).

According to Burns and Leone (2005), the concept of bail dates back to around 1000 AD, when the English criminal justice system classified offenders into two categories: those who were entitled to release on bail and those who were unfit for release prior to the conclusion of their criminal trials. The process did not provide a distinction between felony and misdemeanor penalties (Roth, 2011, p. 26). Therefore, the key factors at the time that dictated who was and was not bailable were "the nature of the offense" and factors like the offender's history of bad repute and the likelihood of conviction based on the "strength of the evidence against the accused as a proxy for the likelihood of flight" (Kalhous & Meringolo, 2012, p. 804).

Contemporary legal criminal justice classification systems do not, however, use social class as a predictive variable because, legally, all men or rather all people are created equal in the eyes of the law. Legally, also, there are no such things as noblemen, commoners, freedmen, or slaves. Rather, contemporary criminal justice systems use labels such as misdemeanor, criminal, convict, sex offender, violent offender, drug offender, and felon, as well as delinquent, incorrigible, or dependent. These factors dictate how each offender ought to be treated within the criminal justice system. In that regard, this chapter briefly discusses judicial assessment and classification, including pretrial assessment, postconviction, and mental disorder classification, as well as the flaws inherent in how legal labels are developed and assigned to offenders.

LEGAL CLASSIFICATION FLAWS

The designation of a behavior or offender under any of the contemporary legal labels or categories is generally informed by prevailing public opinion and sentiment, statutes, court orders, evidence collected at crime scenes, prosecutorial discretion, and court orders. Unfortunately, however, the use of legal variables as a basis for measuring risks and needs and as a method for deciding how an offender is treated sometimes has no scientific grounds, logical basis, or weight of fairness. As a result, legality tends to be at odds with what behavioral sciences teach or even commonsense supports. For instance, legally, there is a clear difference between an offender aged 17 years, 11 months, and 3 weeks and one aged 18 years. If both offenders were to commit premeditated murder on the same day and in the exact same manner with adequate aggravating circumstances, the 17-year-old would not qualify for the death penalty because, according to the U.S. Supreme Court, he would be legally classified as a child. The 18-year-old, however, would qualify for capital punishment because he would be legally considered an adult and thus capable of forming the evil intent that justifies the death penalty.

Similarly, the legal classification of the offender in *People, Plaintiff and Respondent v. Julio Morales* (2013) as a non-sex offender illustrates some of the flaws in legal classification. In this case, the offender entered the dark bedroom of his victim after the victim's boyfriend departed and had sexual intercourse with her while pretending to be her boyfriend. The offender was subsequently charged and convicted of rape. The trial court sentenced him to a term of 3 years in state prison. However, at appeal, the conviction was reversed and the case remanded for a retrial in part because the statute that made it a rape as a result of impersonating a husband only applied to married women. It did not apply in this case since the victim was not married at the time of the sexual encounter (*The People, Plaintiff and Respondent v. Julio Morales, 2013*).

Prosecutors and courts also objectively use legal variables to proportionately match offending behaviors with legal sanctions, such as prison sentences that may be concurrent, consecutive (or cumulative), determinate, indeterminate, mandatory, probation, maximum, or minimum. These legal categories, however, tend to lack the kind of scientific validation that typically drives clinical assessment and classification. The same is true of other important legal variables, such as acquittals, no contest pleas, guilty verdicts, convictions, and aggravating and mitigating factors that are also not scientifically or logically reliable for predicting the risk of criminal or delinquent behaviors. In many cases, these important legal factors have very little clinical value, but each one can instantly move a legal risk level from one extreme to another.

The legal categories of guilty or not guilty, for example, are created by jurors who are purposely selected during a process known as *voir dire* (to speak the truth) based on how they would likely vote at the end of a criminal trial. Studies also show that jurors often fail to comprehend jury instructions, and sometimes they are confused about instructions on the difference between mitigating and aggravating factors. Jurors also generally give in to group dynamics or pressure during jury deliberations, sometimes bargain and compromise their positions, and rely on extralegal factors to draw conclusions about guilt (Meyer & Grant, 2003). These weaknesses do not, however, mean that legal classification is irrelevant. On the contrary, when guided by science or logic, some legal classifications, such as repeat criminal behaviors, documented violent acts, and sexual victimization, play critical roles in the way clinical assessment and classification predict future criminal behaviors, as well as measure the likelihood of future arrests.

JUDICIAL ASSESSMENT AND CLASSIFICATION

Risk assessment and classification occur at every stage of the criminal process, starting from the initial detention to the conclusion of the criminal allegation. The different forms of judicial assessment and classification can, however, be grouped into three distinct categories: (1) pretrial assessment, (2) postconviction classification, and (3) legal mental disorder. Whether a criminal justice institution emphasizes legal assessment or classification over clinical assessment and classification at any of the stages depends on institutional politics, mandates, and goals, which, of course, vary from one agency to another.

The obvious challenge with the variation in risk and needs assessment and classification also depends on what is being measured and the nature of predictive variables that are being used to calculate risk and needs. Consequently, at certain stages of the criminal judicial process, legal variables are emphasized over clinical ones, but during other phases of the process, clinical variables are stressed, while at still other levels, the same criminal justice system may devote more time to clinical variables over legal variables or emphasize legal information over clinical evidence.

When the assessment goals are to identify steps that are needed to mitigate risk to public safety or to ensure proportionality of sanctions, courts and prosecutors emphasize legal variables over clinical ones. When the purpose is to gauge amenability to treatment or to identify steps that are needed to reduce risks and needs, penological institutions and probation and parole departments rely more heavily on the behavioral science approaches that drive clinical assessment and classification. However, when the purpose of the process is to distinguish between offenders who need more intervention from those who demand less therapeutic intervention or supervision, and when the purpose of the process is to identify sex offenders, substance abusers, and violent offenders, penological institutions and probation and parole departments generally use both legal and clinical variables. Furthermore, although judicial, penal, and community-based corrections use legal and clinical classifications, the extent to which each of these agencies emphasizes clinical classification over legal classification, or legal classification over clinical classification, depends on a number of factors, such as legislative guidelines, the nature of criminal behaviors, and whether the overall goals of the institution conducting the classification emphasize physical control over rehabilitation.

The range of judicial classification goes from pretrial releases for low-risk offenders warranted by the offenders' promises to be present in court or third-party releases based on mere promises to present offenders at the next court hearing, to the detention of high-risk offenders without the possibility of bond. The actual process of assessment and classification starts shortly after an offender is detained and continues until all the statutory remedies warranted by the offender's behavior are exhausted. That is, in theory, each time a court reviews the reasons for which an offender is being held and examines the conditions of confinement, the court is, in essence, conducting a judicial assessment and classification that ends up with an extension or in an increased or decreased deprivation of liberty and freedom. There are two levels of such judicial assessment and classification: (1) preconviction and (2) postconviction. Each process is dictated by statutes, precedents, and constitutional principles, and in some cases, judicial assessment and classification are guided by limited behavioral science. For instance, during the initial appearance, as well as during the preliminary hearing stage, offenses that are designated as low risk (misdemeanors) generally tend to be classified as such. Offenders whose behaviors are identified by statute as a felony, habitual, or predatory are judicially presumed to be at high risk of reoffending and thus are likely to be detained without bond or ordered to post a high bond.

Pretrial Assessment

The preconviction assessment and classification process consists of the initial appearance, arraignment, and preliminary assessment and classification. At each of these stages, courts use some combination of the statements in Exhibits 15.1 and 15.2 to make decisions (see Exhibit 15.3) about preconviction detention and release. The purpose of pretrial assessment and classification is, therefore, to establish the suitability of an offender for pretrial release, to identify conditions that the court must impose to guarantee that an offender remains offense-free, and to ascertain specialized conditions that the court must order to ensure the enforcement of court-imposed requirements of pretrial release. The assessment and classification are conducted by pretrial service or probation officers who are charged with conducting investigations and enforcing the pretrial release conditions imposed by courts on offenders.

EXHIBIT 15.1 INITIAL APPEARANCE

		Yes	No
1.	Offender has a criminal record	>	<
2.	Offender supports one or more dependents	<	>
3.	Public opinion of the offense is intensely negative	>	<
4.	Offense is a felony	>	<
5.	Prosecutor is asking for detention without bond	>	<
6.	Behavior is legally violent but not sexual	>	<
7.	Behavior is a sexual offense against a child	>	<
8.	Behavior is a violent sexual act	>	<
9.	Possible sentence is high	>	<
10.	Offender is unremorseful	>	<
11.	Offender is most likely to be convicted	>	<
12.	Offender will likely flee if released	>	<

< = reduces risk and needs > = increases risks and needs

During the initial hearing, courts use the statements in Exhibit 15.1 to assess risk and thus make arraignment decisions regarding detention. At the arraignment and preliminary stages, courts assess the risk of the offender absconding prior to the commencement of prosecution. At each level, the lengthier the possible sentence for an offense, the higher the judicial risk score, and the higher the bail. Therefore, in an effort to ascertain risk level, pretrial service and probation officers typically assign values to legal and social variables, including those in Exhibit 15.2, and then use those statements to calculate risk levels. The higher the risk level, the less likely the offender will be given the opportunity for release, and if the offender is allowed to post bond, then the higher the bail and the stricter the specialized conditions of pretrial release.

EXHIBIT 15.2 ARRAIGNMENT AND PRELIMINARY CLASSIFICATION

		Yes	No
1.	Likelihood of committing new crimes exists	>	<
2.	Defendant statement shows some sense of guilt or remorse	<	>
3.	Offender has prior criminal history	>	<
4.	Offender has strong family and communal ties	<	>
5.	Public favors release in this instance	<	>
6.	Education and employment status or opportunity is good	<	>
7.	Offender's environment negatively affects behaviors	>	<
8.	Prosecutor asks for detention without bond	>	<
9.	Preconviction detention will unfavorably affect health	<	>
10.	Public view of the offense is highly negative	>	<
11.	Detention minimizes further danger to society	>	<
12.	Offender is likely to flee if released	>	<

< = reduces risk and needs > = increases risks and needs

At the arraignment and preliminary stages, courts assess the likelihood of the offender fleeing during the trial. As the names imply, pretrial and preconviction release allows offenders to avoid detention while awaiting the conclusion of their cases. The degree to which a bail amount goes up or down also depends on other social, psychological, and legal factors, such as the relevancy of past history to current criminal behaviors. For example, a 10-year-old DUI record may not significantly increase the risk level for pretrial release, especially if the current offense is unrelated to driving. However, the same DUI history would significantly increase the risk level if the offense is that of driving under the influence of alcohol. If the DUI charge is coupled with allegations of leaving the scene of an accident or child endangerment because of the presence of a minor in the offender's car at the time of the arrest, then the risk level would automatically go up because of the risk of future victimization and the threat to public safety.

EXHIBIT 15.3 INITIAL APPEARANCE CLASSIFICATION

Classification		
1.	Third-party release or own recognizance	Release on "own recognizance" or release to the care of a third party because the offender is not likely to victimize others, tamper with evidence, or escape before the next court hearing
2.	Low bond	Somewhat likely to escape before the next court hearing, victimize others, and tamper with evidence—the higher the likelihood the higher the bond
3.	High bond	Most likely to escape before the next court hearing, victimize others, and tamper with evidence—the higher the likelihood the higher the bond
4.	No bond	Certain to escape, victimize others, tamper with evidence, or escape scheduled court hearing

Courts use the statements in Exhibit 15.1 and 15.2 to calculate risk factors and determine whether to grant a detainee the option to post bail, to order a detainee held in custody without the possibility of posting a bond, or to release an offender based on a verbal promise to return to court as scheduled. The results of the assessment produce one of the conditions in Exhibit 15.3. As indicated, qualification for release on an offender's own recognizance or release to a third party's custody generally requires a trustworthy citizen with good community ties, a good source of socioeconomic support, assurance of law-abiding behaviors, and a strong conviction that the offender will attend or be brought to future court hearings.

Postconviction Classification

More than two thirds of offenders who are convicted or adjudicated are sentenced to probation. In 2013 alone, there were an estimated 3,910,600 adults on probation in the United States (Herberman & Bonczar, 2015). This means that the majority of offenders are subjected to postconviction assessment and classification, primarily to provide advice to trial judges on two questions: whether the offender's risk level qualifies them for probation or any other alternative sanction to incarceration, and if so, what are the most appropriate specialized conditions? Probation officers use responses to statements like those in Exhibit 15.4 to answer these critical questions. In addition, they also consider the effects of community-based sanctions in terms of the positive contribution of offenders' presence in the community to the reduction in the negative effects of confinement, institutionalization cost to society, and prevention of the undue burden borne by innocent family members when the criminal justice process ends with incarceration.

EXHIBIT 15.4 VARIABLE

		Yes	No
1.	Probation or alternative to incarceration is legally allowed	<	>
2.	Probation will produce specific and general deterrence	<	>
3.	Probation offers better opportunity for rehabilitation	<	>
4.	Probation is acceptable in public view	<	>
5.	Offender has prior convictions	>	<
6.	Incarceration will further criminal activity	<	>
7.	Community correctional treatment is desired	<	>
8.	Offender has history of unsuccessful prior probation or parole	>	<
9.	Relevant resources in the community are accessible to offender	<	>
10.	Offender's presence in the community would significantly have a negative effect on victim(s)	>	<
11.	Past adjudication or conviction for similar act	>	<

< = chances of incarceration reduces > = chances of probation increases

The report produced by postconviction assessment and classification traditionally contains comprehensive background information specific to each offender's potential for rehabilitation and community reintegration. Thus the postconviction assessment report (commonly known as the presentencing investigation) typically covers the offender's prior criminal history, financial standing, physical and mental health status, and social history, including family ties, employment potential, and educational levels. The report also highlights offenders' motivations and attitudes in carrying out offenses and any relevant mitigating and aggravating circumstances that inform their delinquent or criminal behaviors.

Indeed, judges have the ultimate sentencing discretion, and they are the most qualified when it comes to determining which offenders statutorily qualify for probation, fines, community service, or incarceration. However, the adjudicatory and regulative nature of judicial functions makes judges less equipped to use psychological, environmental, and social factors as a basis for determining the primary factors that inform a particular criminal behavior and to come up with the right intervention that would minimize future criminal and delinquent behaviors. Judges are also not professionally trained to perform social work duties; thus, they lack the skills necessary for answering questions about the likelihood of recidivism and for measuring the social and psychological effects of incarceration on offenders in particular circumstances.

Probation officers, therefore, perform sentencing assessment and classification at the request of trial courts and recommend one or more of the options in Exhibit 15.5 because they are the most qualified court officials—probation officers have the training, skills, and professional knowledge to appropriately advise courts on matters relating to rehabilitation, supervision, and restrictions. They are equipped to deduce conclusions from the careful assessment of social, biological, and psychological factors that are present or absent in the life of an offender. Further, the process uses both legal and clinical variables for calculating punishment as a form of rehabilitation (specific and general deterrence) and for certain corrective interventions to prevent future recidivism.

EXHIBIT 15.5 POSTCONVICTION CLASSIFICATION

1.	Fines	Minimum risk level
2.	Community service	Minimum risk level
3.	Suspended sentence	Minimum risk level
4.	Restitution only	Minimum risk level
5.	Probation	Medium risk level
6.	Incarceration	High risk level
7.	Statutory sentence	Predetermined statutory risk level

Probation officers are at least expected to perform assessment and classification with the positivist understanding that offenders' behaviors are informed by one or more social, psychological, or biological conditions rather than embrace the freewill explanation that classicalism advances. Hence the report generally contains measurements of future offending behaviors, types of services needed to minimize future criminal behaviors, and appropriate penalty to produce sufficient general and specific deterrents (Abadinsky, 2015). If community-based correction is the best option, then postconviction classification informs the nature of restriction and supervision. Thus the higher the risk level, the more stringent the supervision or options in Exhibit 15.5 would be and the more appropriate and imminent incarceration becomes. Except in situations where a specific statute demands, low-risk scores result in the recommendation of probation with less intrusive alternative sanctions, such as fines, restitution, and community service.

Legal Mental Health Disorders

The American legal system often uses the legal insanity classification to distinguish between offenders who are mentally culpable and those who are legally insane. Four common legal tests govern the process: (1) the M'Naghten rule, (2) the "irresistible impulse" test, (3) the Durham rule, and (4) the Model Penal Code. Offenders and defense teams adore the legal insanity classification because "not guilty by reason of insanity" relieves defendants of criminal responsibility (Criminal-Mental-States, 1959). Prosecutors, on the other hand, may see mental health classification as a license for offenders to escape the full weight of the criminal justice system, and the public may view the classification suspiciously as a defense that could be easily abused.

The root of the insanity defense can be traced to a case in 1843, *Queen v. Daniel M'Naghten*. In this instance, the defendant, Daniel M'Naghten, sought to kill Prime Minister Sir Robert Pell on the presumption that the prime minister was involved in a conspiracy to kill him. M'Naghten, however, shot and killed the prime minister's private secretary, Edward Drummond, thinking that he was shooting at Prime Minister Peel. M'Naghten was subsequently charged with murder. At trial, M'Naghten pled not guilty and called witnesses who testified that he was mentally defective. The defense argued that M'Naghten was insane and thus his delusions caused him to engage in the murderous act. The jury accepted the argument and found the defendant not guilty by reason of insanity.

The M'Naghten test inspired by this case states that an offender is not criminally liable if the court finds they didn't know what they were doing, or the offender knew but could not fully comprehend the wrongfulness of the action at the time of the offense because of mental illness. The test argues that a disease of the mind can cause a defect of reason in ways that make it impossible for an offender to fully understand the wrongfulness of their actions. The mental defect or disease of the mind makes it impossible for the offender to form the evil intent necessary for committing a criminal act. This rule also requires that the offender advance evidence to support any claim of suffering from a disease of the mind, and as a result, the offender must show that they were unable to appreciate the true nature and quality of the wrongful act (*Queen v. M'Naghten, 1843*).

The Durham rule, used in New Hampshire, broadly recognizes mental disease or defect at the time of the incident as a legitimate defense but fails to demand a medical diagnosis of mental illness or disorder. The "irresistible impulse" test is used by most states in combination with the M'Naghten rule. The test accepts the mental health defense in cases where the offender knows that the action is wrong but engages in it because they feel compelled as a result of their mental illness to commit the offense. The Model Penal Code, sometimes called "all defense" or "the substantial capacity" insanity defense, borrows from the M'Naghten rule and irresistible impulse but rejects the diagnosis of psychopath or sociopath as grounds for an insanity defense.

John Hinckley successfully used elements of the Model Penal Code test in his trial for the attempted murder of President Ronald Reagan. Hinckley was found not guilty by reason of insanity. In response to the case, the U.S. Congress passed the Insanity Defense Reform Act of 1984 (2018). The act principally transfers the burden of proof from the prosecutor to the defense and demands that the person claiming mental illness must clearly and convincingly show that at the time of the offense, they were unable to appreciate the wrongfulness of the prohibited act. Offenders who successfully make such cases and subsequently are acquitted and relieved of criminal responsibility must be committed to psychiatric facilities until they are declared healthy enough to live in society.

Hate it or like it, the insanity defense is widely invoked by offenders and rarely accepted by courts or jurors as a legitimate defense. Studies also show that the insanity-plea tests discussed thus far can benefit from some revisions. The tests also provoke debates about whether the majority of people who plead legal insanity falsely do so to gain acquittal (Daftary-Kapur et al., 2011). It is also important to note that whether these claims of insanity are legitimate or not, they do affect public opinion and decisions made by criminal justice professionals. Consequently, the chance becomes great for disregarding legitimate mental health conditions or diverting resources to an offender who may not need such help.

CONCLUSION

The purpose of pretrial risk assessment and classification is to measure the offender's risk level as it applies to failure to attend future court proceedings and the ability to live a crime-free life, at least until the conclusion of the current criminal justice process. The primary purpose of postconviction or adjudication classification is to ascertain the most appropriate sanctions within the court's statutory authority—that is, the determination of whether offender qualifies for secure care or community-based intervention and sanctions. The results of these two assessment processes guide the courts (mainly judges) in regard to the most appropriate sanctions and interventions that will protect society from any antisocial behaviors undertaken by the offender.

Generally speaking, legal classification complicates the categorization of probationers, parolees, and, in some instances, detainees because the process primarily uses the classical approach and retributive and procedural responses to criminal behaviors. Hence legal classification uses a legal, objective scale that blindly classifies offenders without reference to the subjective histories that explain most of their thinking and behavior. Of course, this approach is not very helpful when the focus of assessment and classification is rehabilitation or the prevention of future acts of deviance and criminality.

Clearly, there are instances where certain offenders may be erroneously classified as violent offenders, while actual violent offenders may turn up in a different category of offenses, such as substance abuse offending behavior. For instance, an offender who uses a weapon to rob a convenience store to finance a drug habit will unmistakably be classified as a violent offender by a legal classification system. However, a properly conducted probation or parole classification system would easily categorize the same offender as a substance abuser with a high need for substance abuse treatment and lower need for anger management or treatment for violent behavior.

DISCUSSION QUESTIONS

1. Why would a legal classification not be a good predictor of recidivism?

2. What are some weaknesses and strengths of legal classification in comparison to positivist and clinically driven classifications like the ones that probation and parole officers attempt to conduct?
3. There is strong evidence that legal classification generally favors those who are economically well placed in society. What aspects of the legal classification system support or disprove such a claim?
4. How much weight should be given to mental illness when calculating both risk and needs levels, keeping in mind that almost every person has one or more forms of mental health disorder in the *Diagnostic and Statistical Manual of Mental Disorders, Fifth Edition*?

REFERENCES

Abadinsky, H. (2015). *Probation and parole: Theory and practice*. Pearson.

Burns, R., & Leone, P. K. M. C. (2005). Bounty hunters: A look behind the hype. *Policing: An International Journal of Police Strategies & Management*, *28*(1), 118–138. https://doi.org/http://dx.doi.org/10.1108/13639510510581011

Criminal-Mental-States. (1959). Admissibility of subjective abnormality to disprove criminal mental states: Criminal law. Homicide. Criminal procedure. Evidence of mental abnormality other than legal insanity. *Stanford Law Review*, *12*(1), 226–235. https://doi.org/10.2307/1226740

Daftary-Kapur, T., Groscup, J. L., O'Connor, M., Coffaro, F., & Galietta, M. (2011). Measuring knowledge of the insanity defense: Scale construction and validation. *Behavioral Sciences & the Law*, *29*(1), 40–63. https://doi.org/10.1002/bsl.938

Herberman, E. J., & Bonczar, T. P. (2015). Probation and parole in the United States, 2013. *Bulletin*. http://www.bjs.gov/content/pub/pdf/ppus13.pdf

Insanity Defense Reform Act of 1984 (2018): United States Department of Justice, Criminal Resource Manual, Retrieved from: https://www.justice.gov/archives/jm/criminal-resource-manual-634-insanity-defense-reform-act-1984.

Jones, M. E. (1998). *The end of Roman Britain*. Cornell University Press.

Kalhous, C., & Meringolo, J. (2012). Bail pending trial: Changing interpretations of the Bail Reform Act and the importance of bail from defense attorneys' perspectives. *Pace Law Review*, *32*(3 (Summer 2012), 800–855.

Meyer, J.A.F., & Grant, D. R. (2003). *The courts in our criminal justice system*. Prentice Hall.

People, Plaintiff and Respondent v. Julio Morales, 212 Cal. App 4th 583 (2013).

Queen v. M'Naghten, No. 10 Clark & F.200, 2 ENG, rep. 718 (H.L. 1843) (1843).

Roth, M. P. (2011). *Crime and punishment: A history of the criminal justice system* (2nd ed.). Wadsworth Cengage Learning.

CHAPTER SIXTEEN

Community and Correctional Classification Labels

LEGALLY, ALL OFFENDERS, including those serving time in jails and prisons and those under the supervision of community corrections, are criminals and threats to society. Clinically, however, most community corrections offenders pose little or no specific threat to public safety. In fact, most offenders come from the so-called good citizen category, the population one encounters on school grounds, at religious services, at work and social gatherings, and at public places and events. People also commit crimes for different reasons and under different financial, mental, physical, pathological and environmental conditions and circumstances.

It is also worth noting that although crimes have specific elements irrespective of who commits them, each offender is unique, with different sets of criminogenic risk and needs factors. For example, the element of theft law consists of taking something of value belonging to another person or entity without permission and with the intention of permanently depriving that person or entity of the lawful use of the stolen property. Although these statutory requirements are the same for every theft case, each offender is also unique. For instance, offenders with prior convictions for theft are different than those with no such history. Offenders who steal for the purpose of accumulating wealth are obviously different than those who steal for the sole purpose of acquiring food, security, shelter, and basic psychological needs. Similarly, first-time offenders are different than repeat offenders.

How the public reacts to specific crimes is also very important. In this respect, however, the public, unfortunately, discriminates against certain crimes. For example, crimes such as child molestation, rape, and possession of child pornography generally attract harsher condemnation than the crime of resisting arrest, perjury, tax fraud, obstruction of justice, and most white-collar crimes. All of these factors inform sentencing outcomes or dictate whether incarceration, probation, or placement in a treatment program is an option. It is, therefore, logical that criminal justice practitioners use specific labels to separate or distinguish one offender from another, even when the statutory offenses are similar or identical.

This chapter discusses the contexts within which criminal justice practitioners assign and use classification labels to distinguish between offenders in terms of risk, needs, security, and public safety. Specifically, this chapter talks about the classification labels pretrial, probation, parole, and corrections officers use to distinguish between juvenile and adult offenders; low-risk and high-risk offenders; and those who do and do not qualify for certain privileges, such as pretrial release, probation, or parole status; and those who should be housed with inmates in institutional settings. The assumptions are that as the risk level of an offender increases, security levels go up and so does the need to prevent further harm to society.

COMMUNITY CORRECTIONS SUPERVISION LEVELS

From the standpoint of treatment of offenders, labels for supervision, pretrial release, and probation and parole are typically incomplete without classification labels, such as low risk, medium risk, and high risk. These labels represent individual offenders' risks of not following laws and rules, the security of the public, and the level of treatment needed to address criminogenic risk factors. Hence the labels dictate which offender qualifies for what type of community corrections supervision, who should be ordered to perform community service, who should be held under house arrest, who should be placed in a halfway house program, who should participate in counseling, who needs intensive supervision, and which pretrial releasees, probationers, parolees, or inmates merit minimal supervision.

Pretrial, probation, and parole departments use unique labeling systems to identify those offenders who are low risk, medium risk, and high risk and to separate offenders who need intensive supervision from offenders who require low supervision, with the goal of properly managing offenders' thinking and behavior. In some jurisdictions, the level system of Level 1, Level 2, Level 3, and sometimes Level 4 is used instead of the traditional minimum-, medium- and high-risk levels. It should, however, be noted that in some jurisdictions, the lower the number attached to a level, the higher the risk. For example, in certain jurisdictions, Level 1 is the highest risk level and Level 4 is the lowest risk level.

Minimum-Risk Offenders

The majority of community corrections offenders are at minimum risk of violating their status, committing new offenses, or continuing to participate in antisocial activities. This finding is not, however, surprising because the majority of offenders who enter the criminal justice system do so as a result of low-level felonies and low-level misdemeanor types of offenses, such as DUI, domestic violence, minor acquisitive and white-collar crimes, and controlled substance possession offenses. Generally, most offenders in this category do not have prior convictions or criminal records, and the periods of probation and parole are more likely to be shorter than for medium-risk offenders.

In some jurisdictions, and in certain cases, minimum-risk offenders are not required to contact their supervising officers as long as they don't commit new offenses. Even in situations where minimum-risk offenders are required to make contact with their supervising officers monthly to enforce their compliance with standard and specialized conditions of release, particularly the provision requiring probationers and parolees to totally refrain from committing new crimes, the likelihood of a new offense or technical violation is low. Indeed, minimum-risk offenders are more likely to successfully complete their terms of probation and parole than offenders in the upper categories of risk. The high number of successful completions of parole and probation by minimum-risk offenders does not, however, mean that this group of offenders commits fewer crimes. The reality is that minimum-risk offenders are less likely to get caught since they are monitored or supervised less than medium-risk offenders.

Even when they are caught, minimum-risk offenders are more likely to enjoy the benefit of the doubt than offenders in higher risk categories.

Medium-Risk Offenders

The second largest group of community corrections offenders are medium-risk pretrial releasees, probationers, and parolees with moderate chances of violating their conditions of release or engaging in new criminal activities while under correctional supervision. This group has a medium risk of continuous criminal activity. The majority of these offenders commit violent felonies, sex crimes against children, and gang-related offenses, and they are repeat offenders or have histories of not following lawful orders or directives by their supervising officers. As a result of their reduced risk of committing new offenses, medium-risk offenders are generally only required to make at least one face-to-face contact with their pretrial, probation, or parole officers in a month. Under normal circumstances, a face-to-face meeting is designed to prove that an offender is not outside the supervising jurisdiction, to examine the offender's progress and lapses, and to enhance conditions of release.

High-Risk Offenders

Certain groups of offenders under community corrections supervision are high-risk offenders whose chances of violating conditions of release are greater than most community corrections offenders. Many high-risk offenders are sexual and violent offenders with a history of serious criminal offending behaviors. Consequently, these offenders are subject to more restrictions and are more strictly supervised than medium-risk offenders. For example, this category of offenders is required to make weekly contact with their supervising officers, are subject to frequent and unannounced home inspections, and, where necessary, are also required to submit to regular drug testing. Consequently, high-risk offenders are more likely to be violated for both technical and new offense violations since they are diligently monitored. When there are allegations of violations, they are likely to receive a stricter application of the rules that govern pretrial release, probation, and parole revocation.

Intensive Probation and Parole

In comparison to those who are incarcerated, pretrial releasees, probationers, and parolees are by definition low-risk offenders who are apparently less dangerous than those who are incarcerated. In fact, it is their reduced chance of violating standard conditions of release, recidivating, or engaging in criminal activities while under community supervision that qualifies them for pretrial release, probation, or parole. In some instances, however, a high-risk offender who qualifies for custodial corrections may receive pretrial or probation status for the purpose of preventing the suffering of innocent dependents if such an offender were to be incarcerated. The brief summary of the case in Box 16.1 serves as a good example.

BOX 16.1 PROBATION AFTER SEXUALLY MOLESTING 6-YEAR-OLD DAUGHTER WITH CANCER

Jeremy Schwer, a 41-year-old Indianapolis man, was charged with and pled to felony child molestation charges involving his own daughter. This case is an example of an instance where some people would think an offender deserves a prison term instead of probation, yet a compelling case is made for the latter.

The victim in this case was diagnosed with cancer in 2013 when doctors found a brain tumor. After spending several months in the hospital, she began to undergo a year of chemotherapy. During this period, the girl told her mother that her father was sexually molesting her.

According to court records, the girl alleged that the abuse "happened every night when she slept with her father." Each time the father told his 6-year-old daughter that she should not tell anyone because if she did, he would go to jail.

When the time came for sentencing, the Marion Superior Court gave Mr. Schwer 12 years of probation and ordered him to register as a sex offender, continue to receive treatment for sex offending behaviors at a counseling center, and leave the family home until he was properly treated for sexual offending behaviors. The sentence of probation was drastically less than the 9 years of imprisonment and 3 years of community corrections supervision the deputy prosecutor asked the court to impose on Mr. Schwer.

Obviously, Mr. Schwer did not receive any jail time at sentencing for molesting his sick 6-year-old daughter; instead, the judge gave him probation against the urging of the public prosecutor's office. The reason for the drastic departure was that the girl's mother, who filed for divorce, wrote a letter to the court asking that Mr. Schwer not be sent to prison because she hoped he would help support their children financially.

Of course, the court was not obligated to comply with such a request, but the judge looked at how Mr. Schwer's incarceration would impact the lives of his children, including the victim. It is clear that the court was concerned that incarceration will negatively impact Mr. Schwer's children, including the victim.

There are many cases like the example in Box 16.1 in which the absence of an offender from society will create hardships for other innocent members of society. In those cases, a high-risk offender who meets the requirement for some level of custodial placement may be granted pretrial release or probation. However, to compensate for the alleged compromise of public safety, pretrial and probation agencies place such offenders on an intensive supervision level. The main difference between a high-risk offender and an intensive supervision offender in this respect is the level of supervision and restriction, which are much more severe for intensive pretrial releasees, probationers, and parolees than for high-risk offenders.

As a matter of policy goals, intensive supervision programs have tangible benefits. For example, intensive supervision programs are supposed to reduce the cost of incarceration and the number of offenders behind bars because they allow offenders who are allegedly eligible for incarceration to live in the community at their own expense. In some limited ways, offenders are also allowed to perform normal functions, such as reporting to work, attending school, and socially interacting with the public just like any other member of society while at the same time being prevented by their supervising officers from causing further harm in society. Most importantly, community corrections reduces overcrowding and saves public resources that can be used for other community safety programs.

Unfortunately, however, studies have shown that the anticipated policy result has hardly materialized (Abadinsky, 2012; Petersilia & Turner, 1991; Seiter, 2020). For example, in comparison to standard supervision, intensive supervision programs drive up incarceration numbers, as well as supervision costs. Indeed, as with most intensive sanction-based interventions, studies show that intensive probation does "not decrease the frequency or seriousness of new arrests" but instead actually "increases the incidence of technical violations and jail terms" (Petersilia & Turner, 1993, p. 281). In other words, increased surveillance and restrictions actually increase incarceration rates. However, when the intensive supervision involves participation in an evidence-based program, the outcome can be different for certain categories of offenses, such as substance abuse, sex offending, and violent crimes (Barnes et al., 2017; Barta et al., 2017).

CUSTODIAL SECURITY CLASSIFICATION LABELS

Humans love freedom. People want to sit when they want to sit. They want to use the restroom when they feel like it, to sleep when they want to, and to speak when they want to speak. Painfully, however, the power and right to exercise these and other rights and desires become significantly limited when someone is detained by the criminal justice system. In such situations, the likelihood of a detainee wanting to escape into the free world and the chances of becoming depressed and engaging in self-abusive behaviors go up. Consequently, custody classification measures factors that may warrant the placement of offenders at a specific security level. The factors include (1) a history of past escape or attempts, (2) the severity of current charges in terms of the nature of violence involved and the corresponding prison or jail time, (3) a history of violent crimes, (4) allegations of sex crimes, (5) offenders' disabilities, (6) disciplinary history while in custody, and (7) membership in a security threat group or criminal gang, especially prison gangs.

Security risk levels represent the level of resources and control an offender needs in order to safely serve the entirety of a sentence. In this regard, when talking about offenders' likelihood of escape or violation of security rules and the likelihood of successfully participating in therapeutic activities, federal and state prisons and jails use three- or four-level systems: minimum-, medium-, and high-risk, or minimum-, medium-, high-risk, and supermax security levels (Krisberg et al., 2019). Irrespective of the level systems, risk levels are periodically reviewed for upward or downward adjustment. This also means that a minimum-risk offender can qualify for the high-risk level within minutes, although movement from a high-risk level to low-risk level requires more effort and time.

Legally and therapeutically, inmates are presumed to be at minimum security risk levels unless there exist specific reasons to warrant a change in the level. Hence, an offender's risk level is reviewed each time there is a major incident to warrant such changes. Common factors that call for a review of existing security classification are new felony charges, significant increase or decrease in the time sentenced, and serious custodial rule violations. In most cases, however, custodial rule violations are responsible for level reviews and significant changes in security or risk level. For example, a minimum-risk offender who attempts an escape; who assaults a correctional staff member, visitor to a correctional facility, or another offender; or who damages correctional property or is found in possession of dangerous contraband can be subjected to an immediate review that may result in a significant change in risk level.

Minimum-Security Offenders

Offenders who are assigned to minimum risk levels require minimum supervision because they are less likely to try to escape, cause harm to themselves or others, or require intense supervision to complete their custodial sentences. As a result, this category of offenders poses the least threat to the smooth running of correctional facilities; hence, they are housed in the least restrictive environments and subjected to fewer restrictions. For example, in some institutions, minimum-risk offenders can wear their own clothes, enjoy the luxury of interacting with more offenders under relaxed conditions of supervision, and make physical contact with their visitors (Champion, 2008; Krisberg et al., 2019).

Since most minimum-security-level offenders also have less than a year to complete their sentences, the fear of having their remaining probation or parole status revoked provides good motivation for obeying institutional rules (Siegel & Bartollas, 2016). Consequently, in minimum-risk environments, correctional officers are mainly concerned with minor rule violations and low security threats. Detention-based treatment programs are also rarely present in these environments because the chances of future crimes being committed by minimum-risk offenders are minimal, and most offenders who are housed in minimum-risk facilities transition out of the correctional facility more quickly than offenders in the higher risk levels.

Medium-Security Offenders

A sizable number of custodial offenders are housed at the medium-security level. In comparison to minimum-security offenders, medium-risk offenders enjoy less freedom, but at the same time, they enjoy more freedom than high-security-level offenders in institutional settings. The daily routine for a medium-security offender is also much more regimented than the security protocols applied to minimum-security offenders. Consequently, this category tends to have a higher number of correctional staff members per offender than the minimum- or low-security-level facilities. The reason for the difference is that most offenders in this category tend to have one or more felony convictions or allegations of committing violent or sexual crimes.

Medium-risk offenders are, nevertheless, good candidates for parole and detention-based therapeutic activities, especially considering that they spend more time in detention than minimum-risk offenders and have moderate histories of antisocial thinking and behavior that are arguably more correctible during the term of their incarceration than for higher level offenders. Unfortunately, however, in the absence of adequate therapeutic resources at correctional facilities around the country, security is the main concern in medium-security facilities (Champion, 2008; Krisberg et al., 2019). Indeed, correctional authorities are more concerned about the smooth running of their facilities or the successful prevention of escape and the safety of staff, visitors, offenders, and property than the provision of evidence-based therapeutic interventions.

Maximum-Security Offenders

Only a handful of offenders who are sentenced to jail or prison qualify for the maximum-security label. Maximum-security-level offenders consist of some of the worst in correctional institutions. Offenders with this label tend to have violent criminal histories and are likely to pose a significant threat to the safe running of correctional institutions. In many jurisdictions, maximum-security offenders generally consist of people on death row, verified prison gang members, murderers, and other extremely violent and dangerous individuals. Not surprisingly, therefore, institutions employ tighter security control over maximum-security offenders; thus, institutional safety and the physical safety and containment or control of offenders' thinking and behavior for the duration of their stay are the main concerns for correctional authorities (Champion, 2008; Krisberg et al., 2019).

Maximum-security risk level offenders spend up to 23 hours in their individual cells with little physical interaction with correctional officers or other offenders. People with this security level would not be able to even shake another person's hand for as long as they remain in this category. For example, each time maximum-risk-level offenders must step outside their cells for whatever reason, they first have to be handcuffed through an opening in the doors before they exit. Once the doors are open, the offenders are further restrained with additional security belts and chains before being escorted by at least two officers under the cautious observation of other officers in the control room where movements within correctional facilities are remotely monitored via security cameras.

Supermax Security Level

Murderers on trial or serving longer prison sentences, offenders on death row, and the most dangerous and violent offenders are housed in supermax facilities in jurisdictions with such security levels. As Palmer noted, "supermax" prisons are maximum-security facilities with highly restrictive conditions designed to segregate the most dangerous prisoners from the general prison population" (Palmer, 2010, p. 113). Obviously, supermax correctional facilities house supermax offenders with supermax classification labels. Often, the label is also assigned to the most disruptive and violent institutional threat groups, which generally consist of prison gang members with established histories of violence and offenders who intentionally obstruct the smooth operation of correctional authorities. Without a doubt, offenders with this classification level are among the most dangerous with extensive criminal histories of violence and disruptive institutional behaviors (Champion, 2008; Krisberg et al., 2019).

Offenders at the supermax security level pose the largest threat to penological operations because they are more likely to try to escape; to want to inflict harm on other offenders, correctional staff, and visitors; and least willing to alter their antisocial way of thinking and behaving. Consequently, offenders with this security classification level spend 23 hours of their days locked up in their cells without any physical contact with other offenders or with correctional officers. These offenders communicate with corrections officers on a regular basis but go without shaking hands with another human being for months or years. Often, the only time they are physically touched by another person or their bodies make contact with another person is when they are being handcuffed and moved from one location to another by correctional officers (Champion, 2008; Krisberg et al., 2019).

Punitive Isolation

Prisons and jails have areas designed as isolation units or cells to house offenders with a punitive isolation classification label. The isolation facility houses offenders who violate serious institutional rules, such as participating in physical fights or riots, actively taking part in gang activities, or making serious threats of causing harm to staff members or other offenders. Isolation units are, therefore, used strictly as punishment for past deeds within the facility and as a deterrent of future violations of institutional rules. The decision to house or move an offender into an isolation cell or unit is made by correctional staff in response to serious rule violations. As a result, decisions are made after full compliance with due process requirements.

The process by which offenders are placed in punitive isolation has been repeatedly reviewed by courts, especially with regard to compliance with due process requirements and the length of time an offender spends in isolation. In general, however, the courts have consistently taken the view that the policy furthers legitimate penological functions. That is, the "courts view the proper purpose of isolated confinement to be the maintenance of order within the institution;" therefore the courts consider the policy to be constitutional as long as a period of isolation is proportionate to the violation that warrants the isolation and the isolation does not involve unnecessary punishment that is cruel and unusual or that violates the Eight Amendment of the U.S. Constitution (Palmer, 2010, p. 107).

Administrative Segregation

Prisons and jails are by definition dangerous and violent environments with many violent offenders and vulnerable targets for victimization. Hence while everyone can be a target of victimization, people with disabilities, people who are charged with sex and violent crimes against children and women, juvenile offenders, the elderly, homosexual males who are overtly feminine and sexual, celebrities, law enforcement personnel, and public figures are particularly vulnerable to violent and sexual victimization. Indeed, for these populations, administrative segregation serves as a protective shield against victimization by other offenders. This practice explains why some jurisdictions refer to segregated populations as "protective custody" offenders.

Of course, not all segregated offenders are held in seclusion simply for their own safety. Some celebrities are housed in administrative segregation because their mere presence in general population causes security concerns. For example, a celebrity could create major security issues in correctional institutions they were housed in general population where a large number of offenders would have access to them, congregate around them, or try to attract the celebrity's attention. Of course, such attention becomes a serious threat to the smooth running of a correctional facility or management of the prison population. At a minimum, two main security concerns emerge: (1) the safety of the celebrity and (2) the likelihood of the celebrity using their influence to control the thinking and behavior of a large pool of the prison or jail population. Indeed, with the backing and support of more offenders, a celebrity can successfully challenge correctional authority and obstruct the ability to maintain security.

JUVENILE INSTITUTIONAL LABELS

Juvenile detention centers are not prisons or jails, which is why they are commonly known by names such as juvenile hall, school, detention center, or juvenile correctional institution. Irrespective of the different names, juvenile facilities also use level systems that are often similar to the ones adult community corrections use (i.e., minimum-, medium-, and high-risk levels). Some juvenile detention centers, however, use unique labels, such as orientation, freshman, sophomore, junior, and senior to distinguish between offenders based strictly on their criminogenic needs and not security risks, although the treatment of criminogenic needs also addresses criminogenic risk factors and vice versa. Some jurisdictions use "intake" or "orientation" to label new juvenile arrivals who are still undergoing the risk-assessment and classification process. Every juvenile justice institution, however, uses labels to identify the correctional needs of each probationer, juvenile detainee, or parolee.

Orientation

It takes time for correctional institutions to gather all the necessary information and documents to assess and classify offenders appropriately. The importance of assessing an offender correctly and the length of time it takes to complete the risk assessment and classification process explains why new juvenile arrivals at correctional facilities are held in intake facilities while they undergo the orientation process, which takes a week to a month depending on institutional policies and the individual case. During that period, orientation offenders are required to participate in a variety of therapeutic activities designed to help criminal justice professionals working with those offenders identify the specific goals that must be achieved prior to their release from custody.

Freshman Level

Once juvenile offenders are out of the orientation process, they start out as freshmen and work their way up the level ladders. Hence, the freshman level is the equivalent of the high-risk level. Offenders at the freshmen level, therefore, generally work on accepting responsibility for their criminal or delinquent behaviors. That is, at this stage, offenders must accept that they have committed the offenses for which they are being held. Consequently, these offenders spend the bulk of their time in therapeutic activities. In terms of privileges, freshman-level offenders receive the fewest privileges in comparison to the rest of the levels. Specifically, freshmen may not receive visitors, and even if they do, such visits are usually brief and involve only one or two family members. Offenders at the freshmen level also receive one short phone call per week.

Sophomore Level

Offenders who make it to the sophomore level are generally expected to demonstrate an in-depth understanding of their own behaviors. Specifically, they are required to articulate the actual and possible effects of their behaviors on victims, society, and themselves. The capacity to do so is required to qualify for promotion to the junior level. With regard to incentives, offenders at the sophomore level receive fewer privileges in comparison to junior-level offenders but enjoy more privileges than those accorded to offenders at the freshman level. This means that sophomore-level offenders receive a lower number of visits, shorter phone calls, shorter movie time, and shorter recreational time.

Junior Level

Offenders at the junior level are expected to apply what they have learned about themselves and their thinking and behavior, as well as the skills they have acquired for preventing and avoiding future opportunities for delinquency and criminality. It is, therefore, a common practice in correctional facilities for staff members to occasionally delegate some of their duties to junior- and senior-level offenders, although no matter what, all offenders live under the constant observation and supervision of their correctional staff. With regard to privileges and incentives, junior-level offenders receive a lower number of visits and phone calls, less movie time, and fewer recreational activities in comparison to senior-level offenders.

Senior Level

Offenders at the senior stage of their rehabilitation are required to demonstrate that they have learned new ways of thinking and behaving in preparation for their release into the community. Readiness in this case can be demonstrated by a consistent show of leadership, the ability to comply with existing rules, and the capacity to appropriately resolve personal and interpersonal conflicts. Seniors are also expected to serve as role models for lower level offenders and to assist correctional staff with the collective supervision and management of lower-level offenders. Senior-level offenders also receive longer visits, longer phone calls, longer movie time, longer access to recreational activities, and longer free time than lower level risk offenders. The extent to which a senior responsibly uses the privileges accorded to them is also taken into account when gauging their preparedness for release into the community.

CONCLUSION

Since offenders are assigned labels for specific legal and clinical reasons, they must provide reasons, by way of acceptable behavior, to move up or down the level ladder. For example, if an offender gets to a higher level for physically attacking a corrections officer, the level remains high until that offender has demonstrated sufficient behaviors to indicate that they are no longer a threat to others. The use of classification labels is, therefore, helpful, especially in situations where a correctional officer is encountering an offender for only a brief moment. In such situations, the risk label communicates vital security information, as well as details about that offender's criminogenic risk and needs levels. Such knowledge can be helpful to criminal justice professionals who wish to develop and use the most appropriate behavioral interventions and techniques for rehabilitating, managing, and supervising an offender.

Risk levels can go from minimum to maximum in a matter of minutes, but the reverse generally takes longer to materialize. Hence community corrections and custodial classifications are not permanent because risk levels often fluctuate each time an offender's behavior or circumstances change. For example, if a minimum-risk offender assaults another inmate, they can go from minimum-risk level to supermax level depending on the extent of the harm the offender causes to victims. Similarly, a medium-risk offender can end up on high-risk status if they are caught trying to escape.

Risk levels are specific to certain factors or behaviors; therefore, no one is truly at minimum, medium, or high risk in every sense. For example, an offender can be classified as high risk with regard to escape but remain at a medium-risk level in terms of safety, while at the same time scoring minimum risk in terms of treatment. An offender serving time in jail or prison for driving while under the influence of drugs may not pose any serious threat to the safety of the facility and its occupants, but if they are at a high risk of escaping, then the correct classification is high risk because the prevention of escape is one of the three core penological responsibilities for any correctional institutions.

DISCUSSION QUESTIONS

1. Do security labels effects individual offender's thinking or behavior in a positive or negative way?
2. Why is no one at zero risk of offending, and why are even the best-behaved citizens at minimum-risk levels?
3. How might an increased restriction on high-risk offenders increase their chances of reoffending?

4. Should offenders who qualify for intensive parole be granted parole? Why or why not?
5. Each risk level within the juvenile justice system demands specific behavioral changes by juvenile offenders. Should the same approach be applied to adult offenders?

REFERENCES

Abadinsky, H. (2012). *Probation and parole: Theory and practice.* Pearson.

Barnes, G. C., Hyatt, J. M., & Sherman, L. W. (2017). Even a little bit helps: An implementation and experimental evaluation of cognitive-behavioral therapy for high-risk probationers. *Crime & Delinquency, 63*(1), 3–38. https://doi.org/10.1177/0093854816673862

Barta, W. D., Fisher, V., & Hynes, P. (2017). Decreased re-conviction rates of DUI offenders with intensive supervision and home confinement. *American Journal of Drug & Alcohol Abuse, 43*(6), 742–746. https://doi.org/10.1080/00952990.2016.1237519

Champion, D. J. (2008). *Probation, parole and community corrections.* Prentice Hall.

Krisberg, B. A., Marchionna, S., & Hartney, C. (2019). *American corrections: Concepts and controversies.* Canada. SAGE Publications.

Palmer, J. W. (2010). *Constitutional rights of prisoners* (9th ed.). Anderson Publishing.

Petersilia, J., & Turner, S. (1991). An evaluation of intensive probation in California. *Journal of Criminal Law and Criminology, 82*(3), 610–658.

Petersilia, J., & Turner, S. (1993). Intensive probation and parole. *Crime and Justice, 17,* 281–335. http://www.jstor.org/stable/1147553

Seiter, R. P. (2020). *Corrections: An introduction.* Pearson Education, Inc.

Siegel, L. J., & Bartollas, C. (2016). *Correction Today,* (3rd ed.). Cengage Learning.

SECTION V

Correcting and Preventing Criminal Behaviors

CHAPTER SEVENTEEN

Pretrial, Probation, and Parole Investigative Reports

INVESTIGATIVE REPORTS PRODUCED by pretrial, probation, and parole officers remain a critical part of the American criminal justice process (Macallair, 2002). At the same time, the act of investigating and writing reports for the denial of a pretrial release, probation, or parole involves tedious efforts motivated by a desire to uncover relevant information about each offender's family, educational achievement, criminal history, employment and financial achievement, and mental and physical health. These reports also cover an offender's social history and any factors that may affect thinking and behavior and that may be helpful in imposing an appropriate sentence or passing judgment (Abadinsky, 2012; Macallair, 2002). The purpose of an investigative report is, therefore, to give judges well-reasoned options for denying or granting pretrial release, ordering incarceration, or granting probation. With regard to sentenced offenders, preparole investigative reports give parole boards reasons to grant or deny parole.

Pretrial and presentence investigative reports are written by pretrial and probation officers and submitted to the court before rulings on pretrial release, sentencing, plea bargaining, or an offender's plea of *nolo contendere*, or no contest, to criminal charges. Preparole investigative reports are written by parole officers for parole boards to use as guides for granting or denying parole. This practice of writing reports for criminal justice authorities, including indeed for parole boards, with the aim of informing appropriate decisions regarding pretrial detention and release, incarceration, and parole has a history that is more than a century old. Indeed, beyond the management and supervision of offenders, the core function of pretrial, probation, and parole officers is to investigate offenders and write reports for judges.

This chapter talks about investigative reports in general and specifically pretrial, presentencing, and preparole reports, as well as the content and function of those reports, the sources and use of information, and the ethical challenges associated with producing such reports. The goal of this chapter is, therefore, to provide an overview of the investigative reports produced in criminal justice institutions and the characteristics, definitions, structures, sources, and content commonly associated with pretrial, presentence, and preparole reports.

INVESTIGATIVE REPORTS

The history of investigative reports by pretrial, probation, and parole officers for the purpose of guiding judges in making appropriate decisions about pretrial detention and sentences is one that is strongly linked to the important work of John Augustus in the early 1940s (Macallair, 2002). The father of probation, as he is known, had the positivist belief that individual offenders could be rehabilitated and that the core role of the criminal justice system was to correct antisocial behavior and to prevent future criminal behavior. Augustus also believed that courts had a duty to rehabilitate offenders. Hence he interviewed suitable candidates for his services and collected information relevant to the determination of offenders' suitability for rehabilitation. He then wrote reports about those individuals whom he considered capable of benefiting from community correction. He submitted his reports to trial courts and recommended that those suitable for his services, based on his assessment, be released into his custody.

At the initial stage, Augustus used his reports to convince judges to grant his selected offenders pretrial release. Once the chosen offenders were released into his custody, Augustus helped them find jobs and housing and to reform their behaviors. When the time came for sentencing, he appeared in court with the offenders and supplied reports detailing the specific efforts made by each offender to live a prosocial life and how much the offender had been reformed under his supervision (Macallair, 2002). It was through such practices that Augustus established the process of gathering and analyzing information and writing reports about the suitability of offenders for community corrections (Abadinsky, 2012). In the contemporary era, this practice of investigating and writing reports continues to be a key function of pretrial, probation, and parole officers.

The methods Augustus used were further entrenched in the American judicial process by the rise of the reformatory movements in the 1870s calling for individualized therapeutic approaches to recidivism. The most impactful and critical contributions, however, were certainly the acceptance of the medical model for viewing criminal behavior in the 1920s and 1930s by criminal justice communities. Indeed, the adoption of the belief that criminal behaviors were symptoms of individual pathology and, therefore, criminality could be diagnosed and treated like most medically known diseases was a major contribution to the use of investigative reports in the criminal justice system. The development reduced the job of a pretrial, probation, or parole officer to simply informing judges or parole boards about offenders' symptoms, the severity of the symptoms or risk, the availability of treatment, and the sentencing options available to the court (Macallair, 2002). This departure from the classical model, the notion that criminality is a conscious choice between good and bad behavior by the offender and that, therefore, punishment is the right response to criminality provided the impetus for relying on pretrial, presentencing, and preparole reports as sources of information for therapeutic responses to antisocial and prosocial behaviors.

INSTITUTIONAL APPROACHES TO INVESTIGATIVE REPORTS

The exact content, sources, and uses of investigative reports are dictated by whether an agency is driven mainly by a classical, positivist, or neoclassical approach to the measurement of an offender's behavior after an arrest or indictment. The jurisdiction guided by positivism uses the offender-focused approach. Institutions that are guided by classical responses to crimes use mainly an offense-focused approach, while neoclassical institutions use mixtures of offender-focused and offense-focused approaches. Table 17.1 shows the differences between the two core areas of investigative report concentrations.

TABLE 17.1 *Content of Classical and Positivist-Based Reports*

OFFENDER-FOCUSED REPORT	OFFENSE-FOCUSED REPORT
1. Offense	1. Offense
Current charges and statements by arresting officers, offenders, co-offenders, witnesses, and victims	Current charges or conviction, statements of facts about current charges and offender's compliance with investigating and arresting officers
2. Criminal History	2. Criminal History
All involuntary contact with the criminal justice system and where necessary the circumstances for each contact	Past charges, convictions, adjudications, and acquittals
3. Sentencing Options	3. Sentencing Options
Statutorily mandated sentencing options, including custody, supervised release, probation, jail, fines, community service, and suitable treatment	Statutorily mandated sentencing options including custody, supervised release, probation, jail, community service, or fines
4. Social History	4. Social History
Relevant information about an offender's parents and siblings, marital status, educational level, financial standing, drug use, and relevant antisocial behavior	Offender's family ties, family responsibilities, community ties, education level, and financial standing
5. Employment History	5. Employment History
Summary of past employment, length of past and current employment, and summaries of past terminations, reasons for terminations, and work ethic	Summary of past employment and length of past and current employment. This section focuses on whether the offender is currently employed or is employable
6. Mental and Emotional Health	6. Mental and Emotional Health
Summary of any relevant mental and physical health problem, diagnoses, and, where applicable, compliance with a treatment plan	Summary of any mental and physical health problems relevant to current charges, public safety, and safety of the offender in detention and in the community
7. Recommendation	7. Recommendations
Recommendation for supervised release, detention, fines, jail, prison, community service, and treatment programs	Recommendation for supervised release, detention, fines, jail, prison, and or community service

Offender-focused and offense-focused approaches collect similar information; however, there are clear differences between the two approaches with respect to what offender-focused institutions emphasize and what offense-focused institutions emphasize when making final decisions about pretrial release, sentencing, and parole. For example, offender-focused institutions pay less attention to the offense itself but closely examine each offender's social history, particularly family history, employment potential, educational achievement, and financial standing or prospects. Also important to offender-focused reports are the circumstances under which offenders' criminal activities take place. These circumstances provide a clearer understanding of the extent to which an offender's criminogenic needs are to be served and what treatment interventions can best keep each offender from future criminal activities.

The offense-focused approach assesses each offender's culpability, prior criminal record, and personal background with the underlying assumption that those with extensive criminal histories pose a higher threat to public safety than those with little or no significant criminal history (Macallair, 2002, p. 1449). Offense-focused institutions, therefore, focus more on the offender's criminal activities and less on why an offender engages in such activities. This approach also means that jurisdictions emphasizing offenses over offenders pay greater attention to victims, impact of offenses, and public opinion about offenses. As such, this approach obviously tends to err on the side of punishment.

The actual weight that each agency places on any specific point of information, however, varies from one to another depending on the correctional philosophy informing the report. For example, it makes a big difference when the goal of requesting a pretrial, probation, or preparole report is to ascertain the right treatment for a particular offender. Obviously, the agencies that emphasize retribution and procedural justice give more weight to prior criminal history and an offender's risk of future acts of criminality. Agencies that emphasize distributive and restorative justice or positivist responses to crime, however, pay more attention to offenders' social and criminal histories with the goal of finding out why criminal activities occurred in the first place. Interestingly, the key goal of both offender-focused and offense-focused approaches is to prevent future crimes or recidivism.

SOURCES OF REPORTS

Pretrial, presentencing, and preparole investigative reports produced by pretrial, probation, and parole officers commonly contain specific information from sources such as the offenders, arresting officers, witnesses, codefendants, and community corrections officers who also compile such reports. The final analysis of the community corrections officer conducting the assessment, however, depends on the vital criminogenic risk and needs scores and whether the jurisdiction in which the criminal justice practitioner operates emphasizes an offender-focused or offense-focused approach.

Table 17.2 shows that most information contained in pretrial, presentencing, and preparole investigative reports comes from criminal justice agency records, clinical or psychological and psychiatric evaluation reports, direct interviews of offenders and relevant third parties, and risk-assessment tools. Popular media-based information is also becoming more useful.

Every time a person makes involuntary contact with the criminal justice system, even during a traffic stop, the system generates a report that is saved in both federal and state criminal justice databases that are accessible by other law enforcement personnel, including pretrial, probation, and parole officers around the nation. These agency records generally contain biographic information. Similarly, other agency records, such as court documents, local police reports, and old pretrial, presentencing, and preparole investigative reports, all contain vital information for current pretrial, probation, and parole investigative reports.

The second category of major informative sources includes psychological evaluation reports, psychiatric evaluation reports, and psychosocial reports. Psychological reports are generated by psychologists and usually contain the results of assessment tools and rich

TABLE 17.2 *Core Sources of Investigative Reports*

	INFORMATION	POSSIBLE SOURCE
1.	Biographic data	Interviews and/or agency records
2.	Prior criminal records	Interviews and/or agency records
3.	Past custodial behavior	Interviews and/or agency records
4.	Statements from arresting officers	Interviews and/or agency records
5.	Statements by offenders	Interviews and/or agency records
6.	Statements by victims	Interviews and/or agency records
7.	Prior correctional behaviors	Criminal justice detention records
8.	Compliance with prior supervision	Prior community correction reports
9.	Social history	Interviews and clinical records
10.	Substance use/abuse/dependence	Interviews and clinical records
11.	Employment history	Interviews and clinical records
12.	School performance and conduct	Interviews and clinical records
13.	Financial stability and standing	Interviews and clinical records
14.	Residential stability	Interviews and clinical records
15.	Existing family responsibilities	Interviews and clinical records
16.	Mental health needs status	Interviews and clinical records
17.	Medical health needs	Interviews and clinical records
18.	Educational achievement	Interviews and clinical records
19.	Ability to pay fines and restitution	Interviews and clinical records
20.	Abuse of alcohol or drugs	Interviews and clinical records
21.	Overall risk and needs scores	Interviews and clinical records
22.	Overall risk and needs levels	Interviews and clinical records
23.	Recommended treatments	Interviews and clinical records
24.	Suitability for treatment	Interviews and clinical records
25.	Statements by family members	Interviews and clinical records
26.	Statements by community leaders	Interviews
27.	Statements by employers	Interviews
28.	Consequences of offenses	Officers' judgments
29.	Criminogenic needs scores	Risk assessment instruments
30.	Criminogenic risk scores	Risk assessment instruments
31.	Recommendations	Officers' judgments

documentation of the offenders' social history covering the offenders' childhood, jobs, family structure, criminal history, education, and information about family members, mental health conditions, past deviant thoughts and behaviors, antisocial and prosocial behaviors, and other relevant information. Similarly, psychiatric reports are written by psychiatrists and contain rich information about offenders, including their medical information.

The last core sources of information are interviews of pertinent persons associated with offenders. In most cases, relevant persons include victims, close family members, and people knowledgeable of the offender's thinking and behavior. Beyond these sources, cyber-mediated communication technologies provide many good sources, such as social media postings and news coverage about certain offenders. Indeed, Facebook, Instagram, and Twitter postings can provide rich and reliable information about an offender's attitudes, character, and antisocial and prosocial behaviors and tendencies. These outlets can also provide critical information about an offender's circle of friends and state of mind.

PRETRIAL INVESTIGATION REPORTS

On a daily basis, thousands of people are arrested for crimes ranging from first-degree murder to minor offenses, such as public intoxication and disturbing the peace. This large daily number of detainees means that pretrial service officers play critical roles. At a minimum, pretrial officers assist courts with the separation of those who must remain in detention until the conclusion of their trials from those who should be released into society at least for the duration of their criminal cases. Pretrial officers investigate alleged offenders by gathering and verifying information about their backgrounds, including information about families, education, employment, finances, physical and mental health, controlled substance abuse, and criminal background checks. Officers also interview third parties who are knowledgeable of offenders' thinking and behavior and supervise pretrial releasees with the goal of protecting the community and helping courts administer the most appropriate sentence.

Pretrial investigative reports recommend whether to release an alleged offender before trial based on the degree to which the offender is likely to stay out of trouble by obeying all laws and complying with standard and specialized conditions of pretrial release. Pretrial investigative reports are, therefore, completed at the beginning of the criminal judicial process, right before an offender's initial appearance or bail hearing. Options available to initial appearance and trial judges include pretrial release without supervision and with a surety bond, detention without bail, release on bail, and release with specialized conditions.

Pretrial officers are not expected to discuss pending or alleged criminal offenses, nor are they allowed to give legal advice to offenders because pretrial defendants are presumed innocent until proven guilty beyond a reasonable doubt. Pretrial service officers are, however, expected to educate offenders about the criminal judicial process and standard and specialized conditions of release.

PRESENTENCING INVESTIGATIVE REPORTS

A small number of offenders are discharged from the criminal justice process because of acquittal at trial or dismissal of their cases at some point. The overwhelming majority, however, move through to the sentencing phase because of guilty pleas, pleas of no contest, or conviction at the end of their trials. Pretrial sentencing investigative reports are, therefore, needed to guide the administration of justice, to aid the accurate imposition of restrictions on offenders, and to protect members of the public from future victimization by offenders.

The original purpose of presentencing investigative reports was to provide "information to the court on the defendant's personal history and criminal conduct to promote individualized sentencing" (Macallair, 2002, p. 1449). The presentencing investigative report is designed to provide sentencing judges with comprehensive and specific background information about each offender's suitability for rehabilitation and community reintegration, a list of possible interventions or sentences, the level of risk an offender poses to public safety, the degree to which an offender is likely to recidivate, the level of assistance an offender needs to be successful in the community, and an in-depth understanding of the offenders' life, behavior, and place in society.

Unfortunately, although every offender can benefit from a pretrial sentencing investigative report, not every offender gets one because in most cases, the report is completed only if the sentencing judge orders it, and often the courts only do so in cases where community corrections is both a possible and a suitable alternative to jail or prison. Understandably, only in cases where significant punishment is an option, courts may order a presentencing investigative report. In misdemeanor and low-level felony cases, for example, courts rarely request presentencing investigation reports. In fact, the majority of such cases are regularly resolved without supervised release or incarceration.

The number of courtroom trials that take place and result in conviction is relatively small because most cases end with plea bargaining. In that regard, although the precise number of cases that end in plea bargaining is debatable, studies show that between 85% and 97% of all criminal cases end in plea bargaining (Walsh & Stohr, 2010). The *New York Times* reports that in the world of prosecutors, defense counselors, and judges, "ninety-seven percent of federal cases and 94 percent of state cases end in plea bargains, with the defendants pleading guilty in exchange for a lesser sentence" (Goode, 2012). A U.S. Department of Justice report shows that the "overwhelming majority (90 to 95 percent) of cases result in plea bargaining" (Devers, 2011). As a result, the large number of cases resolved through plea bargaining means that the number of offenders under community supervision is far higher than the number of offenders in correctional facilities (Walsh & Stohr, 2010). Consequently, pretrial, probation, and parole officers spend a significant amount of time collecting and analyzing information and writing presentencing reports.

The presentencing investigative report is written with probation and parole plans, as well as institutional supervision and offender rehabilitation, in mind because each of these issues relies on the presentencing investigative report as a source of information. The report is, therefore, "considered among the most important documents in the criminal justice field" and "has been the central source of information to sentencing judges since the 1920s" (Macallair, 2002, p. 1449). Correctional institutions use the document when assessing inmates' institutional security levels and treatment needs. Parole officers use the documents to gauge what community life will be like for a particular parole candidate. Obviously, the popularity of presentencing investigative reports in terms of wide use and usefulness to preparole investigations, future treatment planning and delivery, and assessment and characterization of thinking and behavior can be credited to the valuable information they capture, especially when the reports are well researched and written.

CORE SECTIONS IN INVESTIGATIVE REPORTS

Each point of information about an offender belongs to a specific section in the investigative report, irrespective of who the offender is, what crime was committed, which community corrections officer is writing the report, and in which jurisdiction the report is being written. That is, the sections and corresponding information listed in Table 17.3 are common

TABLE 17.3 *Sections of Investigative Reports*

Investigative or psycho-social reports generally cover the following sections	Where necessary, and when the information is accessible, a summary of each section must contain the following details.
Biographic Information	The description of an offender must include the offender's name, personal identification or booking number, alias or nickname, date of birth, place of birth, gender, and, where necessary, weight, hair color, eye color, race, birthmarks, scars, and tattoos. Usually, the cover sheet will contain this information.
Charges	Current criminal behavior should cover, in chronological order, all pending charges or charges for which the offender is in contact with the criminal justice system or pretrial, probation, or parole officer. Each charge must be followed by arrest date, name of arresting agency, relevant penal codes, number of counts, statutory penalties, and current disposition or status. Narratives may include brief information about codefendants, if any. It is generally advisable to use a table in this section if the offender has more than one charge.
Offender Statements	Defendant's version of offense or allegation.
Victim Statement	Victim statement to arresting officers and to the officers conducting the investigation.
Prior Criminal Record	In chronological order, criminal history must include all prior charges and dates of arrests, convictions, and acquittals. Summary must also include prior prison and jail terms; prior parole, probation, and pretrial release status; and probation or parole violations. For each offense or arrest, state the date, specific name of the offense, penal code, applicable jurisdiction, and disposition (outcome). Generally, a table is necessary if there is more than one charge.
Prior Probation or Parole	Summary of prior behavior on probation or parole, including how the offender complied with general and specialized conditions of release.
Educational Status	Last attained academic credential, including behavior on school grounds and whether an offender is currently attending school or has achieved a meaningful education level.
Employment	Offender's employment history must include whether they are currently employable, employed, or have had a job. The name of the current employer, current position or rank, and number of months or years at the current job must be reported. Information must also include whether current or past employment is or was full time or part time. Where necessary, offender's preparedness for employment in terms of past work experience, current skills, and educational achievement must be reported.
Military Service	Information about military service, especially dishonorable discharge. This information is also necessary when the offenses consist of violence or involve the use of weapons.
Personal History and Characteristics	History of family ties, marital status, number of children, and relevant childhood and current residential history.
Financial Status	The summary of financial status must include current monthly income, expenses, questionable expenses, evidence of unstable income, and if the offender receives direct financial help from the government, such as social security or food stamps. This section also covers offenders' ability to pay fines and restitution, ability to meet other basic financial needs, and to satisfy liability. This section also includes statements about financial viability and liability.

Offense Impact	The summary should describe how the current offense affects victims and society financially, psychologically, and physically.
Medical History	The medical status section must cover current and past serious medical conditions that inform the offender's suitability for available criminal justice interventions, including incarceration and pretrial release, probation, and parole. Include in this section serious chronic illnesses and past traumas, such as serious head injuries. Provide only relevant medical history without unnecessary violation of the offender's privacy. Medical conditions must not be cited as a basis for any retributive action.
Mental Health	The mental health section must include whether the offender has homicidal ideation, is suicidal, or has a history of suicidal behavior, thoughts, or attempts. Also include in this section past mental health diagnoses and mental health treatment, including the names of current psychotropic medications. Details in this section should not unnecessarily violate the offender's privacy rights. Mental health conditions must not be cited or used as a basis for any retributive action.
Alcohol	The summary of the offender's history of alcohol use must cover whether the offender's use is a cause for concern or if the use of alcohol interferes with the offender's ability to perform basic prosocial functions. If alcohol use is of concern, the level of concern must be indicated.
Controlled Substance	Details about controlled substance use must include age at first controlled substance use, type of substance, quantity of use in each instance of use, frequency of use, and effect of controlled substances on the offender's ability to carry out basic prosocial functions, such as work, school, and compliance with social norms.
Peer Relations	This section must cover whether the offenders' friends engage in lawbreaking behaviors, contribute to or influence the offender's delinquent and criminal behaviors, or if the offender engages in criminal acts in the company of their friends. This section must also cover information about the offender having contact with gang members and other criminal groups, including drug dealers.
Community Resources	Summarize the extent to which the offender's residential environment contributed to the offense for which the offender is currently being processed. This section also provides descriptions of suitable resources that can address those risk and needs factors.
Criminogenic Risk Scores	The criminogenic risk score section must report the scores and corresponding levels for violent, sexual, substance abuse, and general offending behaviors.
Criminogenic Needs	The criminogenic needs of the offender must include lists or details of factors that the offender must address to prevent relapse, recidivism, or failure to complete specific programs.
Responsivity	When necessary, this section must report the offender's overall ability and willingness to take part in relevant criminal justice interventions or practices, including incarceration and community correction programing.
Attitudes and Beliefs	This section must answer whether the offender is remorseful, takes responsibility for antisocial behaviors, and if in the eye of the offender the behavior is serious or trivial.
Recommendations	This section must contain recommendations for community corrections (outpatient) or incarceration (inpatient) treatment or pretrial release, probation, parole, incarceration, and specialized conditions. When necessary, justification for overriding risk scores must be informed by sound professional judgment or other evidence-based calculations.

and relevant headings typically found in pretrial, presentencing, and preparole investigative reports. The value, length, and usefulness of each section, however, depends on the purpose of the report or on whether it is for pretrial release, sentencing, or parole.

Obviously, pretrial investigative reports focus more attention on the types of offenses, prior criminal history, employment history and current status, financial standing, and risk of committing other crimes. Presentencing investigative reports focus on the offense and prior criminal history, personal history and characteristics, and history of compliance or noncompliance with standard and specialized conditions of probation or parole. Preparole investigative reports may contain more information about an offender's compliance with prior probation and parole conditions, criminogenic risk and needs scores, and institutional behaviors. For example, offenders who generate too many incident reports for bad behavior while serving time in jail or prison are less likely to qualify for parole than those who obey prison and jail rules and show a genuine interest in correcting their thinking and behavior.

Specialized conditions are dictated by individual offenders' criminogenic risk factors and needs; therefore, conditions are unique and range from requiring offenders to get drug tested, to attending controlled substance use–related treatment, to complying with more restrictive conditions, such as house arrest, electronic monitoring devices, or subjection to other forms of monitoring. Obviously, the most commonly used specialized conditions of parole or probation are requirements to participate in treatment activities. In particular, sex offenders, controlled substance–related offenders, and mental health–related offenders often receive the specialized condition to attend or complete a particular set of treatment programs to reduce the chance of relapse. Consequently, this special condition is becoming more popular as more and more treatment programs become available to criminal justice agencies and practitioners.

PREPAROLE INVESTIGATIVE REPORTS

Anyone who enters a prison, jail, or detention facility ultimately leaves that facility for the community, alive or dead. The questions, therefore, are who is qualified for parole, what should the specialized conditions of parole for each offender be, and what alternative responses to the specific offending behaviors for which an offender is behind bars exist? Preparole investigative reports are, therefore, designed to help parole boards appropriately and justly answer these important questions. Certainly, the answers to these questions can help parole board members make decisions that best serve victims, advance public safety, help parole officers develop the most appropriate treatment and supervision plans for parolees, and increase the chances of offenders' successful completion of the terms and conditions of their parole.

Parole is an earned early release from jail or prison. Although most offenders have the right to be considered for parole, they are not constitutionally entitled to receive it; therefore, only those offenders who behave well behind bars by complying with all security and treatment expectations earn the privilege of being released from jail or prison prior to the completion of their sentences. In this respect, the behavior of offenders behind bars is regularly documented by corrections officers. Certainly, incident reports generated by correctional facilities are vital, which is why they are regularly used as one of the core bases for recommending parole release or for denying parole to prisoners. In other words, jails and prisons meticulously document all behaviors, good or bad, and use such records when assessing security classification levels and, of course, when determining offenders' fitness for parole release.

STANDARD AND SPECIALIZED CONDITIONS OF PROBATION AND PAROLE

Pretrial releasees, probationers, and parolees are required to sign standard conditions of supervision, irrespective of the offense. In addition to the standard conditions they are required to obey, offenders are also expected to comply with specialized conditions that are unique to their individual criminal behaviors and circumstances. For instance, sex offenders are more likely to be required to avoid places like schools where children are commonly accessible. Substance users are also more likely to be asked to not visit places were illicit drugs are sold or used. These restrictions target criminogenic risk and needs factors that each offender must address to prevent a relapse or violation of the conditions of release.

Conditions of pretrial release, probation, and parole can vary from one jurisdiction to another and from one offender to another within the same jurisdiction. That said, irrespective of the offender, the offense, and the jurisdiction where the offense occurred, offenders on pretrial release, probation, and parole generally are expected to comply with the standard conditions of probation and parole listed in Table 17.4. These conditions are universal to offenders under community supervision, although items 10 through 14 may not apply in some jurisdictions.

Specialized conditions are extremely useful. For example, specialized conditions can be used by officers to prohibit a gang member from spending time in the company of other gang members, to prevent an offender from continuing to be active in criminal gang activities while on probation or parole, to monitor users through drug tests, and to restrict sex offenders from making contact with potential victims. Certainly, allowing drug users to frequent drug houses increases their likelihood of relapsing. Allowing gang members on probation for gang-related crimes to wear their gang colors would also make it harder for such offenders to avoid participation in gang activities. In such cases, the only therapeutic option available to a pretrial service, probation, or parole officer is simply to prohibit the offender from possessing gang colors or gang paraphernalia. Similarly, a child molester is likely to be prohibited by specialized conditions from living near schools or working with children. A prostitute can be ordered to not be present, during certain hours of the day, in areas known for prostitution.

PRETRIAL, PROBATION, AND PAROLE SUPERVISION LEVELS

Although many people who qualify for community corrections have lower criminogenic risk and needs factors compared to those who are ordered to be incarcerated, pretrial, probation, and parole officers use unique risk-level systems to distinguish between high- and low-risk offenders who require more supervision and management and those who need less, respectively. Indeed, while some pretrial releasees, probationers, and parolees require minimal to no direct supervision, some offenders are high-risk and require intensive supervision, while others are medium-risk offenders who fall between the two extremes and require moderate supervision.

TABLE 17.4 *Conditions of Pretrial Release, Probation, and Parole*

1.	**Contact**	Offenders are required to report to their pretrial service, probation, and parole officers within days following their release from detention or being placed on probation.
2.	**Employment Education**	If physically able, offenders are required to maintain gainful employment. Offenders must also notify supervising officers of employment termination or change of job.
3.	**Residence Travel**	Permission is required to travel outside the local jurisdiction.
4.	**Obedience to Laws**	Offenders are required to obey all laws, especially federal, state, and country or city penal laws.
5.	**Weapons**	Offenders are prohibited from owning, possessing, selling, or being in control of any firearm or dangerous weapon.
6.	**Controlled Substances**	Offenders are required to avoid excessive use of alcohol and are prohibited from possessing, using, transporting or being in control or under the influence of any controlled substance. Obviously, illegal possession of controlled substances constitutes a crime under federal or state law.
7.	**Association**	Offenders are not allowed to frequent others known for breaking laws or places where criminal activities are known to exist. For example, offenders are not allowed to be at "crack houses" or in the company of drug dealers, prostitutes, or criminal gang members.
8.	**Cooperation**	Offenders are at all times required to cooperate and comply with demands from their supervising officers.
9.	**Search and Seizure**	Offenders are at all times required to submit to warrantless searches of their premises and vehicles by anyone authorized by law to conduct such searches.
10.	**Drug Tests**	Offenders are required to submit to drug tests as required by their supervising officers.
11.	**Supervision Fees**	When required, offenders must regularly pay monthly dues, including restitution, fines, and fees for their supervision.
12.	**Participate in Treatment**	When required, offenders must fully participate in mental health counseling or any scheduled treatment activity.
13.	**Financial Liability**	Offenders are required to support their children and to fulfill family responsibilities. This means that offenders must pay child support where applicable.
14.	**Specialized Conditions**	Offenders must comply with any specific behavioral restrictions that uniquely apply to each offender.

Some agencies use an expanded level system that runs from Level I to Level V or even higher. Specifically, there are three common level systems: (1) low-, medium-, and high-risk offenders; (2) Level I, Level II, Level III, Level IV, and Level V offenders; and (3) low-low, low, and low-high; low-medium, medium-medium, and high-medium; and low-high, medium-high, and high-high offenders. Each level is based on criminogenic risk and needs scores, but the factors used to calculate those scores may vary from one jurisdiction to another and usually depend on the purpose of the investigative report.

Levels dictate the supervision needed to prevent the offender from violating conditions of release. In this respect, the highest levels are assigned to categories of extreme high-risk offenders who are comparatively at risk and have more needs that make them potential candidates for violating their conditions of release than lower risk offenders. This group of offenders also has a greater chance of incurring more restrictions or specialized conditions of probation or parole.

Low-risk offenders are presumed to have the lowest risk of violating their conditions of release because offenders in this category have low-risk and needs scores. The majority of low-risk offenders are in the system for minor offenses with low statutory sanctions. Consequently, members of these groups are less likely to require direct supervision and management. Medium-risk offenders are presumed to have moderate chances of violating their conditions of release or of committing new crimes, relapsing, and engaging in specific types of antisocial behaviors than those who are low-risk offenders. Obviously, offenders who require intensive supervision are classified as high-risk, Level IV or V, and low-high, high, and high-high, respectively. These groups of offenders are considered serious threats to public safety. For example, Level IV or V offenders need the most intensive supervision. In the correctional setting, these offenders may be designated as supermax prisoners or closed-custody inmates. In the community, offenders in this category may have curfews, wear electronic monitoring devices, and have to make contact with their pretrial, probation, and parole officers more often than lower level offenders. Hence the difference between a Level IV and a Level V offender would be the amount of direct supervision, the intrusiveness of restrictions, the frequency of contact with supervising officers, and the intensity of the monitory mechanism.

ETHICAL AND LEGAL CHALLENGES

The accurate investigation, assessment, and classification of offenders and the reporting of results trigger many ethical concerns, in part because pretrial and presentencing investigative reports collect and report highly sensitive information, including prosocial and antisocial histories. For example, the information these documents provide can be maliciously used to harm an offender's chances of pretrial release, lenient conditions of release, and sentencing options. The information in these reports can also generate problems for human sources, especially those who provide unflattering, incriminating, or aggravating information. It is, therefore, understandable that criminal justice practitioners make notable efforts to ensure that their actions are guided by certain standards.

Obviously, every aspect of investigative activity and report writing that affects people in such a profound way creates ethical concerns. In this case, ethical challenges include whether to disclose certain information in a report, such as the names of sources, so as to give the offender the option to dispute allegations. In addition, there are cases where a pretrial, probation, or parole officer wants to protect sources of information and consequently errs on the side of withholding such information from offenders and thus denying them the chance to defend themselves against allegations made by the sources. These ethical issues and the right to disclose information that adversely affects defendants, as well as potentially the sources of information, have been ruled upon by the U.S. Supreme Court.

Specifically, in *Williams v. New York* (1949), the Court ruled that the content of presentencing investigative reports is confidential. In this case, a jury found the offender guilty of murder in the first degree and recommended that he be imprisoned for life. The trial judge, however, imposed a sentence of death on the offender after considering additional information provided in the presentence investigation report. The offender appealed the sentence, arguing that he was not given the opportunity to cross-examine informants or rebut the report. The Court disagreed and ruled that the due process clause of the Fourteenth Amendment is not violated when a person convicted after a fair trial is sentenced based in part on a confidential presentencing investigative report and that the offender is not permitted to examine or to cross-examine the author or witnesses as to the accuracy of the evidence relied upon by the court to pass judgment (*Williams v. New York*, 1949).

The U.S. Supreme Court has also ruled that except in the case of the death penalty or statutorily stated exceptions, offenders are not constitutionally entitled to presentencing investigative reports. Specifically, the Court ruled in *Gregg v. United States* (1969) that "presentence reports are documents which the rule does not make available to the defendant as a matter of right. There are no formal limitations on the contents of these reports, and they may rest on hearsay and contain information bearing no relation whatever to the crime with which the defendant is charged," the Court ruled (*Gregg v. United States*, 1969). Thus it is up to the U.S. Congress, state legislatures, and or judges to determine who gets a presentencing investigation report and who does not. The Court's conclusion obviously fails to satisfy the question of fairness as it applies to allowing offenders to review their presentencing investigative reports and to challenge unreliable information. Obviously, the fairness of the right to know and cross-examine sources of adverse information used to justify the denial of pretrial release, probation, and parole do not disappear simply because the Constitution is silent on such issues. It is, therefore, not surprising that steps are being taken to mitigate the effects of unjust information in pretrial, presentencing and preparole investigative reports.

Several ethical interventions have been developed to minimize the effect of unverifiable information upon sentencing. At the core is the need to balance the rights of the offender with the rights of the informant, especially in cases where the safety of an informant or source of information is a concern for reasons that include the unhelpfulness of the collected information to the offender, which calls into question the ethical need to disclose damaging information or the source of the information. For example, despite the ruling in *Williams v. New York* (1949), in the federal system, the contents of the presentencing investigation report are disclosed to defendants. Some states also allow defendants to access the reports, while others give presiding judges the discretion to disclose or not disclose the contents of presentencing investigation reports to offenders (Abadinsky, 2012).

Pretrial, probation, and parole officers are also required legally and ethically to ensure that the information contained in the reports they generate is absolutely accurate and free from impropriety. Undoubtedly, investigative reports are required to be factually free from error and free from rumor, unfounded suspicions, gut feelings, and incomplete statements that could create adverse information that would harm an offender's chance of receiving just treatment by the court or parole board. In other words, officers are expected to identify the sources of all information included in a report, to personally make contact with all sources of information, to physically review all relevant documents that support specific critical allegations, and to carefully identify the strengths and relevancy of every claim, statement, and allegation included in a report.

Officers are also expected to select only information relevant to each offender's risk and needs, including the offender's criminal behaviors being investigated. It is important to minimize the length of the information because the audience of investigative reports are judges, prosecutors, public defenders, and pretrial, probation, parole, and correctional officers who are always busy during the course of their work days and thus do not have hours to spend reading and considering a single report. In this respect, it is unhelpful to include information that is irrelevant or indirectly related to an offender's offense or behavior and thinking in an investigative report (Walsh & Stohr, 2010). Finally, officers are expected to evaluate and manage the information they collect to enable offenders' to benefit from treatment services and to help offenders acquire the skills necessary to live a crime-free life. These goals should dictate the answers to most ethical challenges associated with the completion of investigative reports.

CONCLUSION

Reports generated by pretrial service, probation, and parole officers are widely used across the criminal justice system. Pretrial services reports lay the foundation for presentencing reports, and presentencing reports lay the foundation for institutional classifications, which also lay the foundation for preparole reports. Parole investigative reports draw on information from pretrial and presentencing reports, as well as the behavioral reports offenders generate within correctional institutions. Beyond pretrial, probation, and parole officers, investigative reports are also used by psychologists, psychiatrists, and other mental health providers to develop treatment plans and supervise and manage offenders.

The actual content of each pretrial, probation, and parole investigative report is dictated by state or federal law, policies, and practices. This means that the content of reports varies from one jurisdiction to another, although the core sections, content, and sources of information are almost universal to any investigative report, irrespective of the agency. At a minimum, each state or jurisdiction covers the risk an offender poses to society in terms of the likelihood of creating future victims and the punishment of the offender for their antisocial behavior.

DISCUSSION QUESTIONS

1. Should offenders have a legal right to pretrial, presentencing, and preparole investigative reports instead of individual states, jurisdictions, courts, or departments discretionarily picking and choosing who gets an investigative report and who does not?
2. Should offenders have the legal right to access the content of pretrial, presentencing, and preparole investigative reports, including the sources of damaging information?
3. How does the failure to disclose content and sources of certain information to offenders hinder their ability to rehabilitate?
4. To what extent is the U.S. Supreme Court just in deciding that offenders do not have the right to presentencing investigative reports as a matter of judicial process?
5. To what extent is the U.S. Supreme Court just in deciding that offenders do not have the right to review or respond to content in presentencing investigative reports as a matter of judicial process?

6. Which section of the pretrial investigation, presentencing, and preparole investigative reports is the most critical with respect to the calculation of criminogenic risk and needs factors and why?

REFERENCES

Abadinsky, H. (2012). *Probation and parole: Theory and practice*. Pearson.

Devers, L. (2011). *Plea and charge bargaining: Research summary.* Bureau of Justice Assistance, U.S. Department of Justice. https://www.bja.gov/Publications/PleaBargainingResearchSummary.pdf

Goode, E. (2012, March 22). Stronger hand for judges in the 'bazaar' of plea deals. *The New York Times.* https://www.nytimes.com/2012/03/23/us/stronger-hand-for-judges-after-rulings-on-plea-deals.html

Gregg v. United States, No. 394 U.S. 489 (Supreme Court of the United States 1969).

Macallair, D. (2002). The history of the pre-sentence investigation report. In J. Dressler (Ed.), *Encyclopedia of crime and justice* (2nd ed.). Macmillan Reference, Center on Juvenile and Criminal Justice.

Walsh, A., & Stohr, M. (2010). *Correctional assessment, casework & counselling* (5th ed.). American Correctional Association.

Williams v. New York, No. 337 U.S. 241 (Supreme Court of the United States 1949).

CHAPTER EIGHTEEN

Evidence-Based Correctional Interventions

COMMUNITY CORRECTIONS ARE concerned with the rehabilitation of offenders as a means to promote public safety. Hence, in theory, and legally speaking, probation and parole are therapeutic interventions granted by courts and correctional authorities as part of the rehabilitative process. Pretrial service, probation, and parole officers are, therefore, tasked with repeatedly assessing probationers and parolees to determine their criminogenic needs, the risks each offender poses to society, and the supervision and monitoring of offenders' compliance with conditions of probation or parole. To satisfy those professional obligations, pretrial, probation, and parole officers give offenders drug tests, conduct home visits, help offenders gain access to crucial social services, monitor offenders' compliance with court orders, oversee their overall treatment needs, and prepare reports for and make recommendations to the courts regarding offenders' qualification for community corrections and other forms of sanctions and services (Abadinsky, 2012).

This chapter discusses some of the treatment programs and interventions criminal justice practitioners develop and use to control, correct, and change the thinking and behavior of individuals under their supervision. While specific programs will be discussed as examples of evidence-based programs, the main focus is on interventions used to address core criminogenic risk and needs domains: criminal and antisocial behaviors, antisocial associates, family dynamics, school and work, free time, controlled substance use and abuse, and antisocial cognition. Knowledge about these factors and the interventions that probation and parole officers use in their efforts to change the thinking and behavior of offenders are important correctional goals.

DIFFERENCES AMONG BEST PRACTICES, WHAT WORKS, AND EVIDENCE-BASED PRACTICES

Although the use of evidence-based practices began in the medical field, it is currently the leading approach in corrections that relies strictly on sound empirical evidence rather than on anecdotal or professional experiences as is the case with "best practices" and "what works" interventions (NIC, 2019). In that respect, evidence-based practices are currently more preferred in correctional institutions, although the phrases "best practices," "what works," and "evidence-based practices" are interchangeably used to refer to collective experiences and beliefs about long-held interventions. In some contexts, the phrases are used when talking about nonscientific interventions that have been anecdotally declared "successful" by one or more criminal justice professionals. Note that many actors in the criminal justice system believe that the death penalty works and that the best solution to most social problems is criminal prosecution. Also, not every intervention that "works" is evidence-based or capable of changing offenders' thinking and behavior.

Currently, correctional institutions heavily value evidence-based interventions or practices. According to the National Institute of Corrections (NIC, 2019), "Evidence-based practice is the objective, balanced, and responsible use of current research and the best available data to guide policy and practice decisions." Evidence-based practices are, therefore, different than "best practices" and "what works" because unlike these two approaches, evidence-based programs undergo rigorous quality assurance and evaluation processes. For example, new evidence-based practices and programs are rigorously evaluated by social scientists on more than one occasion to determine their effectiveness. Also, unlike "best practices" and "what works," evidence-based practice implies that an intervention has definable and measurable outcomes with regard to the reduction of recidivism and the general prevention of crime.

BEHAVIORAL CONTROL INTERVENTIONS

Most contemporary correctional interventions in the United States are motivated by the desire to reduce prison populations or to keep offenders outside correctional facilities because of the cost of managing detainees and the belief that punishment or excessive restriction and supervision can reduce the rate of crime. The use of these approaches, therefore, continues despite the established understanding that punishment fails to correct behavior and is thus not a useful therapeutic intervention, especially with regard to criminal thinking and behavior.

Most community corrections interventions are guided by increased levels of restriction and supervision intended to achieve specific and general deterrence by constantly reminding offenders that future criminal activity will attract more pain and suffering. The emphasis on restriction explains why community corrections programs, such as intensive supervision, home detention, electronic monitoring, and even halfway houses and day reporting center programs are popular in pretrial service, probation, and parole agencies. It is important to note that while these practices cost less in comparison to incarceration, their failure to reduce recidivism rates means that they are less useful to the prevention of criminal activities.

Intensive Supervision Programs

In most jurisdictions, intensive pretrial release, probation, and parole are used as alternatives to incarceration, which is a form of punishment, and as a cost-saving practice in comparison to the cost of detention. Consequently, most intensive supervision programs are informed by retributive and procedural justice ideas and are characterized by mainly intense restrictions and supervision, threats of revoking community corrections status, and, of course, high rates of technical violations of pretrial release, probation, and parole status, often for alleged breach of one or more standard conditions of pretrial release, probation, or parole.

Of course, studies show that intensive probation or parole does not reduce the chance of new crimes; rather, they increase the offender's chance of being violated because of the program's emphasis on sanctions and restrictions.

Intensive supervision programs subject offenders to severe and highly structured supervision and restriction with which they must comply to avoid incarceration. For example, intensive pretrial releasees, probationers, and parolees are required to comply with one or more specialized conditions and restrictions, such as home confinement, wearing some sort of monitoring device, compliance with curfew, abstaining from alcohol and drug use, frequent home visits, and random drug testing by supervising officers. Intensive supervision programs also subject offenders to close surveillance, increased frequency of contact between supervising officers and offenders, frequent urine testing for controlled substances, and participation in treatment programs. Consequently, about a third of all intensive probation and parole cases end with technical violations (Abadinsky, 2012; Stevens-Martin et al., 2014).

Halfway House Programs

Transitioning from prison or jail into the free world, especially after a prolonged detention, can be extremely difficult for most offenders who are without a home, employment, or a community to which they can return. At a minimum, the absence of assistance regarding housing, employment, and other basic social necessities can significantly increase offenders' chances of making unwanted contact with the criminal justice system. Hence, halfway houses are designed to help offenders safely transition back into their communities from correctional institutions without the risk of ending up on street corners with no place from which to start new lives.

Life in halfway houses is generally more structured than life in private homes, but at the same time, conditions in halfway homes are less structured than life behind bars. Also, as the name implies, halfway houses are technically midpoints between living in jail or in prison and living in the community under the supervision of parole officers. Consequently, those who comply with their conditions of release and the rules at their designated halfway houses get the opportunity to move out of halfway housing complexes into independent living places in the community, and the status of those who fail to do well in terms of complying with halfway housing rules are generally violated, and they are accordingly returned to jail or prison.

Halfway houses also serve as temporary homes designed to mitigate risks associated with transitioning from dependent living in correctional institutions to independent living in the community where the offenders will have to assume full responsibility for all of their own expenses (Mays & Winfree, 2014). Offenders at these temporary housing facilities are, therefore, closely monitored and helped to reenter society peacefully. For example, halfway house programs typically provide offenders with room, board, and other services designed to help them reintegrate into society without the need to commit crimes. Obviously, such services include learning how to secure gainful employment and a permanent residence. Some jurisdictions run halfway houses as semi-independent places where offenders work outside and pay rent to stay at the halfway house. In some cases, halfway house residents may be required to participate in specific treatment programs, such as counseling and job-related training.

Home Detention

At various stages of the criminal justice process, court-ordered intensive supervision programs, especially for pretrial release cases, use home detention or house arrest as alternatives to standard incarceration. Generally, a person confined to their home is permitted to leave for a certain number of hours during the day or week to report for work, attend religious services, procure food, receive medical services, participate in court-ordered correctional counseling, and attend to other necessities as may be deemed fit by supervising officers (Gainey, 2019). In some cases, home detainees are ordered to remain in their residence at all times, although occasionally an offender in this category may receive permission to carry out necessary functions outside their homes, such as the satisfaction of employment obligations, attendance of school, and participation in religious services.

Home detention offenders are usually violent offenders, drug dealers, high-level white-collar criminals, and offenders at high risk of fleeing court jurisdiction prior to the conclusion of their criminal cases. That is, home detainees are mostly high-risk offenders who are not quite suitable for incarceration but who, for many reasons, including public safety concerns, are not good candidates for reduced supervision in the community, in part because in the view of the court, such offenders pose a significant and measurable threat to the public.

Proponents of home detention programs assume that interventions like house arrest or home confinement are effective because they punish offenders for their bad deeds by restricting them and subjecting them to difficult conditions with the hope that the offenders' fear of excessive restrictions will compel them to avoid future acts of criminality. Furthermore, it is argued that home arrest satisfies the goal of imprisonment without the social and financial costs associated with actual incarceration (Abadinsky, 2012). The extent to which this is true or whether house arrest furthers public safety is not, however, clear. Indeed, in the current era of advanced communication technologies, home arrest does not stop offenders from engaging in most crimes on the books. For example, with the aid of cell phone and Internet technologies, drug dealers can sell, buy, and move drugs from one place to another from the comfort of their detention homes. Similarly, white-collar criminals can engage in various criminal activities from their private homes.

Electronic Monitoring

Another visible characteristic of retributive community correction programs for pretrial releasees, probationers, and parolees is the requirement to wear electronic monitoring devices designed to limit offenders' freedom and to monitor their compliance with conditions of release, including compliance with court-mandated specialized restrictions. In this instance, electronic monitoring technologies are considered capable of offering a full continuum of monitoring and supervising of parolees, probationers, and pretrial defendants as well as high-risk immigrants under the supervision of the U.S. Immigration and Customs Enforcement agency.

There are variations of electronic monitoring devices, but they all perform the simple task of enabling supervising officers to determine the physical location of their pretrial releasees, probationers, and parolees at all times (Krisberg et al., 2019). Knowledge of the precise whereabouts of offenders who qualify for electronic monitoring is important because such offenders are generally high-risk offenders, such as home detainees who are considered the most dangerous group of community corrections offenders. The goals of the restrictions and specialized conditions that come with wearing electronic monitoring devices are, therefore, to hold those offenders accountable while at the same time allowing them to live in their own homes at their own expense but under close community corrections supervision so as to minimize the chances of future criminal activities.

The restricted period for offenders confined to their homes may include certain hours of the day, an entire evening, morning, weekend, day, or other time periods when the supervising agency may find it fit to maintain public safety or to prevent recidivism. Depending on the conditions of release, home detainees may also be permitted to leave their homes for medical necessity, to attend school, report to work, or to drop off and pick up dependents from school and medical appointments. The intensity of home detention explains why in some jurisdictions intensive supervision programs employ surveillance officers who constantly monitor offenders, enforce compliance with conditions of release, drug test, inspect offenders' places of employment and residence, and conduct investigations of parole and probation violations.

Despite the strictness and technological superiority of electronic monitoring devices, empirical evidence suggests that electronic monitoring programs are not effective at rehabilitating offenders' thinking and behavior (Abadinsky, 2012; Brancale et al., 2018). Indeed, while electronic monitoring technologies can help correctional officers pinpoint the exact locations of offenders, they do not capture the actions of those offenders. Hence, in an era of Internet and cell phone technologies, as well as heightened technological interconnectivity, offenders can engage in a wide variety of criminal activities while wearing electronic monitoring devices.

Day Reporting Centers

The primary goals of day reporting centers (DRCs) are to reduce criminogenic risks and needs known to increase the likelihood of recidivism. DRCs provide community-based alternatives to incarceration. Consequently, when fully resourced, DRCs can offer offenders a variety of services, including cognitive behavioral therapy, substance abuse–related counseling, anger management, preparation for general educational development certifications, and employment-related training and services. DRCs can also help offenders gain access to public programs and services and thus are therapeutically useful. In this regard, DRCs are good sources of job training and placement, counseling, educational resources, and other vital social services that can meaningfully reduce offenders' chances of future acts of criminality.

In addition to therapeutic services, DRCs are also expected to enforce conditions of supervision. It is, therefore, normal for DRCs to carry out random drug and alcohol testing and other related enforcement of standard and specialized conditions of parole so as to prevent offenders from engaging in criminal activities, at least while under community corrections supervision (Abadinsky, 2012). How DRCs impact post-release arrests, however, remains mixed, with studies showing that DRC participants are "more likely to be arrested and convicted for a new offense in the short term compared to the control group" (Boyle et al., 2013, p. 119). This finding is not unexpected because although in theory DRCs are designed to provide nonresidential support services to pretrial releasees, probationers, and parolees, many jurisdictions use the program as another outlet for sanctions and restrictions.

In general, punitive responses to most criminal and antisocial behaviors are not therapeutic or clinically helpful. As Andrews and Dowden (2007) reported, studies show that "apart from incapacitation, there is simply no consistent evidence that more severe sanctions are associated with reduced recidivism. Indeed, the meta-analytic evidence is that more severe sanctions are associated with at least mild increases in re-offending" (Andrews & Dowden, 2007, p. 450). Furthermore, "official punishment, in the absence of treatment, has little effect on major criminogenic needs other than to enhance feelings of being mistreated and increase association with offenders" (Andrews & Dowden, 2007, p. 451). In this respect, DRCs that focus on treatment with less emphasis on restriction can make a positive difference in the lives of offenders.

THOUGHT AND BEHAVIOR MODIFICATION INTERVENTIONS

Each criminogenic risk domain requires a unique intervention that targets specific criminogenic needs and individual offenders' abilities to benefit from specific interventions fully (Andrews & Dowden, 2007). In this respect, responsivity demands that criminal justice practitioners match the methods and strategies of treatment with each offender's learning style, motivations, and strength levels and target each key criminogenic risk and need associated with an offender (Andrews & Dowden, 2007). Obviously, the extent to which this approach is feasible depends on the correctional philosophy at work and the physical resources available within an agency.

Certainly, treatment that is conceived from the perspective of retributive and procedural justice is quite different than treatment that emerges out of distributive and restorative justice. Thus the use of evidence-based practice in response to increased risk of criminal activities is helpful because the label indicates that the practice has a strong chance of producing measurable and favorable therapeutic results. This approach also explains why evidence-based practices undergo rigorous vetting to determine that they work better and more reliably than non-evidence-based practices or "best practice" and "what works" methods. Consequently, the criminal justice system uses a wide range of evidence-based cognitive behavioral programs, such as (1) reasoning and rehabilitation, (2) relapse prevention therapy, and (3) Thinking for a Change program to address violent, sex, controlled substance abuse, and general offending behaviors (Hansen, 2008; Milkman & Wanberg, 2007). Although some programs, such as Aggression Replacement Training (ART) and Criminal Conduct and Substance Abuse Treatment: Strategies for Self-Improvement and Change (SSC) are behavior-specific programs, they also address other categories of offending behaviors. These popular programs use cognitive behavioral therapy approaches.

The reasoning and rehabilitation program is a cognitive behavioral modification intervention that is informed by the notion that "offenders suffer from cognitive and social deficits" (Milkman & Wanberg, 2007, p. 25). As a result, this program enhances offenders' self-control, prosocial attitudes, prosocial competence, interpersonal problem-solving skills, and thinking before acting. The program can be used in response to a diverse category of behaviors, including sex, controlled substance, violent, and general offending behaviors. The program is widely used in jails, prisons, and in the community.

As the title suggests, the relapse prevention therapy program was designed specifically for managing and preventing relapse. The program uniquely rejects labels such as "alcoholic" or "drug addict" on the grounds that offenders should look at their addictive behaviors as acquired habits that can be stopped. Consequently, this program teaches offenders self-management and self-control skills, as well as how to take ownership of their thoughts and behaviors. Furthermore, the program covers impulse control; hence, it is used to address anger and violent tendencies.

Specifically, relapse prevention therapy addresses "negative emotional states, interpersonal conflict, and social pressure" or how to cope with negative emotions; react to stressful situations, such as financial difficulties; and how to behave in a dysphoric state (Milkman

& Wanberg, 2007, p. 28). Offenders who participate in this program learn about the process of relapse, how to cope with high-risk situations and deal with urges, and how to implement damage control in the event of a relapse. Offenders also learn specific coping skills, such as how to identify trigger events, correct criminal thinking, and deal with mistakes and occasional relapses.

The Thinking for a Change program is widely used across American correctional facilities and community corrections agencies. In fact, the program was introduced by the National Institute of Corrections in 1997 and has since been adopted by local, state, and federal corrections agencies. In terms of its use, the program teaches offenders problem-solving and social skills as alternatives to antisocial thinking and behavior. Furthermore, Thinking for a Change programs help offenders restructure by introspectively examining their own thinking, behaviors, feelings, beliefs, and attitudes (Bush et al., 1997; Bush et al., 2011).

COGNITIVE BEHAVIORAL THERAPY PROGRAMS

Cognitive behavioral therapy is a goal-oriented psychotherapy that uses hands-on practical approaches with the hope to eradicate or modify specific antisocial thoughts and behavioral patterns. This approach is used by criminal justice practitioners to treat a wide range of thoughts and behavioral deficiencies, including sexual offending behaviors, controlled substance abuse, violent tendencies, general offending behaviors and behaviors that are informed by mental health-related deficiencies (Milkman & Wanberg, 2007).

Cognitive behavioral therapy programs are primarily "based on an assumption that the foundations for criminal activity are dysfunctional patterns of thinking;" therefore, offenders can modify their antisocial tendencies, as well as the consequences of their behaviors (Milkman & Wanberg, 2007, p. 5). As a result, cognitive behavioral therapy programs in general aim at helping offenders recognize the patterns and effects of their behaviors by principally focusing on both observable behaviors and on the thoughts that shape the behaviors. In addition, cognitive behavioral therapy programs address criminal thinking, teach new cognitive skills, show offenders how to improve their ability to generate alternative solutions to social problems, develop coping skills, and teach offenders how to problem solve under certain conditions.

Certainly, many of the behavioral modification programs that use cognitive behavior therapy also help offenders understand factors that led them into antisocial or criminal behaviors and how to set specific goals and learn alternative prosocial solutions to known social problems while providing an understanding of how specific thoughts and behaviors can increase or reduce the chances of future offending behaviors. Of also critical importance is the fact that in both group and one-on-one settings, cognitive behavioral therapy allows offenders to share their thoughts and to receive valuable support and feedback from people with similar thoughts and behavioral problems (Milkman & Wanberg, 2007).

BEHAVIOR-SPECIFIC INTERVENTIONS

Sex offenders, violent offenders, and controlled substance abusers or users receive special attention during risk-assessment and classification processes, as well as during the intervention phase. These three categories of criminal behavior account for the majority of evidence-based treatment programs currently in use within the criminal justice system. For example, the ART program is designed specifically for violent offenders. The Thinking for a Change program is used to address controlled substance use and sex offending behaviors, as well as violent behaviors. In most cases, programs specifically designed for violence or controlled substance use can also be used to correct sex offending and general offending behaviors. Indeed, even behavior-specific interventions for sex offenders and controlled substance users or abusers are informed by one or more of the core criminogenic risk domains. Hence, although ART is a behavior-specific intervention for violence and Criminal Conduct and Substance Abuse Treatment: SSC specifically addresses controlled substance abuse, these programs can be used to address certain aspects of sexual offending behaviors.

Violent Offenders

The grave consequences of violent behavior cause the criminal justice system to respond more aggressively and uniquely to all violent crimes. The attention received by violent offending behaviors has generated a long list of evidence-based programs specifically designed to reduce the chances of violence. One example of such programs is the ART program. With considerable reliability, the ART program teaches anger management skills, improves offenders' ability to control their anger, decreases the frequency of angry outbursts, and increases the frequency of constructive and prosocial behaviors within jails, prisons, and the community (Goldstein & Glick, 1994, p. 9).

The ART program was initially created in response to anger and violent behaviors of adolescents. The program is, however, commonly used to address anger and violence among adult offenders. Indeed, the program is based on the conclusion that social skills deficits can explain most violent behavior expressed by juveniles and adults. As a result, ART focuses on prosocial skills development, teaching offenders how to listen to other views and perceptions and how to act in the face of anger-producing situations, as well as what to do and not to do in high-risk situations. The ART program also teaches offenders how to complain, understand, and express their own feelings; participate in difficult conversations; and deal with another person's anger, accusations, group pressure, and failure. In an attempt to teach self-control competencies, ART also covers areas such as how to recognize trigger events to identify, avoid, escape, and cope with external events that lead to violent responses to social events and challenges.

Controlled Substance Abuse

The Criminal Conduct and Substance Abuse Treatment: SSC program is one of the commonly used evidence-based programs designed to address controlled substance use, abuse, and addiction for both juveniles and adults. Specifically, the SSC is an intensive cognitive behavior-oriented treatment program that "provides a standardized, structured, and well-defined approach to the treatment of clients who manifest substance abuse and criminal justice problems" (Milkman & Wanberg, 2007). The SSC program is widely used by criminal justice agencies to assist offenders who are in the criminal justice system for controlled substance use, abuse, and dependence. This and similar programs target the reduction of substance use, abuse, or dependence and the reduction of personal and interpersonal supports for substance-oriented behaviors.

The SSC program has three phases: (1) challenge to change, (2) commitment to change, and (3) ownership of change. The first phase is based on the assumption "that self-disclosure leads to self-awareness, which in turn leads to self-improvement and change" and thus focuses on helping offenders develop self-awareness through self-disclosure and feedback from other offenders and criminal justice professionals delivering the programs (Milkman & Wanberg, 2007, p. 19). In the second phase, offenders are required to demonstrate the actual act of change. Hence offenders learn to strengthen their coping skills, change their antisocial thoughts and behaviors, communicate their thoughts, and to recognize and manage high-risk situations, including the urge to use controlled substances. The third stage is the stabilization and maintenance phase in which offenders are charged to demonstrate ownership of change and to strengthen their commitment to changes in their thinking and behavior.

Sex Offenders

Offenders in the criminal justice system for sex offenses receive considerable attention from criminal justice practitioners, obviously because of the profound way their behavior affects individual victims and society as a whole. Every state and the federal government has well-established sex offender treatment programs. For example, there are state-sponsored sex offender treatment programs running in all 50 states and the District of Columbia with more than 80% of the programs in operation treating probationers and parolees (Przybylski, 2014). Most of the programs that address sex offending behaviors are cognitive behavioral intervention programs with an emphasis on criminogenic risk factors, needs, and responsivity (Moster et al., 2008).

Since most sexual offending behaviors are actually violent acts that share many risks, such as poor social skills, problem-solving deficits, and criminal thinking, with other offending behaviors, sex offender programs use cognitive behavioral treatments that are similar to those used in response to violent crimes. Sex offender–specific programs try to correct deviant sexual arousal and preoccupation with sex in general and particularly with deviant sex. Programs also address pervasive anger or hostility, impulsivity, antisocial attitudes, criminal thinking, and relationship problems. Sex offender–specific behavior programs also pay attention to sex offense–specific criminogenic factors, such as deviant sexual arousal and poor self-regulation (Marotta, 2017; Przybylski, 2014; Yates, 2013).

MATERIAL SERVICE-BASED INTERVENTIONS

Certain criminogenic risk domains, such as unemployment and lack of education, require material assistance beyond mere recognition of the existence of such criminogenic needs. Some criminal justice interventions, therefore, focus on the delivery of material resources to help offenders navigate social constraints without resorting to criminal activity. Material service needs of offenders are important areas of intervention generally neglected or under-resourced in many criminal justice jurisdictions. This reality is obviously problematic because the majority of people who enter the criminal justice system come from economically and socially depressed backgrounds. These offenders' risk levels actually go up when they are placed on probation or parole without adequate material assistance. It is very likely that the inadequate provision of support for post-release settlement needs and services, such as housing, employment, transportation, and other social assistance necessary for successful participation in communal life and completion of probation or parole, puts many community corrections offenders at increased risk of engaging in prohibited activities.

The majority of material services provided by community corrections to address criminogenic needs are associated with the employment domain, and many only target the achievement of a specific educational level that is required to secure entry-level gainful employment. In cases where poor employment history and not lack of academic achievement indicates an elevated risk of committing crimes or engaging in other antisocial behaviors, material service-based interventions often fall short. What could be helpful is the enhancement of offenders' social and problem-solving skills with a specific focus on individual offenders' core areas of needs, including the need to improve work performance, personal satisfaction with employment, and enhanced work output (Andrews & Dowden, 2007).

Indeed, there are increased needs for material services beyond employment or education achievement. Certainly, adequate material services are needed to effectively move offenders toward the completion of probation or parole, avoiding recidivism or relapse, and functioning within the realities placed on them by the criminal justice system and society. Many offenders could also benefit from supportive and empathic client-centered counseling that provides means for satisfactorily resolving ambivalences. Criminal justice practitioners can achieve many of these goals through empathetic, respectful and optimistic interactions with offenders, and by giving offenders access to information that will help them identify steps to take in various situations (Abadinsky, 2012).

EFFECT OF EVIDENCE-BASED INTERVENTION

Collectively, cognitive behavioral therapy programs can effect change in the areas of antisocial personality, antisocial cognition, family, leisure time, antisocial associates, antisocial thoughts and behaviors, and controlled substance abuse. As every person is behaviorally and cognitively different from others, it is, therefore, important to target each offender's capacity to develop problem-solving, self-management, anger management, and coping skills to aid their individual capacity to productively get along with others. Evidence-based programs in this respect specifically target offenders' ability to recognize risky thoughts and feelings, to exercise self-restraint in the face of high-risk offenders' capacity to build alternative means of dealing with stressful situations, to improve willingness to abandon procriminal friends, to develop prosocial ways of spending leisure time, and to develop prosocial thinking and attitudes.

Offenders with a history of antisocial personality and a criminal history can also benefit from programs that target the development of noncriminal solutions to social problems. Similarly, treatment interventions that focus on the reduction of family conflict, building of positive relationships with prosocial institutions, and enhancement of individual thinking and behavior are extremely helpful. The core aims of these interventions are, of course, to promote prosocial and crime-free activities and interactions with prosocial associates, to minimize association with antisocial peers, and to maximize prosocial association with peers. Indeed, in general terms, effective "cognitive-behavioral programs of all types attempt to assist offenders in the area of identifying and defining factors that led them into making contact with the criminal justice system, to identify achievable behavioral and cognitive goals, develop a new alternative way of prosaically solving social problem, and to engage in behaviors that are likely to facilitate the achievement of such goals" (Milkman & Wanberg, 2007).

CONCLUSION

Treatment, especially when it is evidence-based or informed by sound criminological theory with a clear focus on criminogenic needs and responsivity, can make a difference in all categories of criminal offending behaviors. Indeed, while some behaviors such as sexual offending, substance dependence or abuse, and violent tendencies and behaviors are more difficult to treat than, for example, criminal thinking, family dysfunction, and association with antisocial peers, every behavior can be treated or managed with properly designed and delivered interventions. The extent to which therapeutic intervention makes a difference may in some cases depend on how much of the intervention is dictated by the need to punish rather than to treat or rehabilitate. In this regard, it is important to recall that the oldest societal response to deviant and criminal behavior is punishment, and the least successful intervention in terms of changing thinking and behavior is also punishment.

DISCUSSION QUESTIONS

1. Why, no matter how effective an intervention might be, must treatment be tailored to each offender's criminogenic risk, needs, and responsivity?
2. Do evidence-based treatment interventions therapeutically deliver some form of sanction to hold offenders accountable for their behaviors?
3. Which criminogenic risk domain is more difficult to assess and address, and why?
4. Why is substance abuse treated as a separate domain even though the behavior is one of many that fall under criminal activities?
5. What are the therapeutic benefits and challenges associated with the use of "best practices" or "what works" interventions?

REFERENCES

Abadinsky, H. (2012). *Probation and parole: Theory and practice.* Pearson.

Andrews, D. A., & Dowden, C. (2007). The risk-need-responsivity model of assessment and human service in prevention and corrections: Crime-prevention jurisprudence. *Canadian Journal of Criminology & Criminal Justice, 49*(4), 439–464. https://doi.org/10.3138/cjccj.49.4.439

Boyle, D. J., Ragusa-Salerno, L. M., Lanterman, J. L., & Marcus, A. F. (2013). An evaluation of day reporting centers for parolees: Outcomes of a randomized trial. *Criminology and Public Policy, 12*(1), 119. https://doi.org/10.1111/1745-9133.12010

Brancale, J., Blomberg, T. G., & Bales, W. D. (2018). Electronic monitoring. In H. N. Pontell & G. Bruinsma (Eds.), *Oxford research encyclopedia of criminology.* https://oxfordre.com/criminology/

Bush, J., Glick, B., & Taymans, J. (1997). *Thinking for a change: Integrated cognitive behavior change program.* National Institute of Corrections, U. S. Department of Justice. https://ccoso.org/sites/default/files/import/016672-Curriculum.pdf

Bush, J., Glick, B., Taymans, J., & Guevara, M. (2011). *Thinking for a change integrated cognitive behavior change program* (version 3.1). U.S. Department of Justice, National Institute of Corrections. http://trainercounselor.com/wp-content/uploads/2011/11/016672-Curriculum.pdf

Gainey, R. R. (2019). *House arrest.* Britannica.com. https://www.britannica.com/topic/house-arrest

Goldstein, A. P., & Glick, B. (1994). Aggression replacement training: Curriculum and evaluation. *Simulation & Gaming, 25*(1), 9–26. https://doi.org/10.1177/1046878194251003

Hansen, C. (2008). Cognitive-behavioral interventions: Where they come from and what they do. *Federal Probation, 72*(2), 43–49. https://www.uscourts.gov/sites/default/files/72_2_6_0.pdf

Krisberg, B. A., Marchionna, S., & Hartney, C. (2019). *American corrections: Concepts and controversies.* Sage Publications.

Marotta, P. L. (2017). A systematic review of behavioral health interventions for sex offenders with intellectual disabilities. *Sexual Abuse: A Journal of Research and Treatment, 29*(2), 148–185. https://doi.org/10.1177/1079063215569546

Mays, G. L., & Winfree, L. T. (2014). *Essentials of corrections* (5th ed.). Cengage Learning.

Milkman, H., & Wanberg, K. (2007, May). *Cognitive-behavioral treatment: A review and discussion for corrections professionals.* National Institute of Corrections. https://nicic.gov/cognitive-behavioral-treatment-review-and-discussion-corrections-professionals

Moster, A., Wnuk, D. W., & Jeglic, E. L. (2008). Cognitive behavioral therapy interventions with sex offenders. *Journal of Correctional Health Care, 14*(2), 109–121. https://doi.org/10.1177/1078345807313874

NIC. (2019). *Evidence-based practices (EBP).* https://nicic.gov/evidence-based-practices-ebp

Przybylski, R. (2014). *Chapter 7: Effectiveness of treatment for adult sex offenders.* Sex Offender Management Assessment and Planning Initiative. https://www.smart.gov/SOMAPI/sec1/ch7_treatment.html

Stevens-Martin, K., Oyewole, O., & Hipolito, C. (2014). Technical revocations of probation in one jurisdiction: Uncovering the hidden realities. *Federal Probation, 78*(3), 1–9. https://login.libproxy.csustan.edu/login?url=http://search.ebscohost.com/login.aspx?direct=true&db=aph&AN=100210784&site=ehost-live&scope=site

Yates, P. M. (2013). Treatment of sexual offenders: Research, best practices, and emerging models. *International Journal of Behavioral Consultation and Therapy, 8*(3–4), 89–95. https://doi.org/10.1037/h0100989

Glossary

Antisocial Behavior Antisocial thoughts typically lead to antisocial behaviors or behaviors that are unlawful, unacceptable, and frowned upon by the public. Thus stealing, smoking cigarettes in places where smoking cigarettes is prohibited, skipping school, and hitting other people against established rules are all examples of antisocial behaviors. Indeed, these behaviors also show disregard and a lack of respect for the law and socially acceptable norms.

Antisocial Thought A pattern or set of thought processes that are favorable to violations of rules, norms, or laws or that are likely to enhance the chances of engaging in antisocial behaviors. For instance, believing or thinking that gainful employment is not important, obeying laws is a waste of time, drug use is not all that bad, or selling drugs is a quicker and more fruitful way to make a living are antisocial thoughts because such thoughts or beliefs increase the chances of criminal or delinquent behaviors.

Assessment Systematic examination and analysis of an offender's psychological well-being, thought processes, past behaviors, and socioeconomic standing. Assessment is motivated by the desire to understand an offender's patterns of thinking and behavior, predict an offender's future behavior, identify the most fitting therapeutic interventions for an offender, and appraise an offender's suitability for a specific treatment intervention.

Case Plan A carefully developed blueprint for the rehabilitation of an offender. A case plan is usually developed based on risk-assessment and classification results. Such plans outline actions that must be undertaken by an offender and the services that must be provided by criminal justice practitioners with the goal of correcting an offender's antisocial thoughts and behaviors. Case plans are sometimes referred to as treatment plans.

Classification The purpose of classification is to categorize an offender's behavior (sex, violent, controlled substance, general, or mental health–related offender) and to predict the likelihood of his or her reoffending in a particular behavioral category in any of the five areas of delinquent and/or criminal behaviors.

Clinical Classification The categorization of an offender based on his or her deviant or prohibited act, irrespective of whether such behavior is recorded by law enforcement. For example, an offender with a history of violent confrontation or altercation is clinically a violent offender irrespective of whether he or she is adjudicated or convicted for such acts.

Clinical Staff Typically, clinical staff members are correctional staff members charged or concerned with the rehabilitation of offenders. These staff members are tasked with helping offenders correct their behaviors. Institutional psychologists, therapists, and probation, parole, and correctional staff members who assess and prescribe interventions are clinical staff.

Cognitive Ability The mental capacity of a person in terms of the ability to foresee the consequences of prosocial and antisocial behavior. An example of a healthy cognitive ability is the capacity to articulate the consequences of specific criminal or delinquent behaviors.

Cognitive Behavioral Therapy A treatment approach driven by the belief that antisocial thinking often leads to antisocial behavior. Hence, cognitive behavioral therapy programs seek to correct offenders' thinking and behavior through activities designed to help them reevaluate the mental processes that inform their behaviors. An example of cognitive behavioral therapy is Thinking for a Change.

Commitment A decision by a juvenile court judge ordering the detention of a youth in a secured facility is known as a commitment order. A committed youth is, therefore, a youth who has been ordered to spend days, months, or years in a juvenile detention facility in order to receive treatment for a specific delinquent behavior or to protect such youth from specific adverse conditions that are likely to increase the youth's chances of engaging in consequential antisocial behaviors.

Coping Skills Specific cognitive, physical, verbal, and social skills required to resolve conflict in a manner that results in a desirable outcome. In most cases, the term refers specifically to offenders' ability to deal with emotionally and physically stressful situations appropriately and to resolve conflict in ways that lead to good outcomes.

Criminal Justice Practitioner A trained professional who works for any criminal justice agency and who is charged with or concerned about the rehabilitation of offenders who involuntarily make contact with any criminal justice system.

Criminal Thinking Distorted or illogical thinking or a specific thought process that normalizes, rationalizes, facilitates, or reinforces delinquent and criminal behavior. Common forms of criminal thinking used by offenders are blaming other persons for their own actions, justification of antisocial behaviors, minimization of antisocial behaviors, and claiming to be a victim of their own wrongdoing.

Criminogenic Factors Behaviors and thought processes that increase an offender's participation in criminal and delinquent activities. Criminogenic needs, therefore, refer to resources and interventions that will reduce the offender's risk of future criminal or delinquent behaviors.

Delinquency The violation of a criminal law or the commission of a status offense by a person under the age of 18. The juvenile court judge determines whether an offender is delinquent or criminal in accordance with the offender's deeds.

Deviant Sexual Arousal Sexual stimulation in response to a person or thing that is prohibited by law or social norm from being viewed as a source of sexual gratification. Getting sexually excited by close family members, children, animals, and objects are examples of deviant sexual arousal. Behind most deviant sexual arousals are deviant sexual fantasies.

Dynamic Risk Factor Most factors that predict behaviors are dynamic factors that change as a result of treatment or a decision by an offender to alter or put an end to a behavior or factor. For instance, controlled substance use is a dynamic risk factor because the risk will cease to exist when an offender quits. Similarly, not having a college education is a dynamic risk factor because an offender can easily change that status by simply enrolling in college and pursuing a college education. Unemployment is also a dynamic risk factor because the status of joblessness changes once a person acquires a job.

Evidence-Based Many programs and practices are marketed as being able to correct antisocial thoughts and behaviors. Among such practices and programs, those that have been studied, tested, and found to have the potential to significantly reduce an offender's chances of engaging in specific antisocial behaviors are known as evidence-based programs or practices. The U.S. Department of Justice maintains an up-to-date *Model Programs Guide* listing evidence-based programs.

Grooming A carefully developed plan that is designed to trick a potential victim into going along with acts of victimization. Most grooming, especially by juvenile sex offenders, involves manipulation of the victim, including the coaxing of the victim either to go along with their victimization or to keep their victimization secret. An offender may use tactics such as gaining a victim's trust by giving compliments, attention, or gifts and by progressively victimizing the offender.

Incest Any sexual activity that involves an offender and a family member.

Intake When an offender is detained by police officers, they are initially taken into county jails. Upon arrival, they are interviewed by an intake officer who determines the offender's risk level for the purpose of determining the security and treatment needs of the offender.

Intervention Any criminal justice response to a delinquent or criminal behavior that is intended to end a particular behavior. Thus, commitment, incarceration placement in counseling, and an order to earn the general equivalency diploma or participate in a particular programming activity are examples of criminal justice interventions.

Involuntarily Contact Any contact with the criminal justice system as an offender or suspect or in relation to any incorrigible, delinquent, or criminal behavior

Legal Classification The designation of behaviors or the labeling of offenders in accordance with existing law or classifications created by legislators. Legal classification uses objective scales; therefore, offenders and behaviors are classified without regard to individual circumstances and contexts in which a particular behavior occurs. For example, legally, a person who sells drugs at school is a law-abiding person until they are caught and adjudicated or prosecuted. Offenders with a history of violent confrontation or altercation are not legally violent persons until they are caught and adjudicated or convicted.

Mental Health Disorder Any mental or cognitive condition that enhances an offender's ability to engage in antisocial activities or any serious psychological condition that is characterized by recordable or measurable symptoms of distress, mental impairment, or decreased functioning or that significantly increases the risk of engaging in antisocial behaviors.

Needs Resources and interventions that an offender must have to reduce the risk of criminal or delinquent behavior, as well as to increase the number or strength of protective factors. Common needs include a high school diploma, job, tutoring, transportation, prosocial peers, a safe home, and behavior-specific counseling or treatment.

Needs Factor A set of specific services, skills, treatment, interventions, assistance, resources, and knowledge particularly needed to avoid future participation in delinquent and criminal behavior. Some offenders have needs for developed beliefs and thoughts that are favorable to law- and rule-abiding behaviors. A needs assessment is, therefore, a process that identifies treatment goals, a treatment plan, and the appropriate level of supervision and resources an offender must be afforded to avoid a relapse.

Pedophilia A sexual attraction to children, mostly by older persons. Pedophiles are sexually attracted to or get sexually aroused by the thought of engaging in any sexual activity with children.

Predictive Value The term *predictive value* is used to describe factors that studies show can impact individual ways of thinking and behavior. Factors that have predictive value encompass risk, responsivity level, and protective and needs factors. Examples of factors with predictive value include family, educational, and employment history, as well as the types of friends and acquaintances an offender keeps and the history of any past violent, deviant sexual, substance abuse, general offending, or mental health-related behaviors. Studies show that these factors can be used to predict offenders' future thinking and behavior.

Prosocial Behaviors Behaviors that are consistent with the rules, norms, and values of a society. They are behaviors that are expected by law and that do not conflict with societal expectations. Generally, prosocial behaviors promote noncriminal or nondelinquent behaviors and are more likely to produce a noncriminal or nondelinquent outcomes. Examples of prosocial thoughts are beliefs that education is important, respect for the law is necessary, hard work is beneficial, and crime and delinquency often lead to undesirable outcomes.

Protective Factor A variable in the form of event, behavior, thought process, history, view, or belief that reduces the chance of criminal or delinquent behaviors. Certain characteristics, such as a good academic track record, no history of controlled substance use, supportive family background, and association with nondelinquent and noncriminal peers, are known protective factors.

Psychosocial A comprehensive report generated by clinical staff that details an offender's history of offending and ways of thinking. Psychosocial reports typically cover matters such as an offender's psychological and physical well-being, residential status, employment history, family situation, and social history. Psychosocial reports are written by trained clinical and correctional staff members, such as psychologists, psychology associates, and probation and parole officers.

Recidivism This term is used to describe delinquent or criminal behaviors by offenders who have been treated or addressed for the same or similar behavior in the past.

Responsivity Measurement of an offender's readiness and ability to benefit from interventions that address risk and needs factors. Hence the measurement of responsivity looks at offenders' willingness and readiness in terms of their ability to comprehend and carry out treatment instructions.

Responsivity The cognitive and material readiness of an offender to fully benefit from a rehabilitative intervention. The principle of responsivity insists that cognitive behavioral treatment programs must be tailored to each offender's learning style, motivation level, cognitive and physical abilities, and strengths.

Risk Factor A variable shown by studies to increase the likelihood of a specific future offending behavior or to predict the likelihood of antisocial behavior. Most risk factors are cognitive, behavioral, attitudinal, and historical factors that can increase the likelihood of future delinquent and criminal behaviors. Examples of risk factors are having friends who glamorize criminal activities.

Service The average offender who enters the criminal justice system has a lot of needs, including the need for help with medical attention, education, and future employment. Any of those resources qualify as a service. Common services include medical and mental health services, educational services, and other services such as assistance regarding readiness for employment and/or finding a school.

Sexual Abuse The subjection of a child, especially someone younger than the offender, to any sexual activity. Examples of sexual abuse include child molestation or the use of a child in any sexual activity or in any manner so that the abuser derives sexual gratification or financial benefit.

Sexual Misconduct This term generally refers to any sexual behavior that is viewed as deviant, inappropriate, or prohibited.

Static Risk Factor Although most risk factors can be manipulated or completely eliminated, some risk factors do not change irrespective of efforts by offenders. Such factors are known as static risk factors. Examples of static risk factors include a history of being arrested, spending time in a controlled environment, growing up in a single-parent home, and being physically, sexually, or emotionally victimized by others. Similarly, static protective factors, such as the achievement of a high school diploma and growing up in a supportive and healthy family environment, do not change.

Substance Abuse A pattern of controlled substance use characterized by the repeated use of controlled substances to achieve intoxication despite physical evidence of adverse consequences associated with the controlled substance use behaviors. Examples of negative consequences of controlled substance use include serious and minor behaviors, such as missing classes or work and failing to satisfy social and legal obligations.

Substance Dependence A pattern of controlled substance use characterized by the continuous and increased use of controlled substances to achieve a level of intoxication that allows the user to avoid the discomfort associated with withdrawal symptoms. Another documented symptom of substance dependence is when an offender feels continuously pressured to use higher and higher doses of a controlled substance to achieve similar levels of intoxication.

Treatment This term is used to describe any delivery of correctional service, opportunity, intervention, or assistance or the provision of opportunities and similar services to offenders with the sole purpose of helping them avoid future antisocial thinking and behavior. Examples of treatment are requiring an offender to attend counseling sessions or to acquire a high school diploma.

Violent Crime Unlawful acts that are violent in nature. Violent crimes are often directed at persons or property and include offenses such as murder, forcible rape, armed robbery, kidnapping, and aggravated assault.

Index

www.ingramcontent.com/pod-product-compliance
Ingram Content Group UK Ltd.
Pitfield, Milton Keynes, MK11 3LW, UK
UKHW051509290926
15471UKWH00008B/1512

9 781516 515257